Praise for *Obstacles to Stillness*

Our spiritual trajectories toward salvation or awakening are journeys marked by breakthroughs and great insight but can also be punctuated by setbacks and moments of discouragement. Shodhin Geiman's work brings Evagrius's taxonomy of the passions into conversation with the early Buddhist discourse on "hindrances" to liberation and shows how both traditions engage these inner obstacles and turn them into resources for our spiritual growth. This volume is a great resource for scholars of Buddhist-Christian dialogue, but also for anyone seeking greater understanding of their path to integration and inner freedom.

—Thomas Cattoi, associate professor of Christology and Cultures, Jesuit School of Theology at Santa Clara University and the Graduate Theological Union, Berkeley, and coeditor of *Buddhist-Christian Studies*

Shodhin K. Geiman offers a carefully nuanced, judicious comparison of the paths of renunciant-contemplative life described by Evagrius of Pontus and Shakyamuni Buddha, emphasizing each figure's recommendations for handling obstacles through practices of self-surrender. By sharply distinguishing between the renunciant-contemplative life and service to the world, Geiman offers a thoughtful challenge to socially engaged Buddhists and Christians. Even those who will disagree with his conclusion will find much to ponder in his discussion.

—Leo D. Lefebure, Matteo Ricci Professor of Theology, Georgetown University

Evagrius's description of the eight great "sins" that hinder a Christian's centered, prayerful life with God receives a fresh interpretation with a comparison to analogous concepts in early Indian Buddhism. This deep dive offers a rich vein of analysis for both traditions, and sheds light on what is needed for a contemplative spiritual life that will lead to the attainment of the respective soteriological aims of each religious tradition.

—Kristin Johnston Largen, president, Wartburg Theological Seminary

I0894467

Anyone embarking upon a spiritual path—whether Buddhist, Christian, or other—will soon come across the difficulties strewn across such a way, tempting the aspirant to give up on the good intentions they initially had. Shodhin Geiman is to be congratulated on writing a unique and original book that guides the aspirant through the eight obstacles to the contemplative life as presented by the early Christian "desert father" Evagrius of Pontus. Showing great erudition and experience, he draws upon Buddhist and Christian sources to unlock the wisdom of the ancients for today's spiritual seekers. The book is readable, practical, and learned. I would not hesitate to recommend this to anyone seriously pursuing a spiritual path, regardless of their years of experience.

—Peter Tyler, professor of pastoral theology and spirituality, St. Mary's University, Twickenham, London

Obstacles to Stillness

Obstacles to **STILLNESS**

Thoughts, Hindrances, and Self-Surrender in Evagrius and the Buddha

Shodhin K. Geiman

FORTRESS PRESS
MINNEAPOLIS

OBSTACLES TO STILLNESS
Thoughts, Hindrances, and Self-Surrender in Evagrius and the Buddha

Library of Congress Cataloging-in-Publication Data

Names: Geiman, Shodhin K., author.
Title: Obstacles to stillness : thoughts, hindrances, and self-surrender in Evagrius and the Buddha / Shodhin K. Geiman.
Description: Minneapolis : Fortress Press, 2023. | Includes bibliographical references and index. |
Identifiers: LCCN 2023021871 (print) | LCCN 2023021872 (ebook) | ISBN 9781506481265 (paperback) | ISBN 9781506481272 (ebook)
Subjects: LCSH: Spiritual life—Christianity. | Evagrius, Ponticus, 345?-399. | Gautama Buddha—Teachings. | Spiritual life—Buddhism. | Aesthetics—Religious aspects—Christianity. | Aesthetics—Religious aspects—Buddhism.
Classification: LCC BV4501.3 .G4456 2023 (print) | LCC BV4501.3 (ebook) | DDC 242—dc23/eng/20230712
LC record available at https://lccn.loc.gov/2023021871
LC ebook record available at https://lccn.loc.gov/2023021872

Cover image: Cover art made with Grainy grunge abstract background - stock photo ©Sergey Ryumin | Getty Images
Cover design: Kristin Miller

Print ISBN: 978-1-5064-8126-5
eBook ISBN: 978-1-5064-8127-2

To my teachers, first in the gospel, then in the Dharma,
who spared no kindness in relentlessly drawing attention to
my many obstructions.

Out of his anguish he shall see light; he shall find satisfaction through his knowledge.

Isaiah 53:11

Being rid of all lust, hate, and delusion, purged of flaws, he is worthy of gifts, worthy of hospitality, worthy of offerings, worthy of reverential salutations, an unsurpassed field of merit for the world.

Dantabhūmi Sutra

Contents

Introduction

In Luke's Gospel (15:11–24), we find a tale of a prodigal. It seems a young man had decided it was time for him to lead his own life, so he asked his father for his share of the inheritance and proceeded to set off for distant lands. In the *Lotus Sutra*, we also find a tale of a prodigal.[1] It seems this young man, too, had decided it was time to be on his own, so he left his father and set up shop in another country. In neither case did it go at all well for these fellows, and both ended up miserably destitute. By the end of each parable, however, we find both of these men back home and enjoying the riches of their fathers, freed at last from their self-incurred penury.

But that is where the similarities between the two parables end. Luke's rather terse account has the son simply making the decision to head home without further ado, and the next we hear his father is already meeting him along the road. In the *Lotus*, the son aimlessly wanders for a long period and then happens completely by chance to wind up in the vicinity of his father. He is unaware of his father's identity, however, since he has been away for so many years and had lost track of his father's whereabouts. What follows is a rather lengthy account of how the father, having caught a glimpse of his son as he went about town, begins a gradual process of slowly bringing the son into the realization of his rightful identity. Through a series of skillful actions on the father's part, the son eventually comes to shed his fear and ignorance and in so doing comes to know himself—not as he had fancied himself to be, but as he truly is, his father's son by birthright.[2]

---

1 Burton Watson, trans., *The Lotus Sutra* (New York: Columbia University Press, 1993), 81–86.

2 The marked similarities of the Buddhist and Christian versions of the parable of the prodigal were not lost on some of the earliest European scholars studying Buddhist texts. Both versions capture key elements of the spiritual journey: a self-centered turning away from one's original state, a deep recognition of the misery that follows from it, a decisive change of heart (*metanoia*), and a conscious effort to return to one's original

It fell to subsequent generations of Christians to fill in the details of that journey back to the Father, a journey that, as many of them had come to experience firsthand, was not at all as simple and straightforward as Luke had portrayed it to be. They would have come to experience a deep-seated ambivalence about giving up their much-cherished but ultimately impotent autonomy, experienced as a nagging, persistent hold on their former lives, miserable as they had been, even as they now sought to be free of them. Moreover, they would have seen others who had started on their journey only to be stymied on the road mid-travel, and—even more disconcerting—they would have known of still others who had turned right around and headed back to their familiar, if fruitless, lives. Perhaps surprisingly, though perhaps not, their accounts of that arduous and oftentimes confusing trek would come to bear a rather striking resemblance to the account the *Lotus* provides.

It is in the spirit of exploring that fraught journey that this book takes up what Evagrius of Pontus (345–399 CE), the first systematic taxonomist of Christian contemplative life, called the *logismoi*, or obstructive thoughts, and what in the teaching of the Buddha are referred to as the *nīvaraṇas*, or hindrances. These are, in their respective practice traditions, the great obstacles that thwart an aspirant in coming to stillness (in Greek *hesychia*, or in Sanskrit/Pāli *samatha*),[3] that unfettered equipoise of mind that first makes possible, then complements and helps bring to active fruition, the clear, radiant, and selfless wisdom (*gnōsis* or *paññā/prajña*) toward which contemplative life leads.

Many of Evagrius's eight logismoi—gluttony (*gastrimargia*), fornication (*porneia*), avarice (*philargyria*), anger (*orgē*), sadness (*lypē*), acedia (*akēdia*), vainglory (*kenodoxia*), and pride (*hyperēphania*)—might seem rather familiar,

state. See J. M. Carter, "The Prodigal Son in Its Buddhist Shape," *JRAS* (1893): 333–34, for one such early comparison.

3 In what follows, I will use the word *obstacles* when referring to the logismoi and the nīvaraṇas together. I will leave *logismoi* untranslated, and I will use *nīvaraṇas* and *hindrances* interchangeably, as is custom. I know of no satisfactory translation for *logismoi*. Often it is translated as "bad thoughts" or "evil thoughts," and while they are certainly troublesome, it is not clear that they belong under the economy of sin and redemption as traditionally understood. They may be part and parcel of the human condition, but they are not things of which one could be—or even needs to be—*forgiven* as much as they are things for one to *see into* and *abandon*.

Key terms in the Buddhist tradition I will give in Pāli or, where the Sanskrit differs from the Pāli, first in Pāli, then in Sanskrit. As is convention, general references in the text will use the Sanskrit term; where a direct quote uses Pāli, I will keep the Pāli.

since they were the basis of what would later be recast in the Western church as the "seven deadly sins."[4] Here, however, they will be treated as Evagrius treated them, namely, as banes particular to a form of life that conduces to the attainment of impassability (*apatheia*) and stillness that together open the aspirant to divine knowledge (gnōsis) and a share in the life of God (*theōsis*). This allows them to be viewed alongside the five nīvaraṇas—sensory desire (*kāmacchanda*), ill will (*vyāpadā*), sloth-torpor (*thīna-midda*), restlessness-remorse (*uddhacca-kukkucca*), and doubt/indecision (*vicikicchā*)—which, in the Dharma,[5] are identified as obstacles to the attainment of dispassion (*virāga*), which leads to stillness (samatha) and insight (*vipassanā*). Together, samatha and vipassanā serve as the twofold basis on which wisdom can arise, a wisdom that, in its turn, conduces to the cessation (*nibbāna/nirvāṇa*) of craving (*tanha/tṛṣṇā*) with its attendant suffering (*dukkha*). Some of the obstacles pair up rather straightforwardly, while others point to particular concerns that arose within one or the other tradition. Together they form a comprehensive inventory of the pervasive, deeply rooted ways one can cling to illusions concerning oneself, the world, and the very aim of one's aspiration, even as—and, more to the point, *precisely because*—one will have set oneself resolutely on the path to the realization of that aspiration.

The striking similarities of the logismoi and nīvaraṇas is enough to invite a closer comparative look at them as obstacles inherent to contemplative or meditative practice, and that is the aim of this book. My guiding thesis is that these obstacles are common to both traditions because both traditions call for the surrender of the self on the path to the realization of their respective soteriological aims. Whether cast as "self-emptying" (*kenōsis*) in the Christian tradition, or as "seeing into the emptiness of the self" (*suññatā/śūnyatā*) in the teaching of the Buddha, that process of self-surrender is precisely what the obstacles stand in the way of.

The chapters in part I set the logismoi and the nīvaraṇas within the context of the respective training sequences by which one becomes established in contemplative prayer or meditation. The chapters in part II are devoted

4 The literature on the Evagrian origins of the seven deadly sins is ample enough. See Otto Zöckler, *Das Lehrstück von den sieben Hauptsünden* (Munich: Beck, 1893); Angela Tilby, *The Seven Deadly Sins: Their Origin in the Spiritual Teaching of Evagrius the Hermit* (London: SPCK, 2002); and Richard Newhauser, ed., *In the Garden of Evil: The Vices and Culture in the Middle Ages* (Toronto: Pontifical Institute of Mediaeval Studies, 2005).

5 "The Dharma" is a common way of referring to teachings of the Buddha.

to exploring the various individual obstacles that confront the now readied practitioner, together when applicable and separately when necessary.[6] Before proceeding, however, some words are certainly in order about the advisability of considering the logismoi and the nīvaraṇas in conjunction with each other as well as an indication of what such a pairing could offer.[7] The place to begin is with an understanding of the particular kind of spiritual practice out of which they came to be identified.

Renunciant-contemplative practice is a distinctive form of training, discipline, and life that involves a graduated practice of meditation or prayer grounded in a moderate and sustained ascesis. As a *contemplative* practice, the emphasis is on individual (rather than corporate) and silent (rather than liturgical or ritual) activity. Without necessarily abandoning them altogether, it makes use of these more vocal and communal exercises to the extent to which they support, challenge, and help develop one's otherwise necessarily solitary

---

6 I will not be taking up questions of influence (i.e., whether Evagrius might have had some access to Buddhist teachings), nor will I address the matter of differences in their respective rosters (e.g., why sadness, for instance, appears in Evagrius's list of logismoi but is not counted among the nīvaraṇas, or why indecision is considered a nīvaraṇa but has no parallel among the logismoi).

7 While this is the first extended treatment of the logismoi and the nīvaraṇas together, the similarity of certain elements of Evagrian spirituality and cultivation in the Dharma have not been lost on scholars over the past hundred years or so. In the 1930s, Hans Urs von Balthasar noted the affinities between the two, and he was led to the conclusion that the mystical teaching of Evagrius stood closer to Buddhism than to Christianity. See von Balthasar, "The Metaphysics and Mystical Theology of Evagrius," *Monastic Studies* 3 (1965): 183–95. Von Balthasar's focus was on the purely *metaphysical* similarities between the two more so than on their *practical* similarities as accounts of spiritual development, so his overall assessment needs to be read with some caution. Francis V. Tiso has pointed out connections between certain key elements of Evagrius's work and aspects of Abhidharma literature, though he does so primarily out of an interest in the question whether Evagrian thought might have been influenced by Buddhist sources. See Tiso, "Evagrius of Pontus and Buddhist Abhidharma," *Religion East & West* 5 (2005): 41–71. As interesting as the question of historical influence might be, it is, in the end, rather immaterial to the matter at hand. Finally, David Linge has skillfully drawn attention to particular sutras that have close parallels in Evagrius's writings, and he suggestively compares aspects of Evagrius's reflections on prayer to vipassanā practice. See Linge, "Leading the Life of Angels: Ascetic Practice and Reflection in the Writings of Evagrius of Pontus," *JAAR* 68, no. 3 (September 2000): 537–68. Here, I will proceed on the assumption that, as far as a consideration of the obstacles goes, samatha practice actually provides the closer parallel, because it is in conjunction with the establishment of samatha through the practice of *samādhi*—not vipassanā—that these are dealt with directly.

undertaking. Dedicated periods of concerted prayer or meditation in relative seclusion comprise a good part of the practice, as one might expect, but these are not understood as ends in themselves, nor are they engaged in apart from a broader training regimen and conduct of daily affairs.

Because the quality of one's prayer or meditation is contingent on the degree to which one is no longer assailed internally by the push and pull of one's psychophysical states, or externally by the many and oftentimes conflicting demands of social life, contemplative practice is also by its very nature a *renunciant* practice. But far from being a matter of adopting this or that bizarre austerity, mustering herculean acts of brute will, or inflicting self-harm, renunciation is here understood as a progressive, focused, and ultimately wholesale surrender of the attachments and aversions that give rise to distorted thoughts and unskillful actions that disturb the mind and so cloud the essential truth of things and oneself. As those attachments and aversions are only ever one's own creation, in the end this practice involves nothing short of setting aside everything that bolsters the conceit of the self in thought, word, and deed in order for that essential truth to clearly manifest. Renunciant-contemplative practice is thus the work of a lifetime—indeed, even longer[8]—and it is most assuredly *religious*, as distinct from simply *spiritual*, since it involves a rule of life, a mode of conduct, and submission to the guidance of those more advanced in the practice, even as it conduces to the threshold of the supramundane.[9]

So defined, it is clear that renunciant-contemplative practice is not limited to any one particular religious tradition, though some have certainly been more amenable to it than others. The variety of the names we have for those who adopt this way as their only station in life—anchorite, cenobite, *sādhu*, *śramaṇa*, fakir, *bhikkhu*/*bhikkhunī*, monk/nun, friar, hermit[10]—and

8 In the Christian tradition this is described as *epektasis*, the infinite striving for God; in the Dharma, one is said to course through countless rebirths until all traces of self are extinguished in perfect enlightenment, or *anuttarā samyak-saṃbodhi*.

9 In speaking of renunciant-contemplative practice in this way, I am expressly avoiding referring to it as a *mystical* practice, at least as it is commonly understood. The kind of practice we are dealing with here is not one that welcomes the attainment of visions or special states, for these are still conditioned, transitory phenomena that, should they occur, will also have to be seen as such and set aside.

10 Renunciant-contemplative practice is a broader category than *monastic* or *cenobitic* practice. To be sure, monastic practice affords a singularly effective context for renunciant-contemplative development, but its development is not necessarily bound

for those who do so within the context of family and occupation—oblate, *upāsaka/upāsikā*, a member of a canonical "Third" order or tertiary[11]—attests to its ubiquity as well as its staying power. Despite their (for lack of a better word) *organizational* differences, common to all of these is the commitment to a life dedicated to ego attrition along with everything that process requires.

From its earliest expression in the fifth century BCE, the Dharma of the Buddha was developed and promulgated as just such a renunciative-contemplative practice. The Buddha himself began his quest as a striver (*samaṇa/śramaṇa*), one who belonged to what is called the renouncer (*saṃnyāsin*) tradition that was part of the religious landscape of his time. According to the legend, he began his search in earnest when, one evening, he happened upon a sick person, an old person, a corpse being carried to the charnel grounds, and a renunciant (*śramaṇa*) very much at peace. From the first three, so it is said, he caught his first glimpses of the pervasiveness of dukkha; from the last, his first glimpse of the path to its end. Subsequently entering the company of such homeleavers, he apprenticed himself in succession to two teachers, who were themselves quite accomplished in the practice. From them, he learned the cultivation of some of the highest levels of meditative concentration and awareness, and when the Buddha-to-be eventually parted company with them, it was not because he thought they were *wrong*, but because, having mastered what they had to teach, he was still left with the inkling that there was *further yet to go* on the path to dukkha's definitive end.[12]

While the Buddha decried all forms of mortification, having himself once neared death through extreme fasting, he never flagged in his praise of renunciation and solitude. When Ānanda, one of his senior disciples, once said to him, "Renunciation, Bhante, is the dividing line between the multitude and the bhikkhus in this Dhamma and discipline," the Buddha

up with whether one is settled or peripatetic, begs one's food or farms it, or engages in labor in town or only within the walls of the monastic compound.

11 If it is important not to equate renunciant-contemplative practice with monasticism, it is equally important to distinguish between *everyday* lay practice and *committed* lay practice. One may certainly be counted among the Buddhists or among the Christians without having dedicated oneself to the practice under discussion here. *Being a Buddhist* is not the same thing as *living out the Dharma*, and *being a Christian* is not the same thing as *living out the gospel*.

12 Bhikkhu Ñaṇamoli and Bhikkhu Bodhi, trans., *The Middle Length Discourses of the Buddha: A Translation of the Majjhima Nikāya* (Boston: Wisdom, 1995), 256–59.

replied, "So it is, Ānanda! So it is, Ānanda!"[13] Elsewhere he drew the line more emphatically:

> How is it possible that [one], living in the midst of sensual pleasures, enjoying sensual pleasures, being devoured by thoughts of sensual pleasures, being consumed by the fever of sensual pleasures, bent on the search for sensual pleasures, could know, see, or realise that which must be known through renunciation, seen through renunciation, attained through renunciation, realised through renunciation? That is impossible.[14]

He openly admitted that, even in his own case, it was not until he not only saw the good in renunciation but threw himself wholeheartedly into its pursuit that his mind could finally become placid, settled, and liberated in it.[15]

The Buddha was no less unsparing in his praise of solitude as an integral component of the path. One may learn the Dharma well, devote time to speaking with others about it, recite it at length, and even spend time probing it in some detail; but, he pointed out, only one who "does not neglect seclusion but devotes himself to internal serenity of mind" can be called one who "dwells in the Dhamma."[16] This solitude, however, is not measured so much in terms of the number or kind of one's acquaintances but in terms of the maintenance of an environment free of unnecessary distractions:

> I do not praise bonding with everyone whatsoever, nor do I praise bonding with no one at all. I do not praise bonding with householders and monastics, but I do praise bonding with quiet and noiseless lodgings far from the flurry of people, remote from human habitation, and suitable for seclusion.[17]

One then uses that quiet and noiseless space in order to free the mind from all of those things that had been feeding one's delusions. If one did not take that subsequent step, however, one would wind up even more vexed than before, no matter how secluded one might be:

> Stuck in the cave, densely covered over,
> dwelling immersed in bewilderment,

---

13 Bhikkhu Bodhi, trans., *The Numerical Discourses of the Buddha: A Translation of the Aṅguttara Nikāya* (Somerville, MA: Wisdom, 2012), 1310. In Bodhi's translations of the *Nikāyas*, he uses the Pāli term, *Dhamma*, and I leave it true to the translation when cited. In all other instances, I will use *Dharma*, as is now standard in everyday English.

14 Ñāṇamoli and Bodhi, *Middle Length Discourses*, 990.

15 Bodhi, *Numerical Discourses*, 1310.

16 Bodhi, *Numerical Discourses*, 698–99.

17 Bodhi, *Numerical Discourses*, 1061.

a person such as this is far from seclusion,
for in the world sensual pleasures
are not easily abandoned.[18]

True seclusion, then, means not simply isolating oneself from the daily bustle but—and most importantly—rendering the mind clear of all that would otherwise obstruct it.

The Buddha called what he taught "the teaching-and-discipline" (*dhamma-vinaya*), attesting to the integral unity of contemplation and renunciation both as a training tool and as the very expression of awakened and awakening mind. The teaching is ineffective without the active engagement of the aspirant, and the various activities connected with the practice are pointless without proper aim and aspiration. In short, renunciant-contemplative practice is simply another name for what the *Nikāyas*[19] refer to broadly as the *holy life* (*brahmacariya*).

Unlike its Buddhist counterpart, renunciant-contemplative life was not an inherent aspect of Christian practice from the outset. To be fair, it should not be forgotten that in its earliest beginnings there was no *inherent* aspect of Christian practice to speak of at all—the very first Christians self-identified as Jews and continued to pray together in the temple in Jerusalem. But as the gospel spread out from Jerusalem, and as Christians began to formulate answers to the many questions that Scripture had been unclear about or simply silent on, they rather quickly found themselves moving beyond the parameters of the Jewish framework within which Christianity began, and they took on those conceptual and practical endowments of the surrounding cultures perceived to be congenial to living out the gospel.

One of these endowments was a ready language in Greek and Roman philosophy with which to explore their growing appreciation for what might

18 Bhikkhu Bodhi, trans., *The Suttanipāta: An Ancient Collection of the Buddha's Discourses Together with Its Commentaries* (Somerville, MA: Wisdom, 2017), 292. Once the brahmin Jāṇussoṇi approached the Buddha and expressed his concern for the mental health of the forest-dwelling monks given the difficulties of the practice of solitude they undertook there: "Master Gotama, remote jungle-thicket resting places in the forest are hard to endure, seclusion is hard to practice, and it hard to enjoy solitude. One would think the jungles must rob a bhikkhu of his mind." The Buddha agreed that, indeed, one would "if he has no concentration" (Ñāṇamoli and Bodhi, *Middle Length Discourses*, 102). Even a quiet meditation hall in a city building can feel like a prison cell if one is not actively engaged in the penetrating work of the practice.

19 The *Nikāyas* are the collected discourses of the Buddha. With the exception of the *Mettā Sutra*, all sutras referred to in the chapters below are drawn from the *Nikāyas*.

be called the "interior life" of the practitioner. That inward turn had already been called for in the New Testament. In the Sermon on the Mount, for example, Jesus took the Mosaic commandment against murder and included under it not only the actual taking of life but the very disposition to anger that underlies it. He likewise took the commandment against adultery and included under it not only engaging in illicit sex but the disposition to lust that prompts such behavior in the first place. Instead of looking to reinforce one's position by appealing to heaven or earth, Jesus told the disciples not to invoke such support at all but to speak their own minds directly. And rather than underwriting a standard for meting out a measured, proportional justice, he bid his followers not only *not* to defend themselves from others' harmful acts by retaliating in kind, but to expose themselves even further to such harm, thereby setting aside the very resentment that leads to talk of justice in the first place (Matt 5:21–48). This call to be perfect like the Father meant not only keeping one's outward behavior in check but also examining in detail and setting aside without remainder all those sources of imperfection to be found within oneself as well. The composite nature of the human person as imagined by the philosophers—one that had bodily, affective, and noetic dimensions—came to be pressed into service as a way of describing that sense of inwardness and distinguishing it from more outward appearances and simple conformity to moral norms.

This inward turn called for in the Gospels gave rise to a new understanding of prayer as well. Up to this point, prayer was generally understood to mean *public* prayer—vocal, liturgical, and communitarian.[20] But with the increasing sense of the importance of examining one's own thoughts and states of mind, prayer soon came to be viewed as something primarily carried out in silence, stillness, and solitude in a spirit of wordless watchfulness (*nepsis*). This, too, is commanded in the Gospels. Jesus frequently enough removed himself to a deserted place, and he advised his disciples against placing stock in public displays of religiosity and blind adherence to rites, counseling them instead to go into their room, shut the door, and pray in secret (Matt 6:5–6).

But this practice of silent prayer was not simply a quieter and more solitary version of what had been rather vocal and public: it was the gateway for

20 Pieter W. van der Horst, "Silent Prayer in Antiquity," *Numen* 41 (1994): 1–2; for a fuller treatment of this complex topic, see Brouria Bitton-Ashkelony, "'More Interior than the Lips and the Tongue': John of Apamea and Silent Prayer in Antiquity," *JECS* 20 (2012): 303–31.

entering more fully into the ever-present silent and still presence of God. The divine was not to be simply read or heard about, then discussed and believed in; rather, it was to be approached in all humility through a process of clearly and patiently surrendering one's attachments so as to open oneself up to the truth of oneself and the world, and it was this "commitment to truth and to seeing things as they are that disposed one for contemplation of God."[21]

One who adopted this way of life came to be known as a monk—a solitary one (*monachos*)—a person whose physical solitariness was not nearly as defining as his or her singleness of heart, a heart not divided by competing drives and allegiances in its striving for union with God. We do not have records of the first Christians to adopt this way of life, but by the early fourth century, Athanasius of Alexandria, remarking on their number, could write that the "desert was made a city by the monks."[22] We know some of these men and women today collectively as the Desert Fathers and Desert Mothers, and the tales of their exploits from these early years, collected in the *Apophthegmata Patrum*,[23] the *Historia Monachorum in Ægypto*,[24] and the *Lausiac History*,[25] among others, have been passed down from generation to generation both as testament to their dedication and as a record of their attainments. There were also such clusters of practitioners in Gaza, in Syria, in Cappadocia, and in more urban centers such as Jerusalem as well,[26] so this development was not at all limited to the desert but was to be found wherever there were Christians willing to take up the practice.

---

21 See Columba Stewart, OSB, "The Desert Fathers on Radical Self-Honesty," *Vox Benedictina* 8 (1991): 11.

22 Athanasius, *The Life of Antony and the Letter to Marcellinus*, trans. Robert C. Gregg (New York: Paulist, 1980), 42–43. The desert Athanasius had in mind was the Nitrian Desert in Egypt.

23 See Benedicta Ward, trans., *The Sayings of the Desert Fathers: The Alphabetical Collection* (Kalamazoo, MI: Cistercian, 1975); and John Wortley, *Anonymous Sayings of the Desert Fathers* (New York: Cambridge University Press, 2017).

24 Norman Russell, trans., *The Lives of the Desert Fathers: The Historia Monachorum in Aegypto* (Collegeville, MN: Cistercian, 1980).

25 Palladius of Aspuna, *The Lausiac History*, trans. John Wortley (Collegeville, MN: Cistercian, 2015).

26 On Desert Fathers and Mothers in Gaza, see, for example, Jennifer L. L. Hevelone-Harper, *Disciples of the Desert: Monks, Laity, and Spiritual Authority in Sixth-Century Gaza* (Baltimore: Johns Hopkins University Press, 2014); on those in Syria, see in particular Sebastian Brock, *The Syriac Fathers on Prayer and the Spiritual Life* (Kalamazoo, MI: Cistercian, 1987). Basil established a cenobitic monastery near Neocaesarea around 356 CE. Melania the Elder established a convent in Jerusalem, and Rufinus of Aquileia founded a monastery with funding from Melania on the Mount of Olives.

Evagrius eventually found himself among their number. Born in Ibora in Pontus (northern Asia Minor bordering on the Black Sea) to a Christian family, as a young man he came under the influence of Basil the Great and Gregory Nazianzen, the towering Cappadocian Fathers. He was ordained a lector by Basil and a deacon by Gregory, and he accompanied Gregory to Constantinople for the Second Ecumenical Council in 381.[27] Known for his gifted intellect, Evagrius fell in with the circle of theologians and scholars who were particularly drawn to the writings of the influential (and by then increasingly controversial) theologian Origen. Among them were Melania the Elder and Rufinus of Aquileia in Jerusalem, and their friendship proved instrumental in pointing him toward the swelling settlements of renunciant-contemplatives in Egypt. There he first joined the band of semicenobites in Nitria, where he stayed for two years before installing himself among the anchorites in Kellia, where he stayed for the remaining fourteen years of his life.

Despite the ill fortune surrounding his name and his writings in the centuries following his death,[28] Evagrius would come to exert an indelible influence on the subsequent development of renunciant-contemplative practice in the life of the church. In the West, this followed a line from John Cassian, who relied heavily on Evagrius in composing his writings on the contemplative life, to Benedict, who, inspired by Cassian, established a rule of life for coenobitic monasticism that served as the template for all further monastic developments in the Latin church.[29] In the East, some of his practical words of advice to aspiring monks were transmitted across the centuries either anonymously or under the name of St. Nilus of Ancyra, helping in the process to develop

27 This is the generally received account. Ilaria Ramelli makes a compelling case that it was, in fact, Gregory of Nyssa—not Nazianzen—who is the Gregory in question here. See Ramelli, "Evagrius and Gregory: Nazianzen or Nyssen? Cappadocian (and Origenian) Influence on Evagrius," *GRBS* 53 (2013): 117–37; and Ramelli, "Gregory and Evagrius," *StPatr* 101 (2021): 177–206.

28 For an overview of the twists and turns of the church's engagement with Evagrius's writings, see Gabriel Bunge, *"Évagre le sage." L'image d'Évagre le Pontique dans l'Histoire de l'Église* (Sankt Ottilien, Germany: EOS, 2022).

29 John Cassian (ca. 360–ca. 435 CE) traveled among the settlements in Nitria and Scete as a young man and was quite familiar with Evagrius's work. His *Institutes* and *Conferences* helped spread the spirituality of Evagrius and other Desert Elders to Western Europe. Benedict of Nursia (480–548 CE) was heavily influenced by Cassian's writings in composing his *Rule* (ca. 530 CE). It has been followed more or less strictly by the Benedictines and their offshoots, the Camaldolese, the Cistercians, and the Trappists, since that time.

the distinctive flavor of Orthodox monasticism and spirituality such as we now find expressed in the *Philokalia*.[30]

Whether in its Evagrian or Dharmic understandings, renunciant-contemplative life is undertaken in light of the sense, however dim at the outset, that what one seeks is already laid bare, manifest, and ever accessible—if only one were to stop getting in the way of it. The first significant stride on the path to the realization of that inkling's truth—and the first sure sign of the attrition of the self that has ever occluded it—is the establishment of what in both traditions is called *stillness*. This stillness is far from being some kind of fleeting psychophysical state or condition one hopes to be able to access and, as it were, enjoy for its own sake from time to time. Instead, it is the perduring quality of one's life through and through, once one has begun to see things as they really are, rather than as one has hitherto taken them to be.

Hesychia was the name by which this stillness was known among early Christians. Originally used as a term to describe the contours of anchoritic life generally, it slowly came to describe as well the overall state of one who had come to live that life successfully:

> *Hesychia* . . . has to do with the outset, with the conditions necessary for the spiritual life to flourish [but] it becomes clear that—in a sense—*hesychia* is also the hallmark of the envisaged end of ascetic living: it represents the peace for which the ascetic longs. *Hesychia* is the door that leads to contemplation, to the vision of God, to the end of the mystagogical process. Thus, it points to both the beginning and the end of the journey.[31]

Whether at the beginning or at the end or somewhere in between, hesychia involved "an isolation of oneself, in person and in thought, from the things of this world, in a conscious awareness of the presence of God," an isolation that led to "a tranquil acquiescence in the will of God, producing a profound calm and great peace within."[32] It is perhaps best summarily described as a

30 The *Philokalia* is a compendium of writings on the contemplative life from the fourth through fifteenth centuries and compiled in the eighteenth century for the training of Orthodox monks in stillness.

31 Nienke Vos, "Seeing *Hesychia*: Appeals to the Imagination in the *Apophthegmata Patrum*," *StPatr* 64 (2013): 35.

32 John Wortley, "What *hêsychia* Meant to the Desert Fathers," *Cistercian Studies Quarterly* 54 (2019): 169.

life permeated with a "graced depth of inner stillness,"[33] unbuffeted without and unagitated within because it is a life that has become increasingly receptive to the spirit of God.

Hesychia is the profound stillness of the mind, but its entry point is apatheia, the stilling of the appetitive drives of the body. Much like the fate hesychia was to suffer in the subsequent history of the church,[34] apatheia, too, was subject to misunderstanding and derision. Jerome's broadside set the tone for any who would also want to cast scorn on it:

> Evagrius of Ibera in Pontus, who sends letters to virgins and monks and among others to her whose name bears witness to the blackness of her perfidy,[35] has published a book of maxims on apathy, or, as we should say, impassivity or imperturbability; a state in which the mind ceases to be agitated and—to speak simply—becomes either a stone or a God.[36]

But in Evagrius's understanding apatheia actually renders one *more fully* human rather than less so. It is the fruit of discretion, of wise choices, of a right understanding of the nature of oneself and the world and God—and it issues forth in love,[37] something a stone is utterly incapable of. That it should serve to render one more like unto God, who is love, then, is not an easily dismissible bit of questionable theology but a robust expression of thoroughgoing orthodoxy.[38]

For its part, the practice of the Dharma has but one aim: the "unshakable deliverance of mind" from all that has hitherto obstructed it.[39] This deliver-

33 William Harmless, SJ, *Desert Christians: An Introduction to the Literature of Early Monasticism* (New York: Oxford University Press, 2004), 228.

34 The controversy surrounding hesychia came to a head in the fourteenth century with the attacks on it undertaken by Barlaam of Seminara, which prompted Gregory Palamas's *Triads* in response to them. The Fifth Council of Constantinople vindicated Palamas on the matter.

35 Jerome is playing on Melania the Elder's name, which means "dark" or "black."

36 Jerome, *Letter* 133.3, to Ctesiphon, in *NPNF*[2] 6:274.

37 Evagrius, *Praktikos* 81; in *The Greek Ascetic Corpus*, trans. Robert E. Sinkewicz (New York: Oxford University Press, 2003), 110. Hereafter, all citations from this work will follow the form Evagrius, *title of text* and section number; Sinkewicz, page number.

38 Leszek Misiarczyk points out that part of Jerome's critique of Evagrius here stems from Jerome's mistaken identification of apatheia with *sinlessness*. See Leszek Misiarczyk, "*Impassibilitas et impeccantia*: Jerome's Misunderstanding of Impassibility and Sinlessness in Evagrius Ponticus," *Bogoslovni vestnik* 81 (2021): 271–81.

39 Ñāṇamoli and Bodhi, *Middle Length Discourses*, 290.

ance is made possible, though not completed by, the cultivation of serenity or stillness (samatha) and the development of insight (vipassana):

> Bhikkhus, these two things pertain to true knowledge. What two? Serenity and insight. When serenity is developed, what benefit does one experience? The mind is developed. When the mind is developed, what benefit does one experience? Lust is abandoned. When insight is developed, what benefit does one experience? Wisdom is developed. When wisdom is developed, what benefit does one experience? Ignorance is abandoned.[40]

While these two techniques are not at odds with each other[41] and can be practiced more or less simultaneously,[42] one will generally establish the mind in samatha through meditative concentration (*samādhi*) first and then, once settled, proceed with vipassanā and the path of insight. Whatever clarity and vision vipassanā might afford is likely to be quickly dissipated and lost if the practitioner has not established the ground of stillness in which it might take root.

Here, too, the cultivation of dispassion toward both psychophysical experiences and external circumstances is key to the aspirant's cultivation of stillness. In the *Nikāyas* this is captured by the related terms *nibbidā* and *virāga*. *Nibbidā* is frequently rendered "disenchantment" or "revulsion," and while that sounds a bit harsh,

> what is intended by this is not a reaction of emotional disgust, accompanied by horror and aversion, but a calm inward turning away from all conditioned existence. . . . Revulsion arises from knowledge and vision of things as they really are (*yathābhūtañāṇadassana*), and naturally leads to dispassion (*virāga*) and liberation (*vimutti*).[43]

The enthralling character of a given conditioned phenomenon, which up until now held the aspirant in its grip, begins to be seen for exactly the delusion it is. Just as in the case of a mirage, once one sees that it is not as it appears,

---

40 Bodhi, *Numerical Discourses*, 152. There is some debate as to whether these two meditative practices reflect an early differentiation in the tradition between two camps of bhikkhus, but, whatever the origins, it has long been held that the path to liberation requires both.

41 See, for example, R[upert] M. L. Gethin, *The Buddhist Path to Awakening* (Oxford: One World, 2007), xiv.

42 See Bodhi, *Numerical Discourses*, 1404–5.

43 Bhikkhu Bodhi, trans., *The Connected Discourses of the Buddha: A Translation of the Saṃyutta Nikāya* (Boston: Wisdom, 2000), 53.

one will no longer continue to approach it as if it were water. *Virāga*, as here, is generally rendered "dispassion"; once one realizes that not just that shimmering mirage but *all* phenomena are of this illusory nature,[44] one finds oneself disinclined to run toward *any* of them. Tṛṣṇā, that craving that sends one chasing after them, begins to abate, and "the wavering or trepidation of the mind is subdued and brought to an end."[45] There is still further yet to go on the path to the final cessation of tṛṣṇā and its attendant dukkha, but without this much having been accomplished, no further steps on the path will be possible.

Obstructing the establishment of hesychia and samatha are the logismoi and the nīvaraṇas, which emerge at parallel points in the training trajectories outlined by Evagrius and the Buddha. These obstacles become the express focus of contemplative practice once the aspirant has become rather firmly established in dispassion. It is only then that an individual is capable of dealing with them effectively, thanks to the discernment that has been cultivated up to that point through ascesis. The stilling of the body, guarding its comportment, and restraining its impulses are the first—and *necessary*—steps to stilling the fearful and fretting mind. But unless that mind is stilled as well, one will be at a loss to make sense of—and will lack the resolve to keep at—the practice of ascesis by which one first undertakes this path and sustains it to the end.[46]

The logismoi and the nīvaraṇas emerge as the focus of meditative practice at this stage in both traditions because of two specific ways in which they hinder the aspirant. First, the logismoi and the nīvaraṇas are fundamentally *deceptive* in what they conjure up in the aspirant. They are tenacious habits of mind (as opposed to something like momentary feelings) that compel one to view as important that which is unimportant, as lasting that which is transient, as skillful that which is unskillful, and as essential that which

44 In the *Diamond Sutra* it is put like this: "As a lamp, a cataract, a star in space / an illusion, a dewdrop, a bubble / a dream, a cloud, a flash of lightning / view all created things like this." Red Pine, trans., *The Diamond Sutra: Text and Commentaries Translated from Sanskrit and Chinese* (Washington: Counterpoint, 2001), 27.

45 Bhikkhu Bodhi, ed., *A Comprehensive Manual of Abhidhamma: The Abhidhammattha Sangaha of Ācariya Anuruddha* (Onalaska, WA: Pariyatti, 2000), 329.

46 Colm Luibhéid points out that too great an emphasis on the mere act of separating oneself from society and engaging in ascetic practice does not begin to account for why one would *keep at it* for decades. See Luibhéid, "Antony and the Renunciation of Society," *ITQ* 52 (1986): 305.

could never be. One who falls prey to them suffers from a kind of "stupidity," as Nāgārjuna, the great scholar and monk of the Madhyamaka school, later pointed out.[47] That said, it is not at all an *obvious* stupidity, and much of the work at this stage of practice involves coming to see just how stupid they are. So, in addition to identifying and describing the obstacles, the Buddha and Evagrius offer a number of strategies by which the aspirant might come to see them as so many forms of self-deception. Specifically, they suggest that one at this stage of the training is well-served by relying on the Scriptures or the sutras, listening to talks given by those more developed in the practice, and, above all, submitting to the corrective guidance of a trusted teacher.[48]

Second, the obstacles are nothing if not *tempting.* Evagrius frequently refers to them as *demons*, and the Buddha counted them among the *armies of Māra*, the tempter or "Dark One."[49] We need not dwell on the ontological status of such beings ("Are they real?") in order to appreciate their power; a better place to look for an explanation of their hold would be in the nature of the very aspirational aim they seek to subvert. The point where the obstacles begin to emerge with full force—that is, where the demons and hosts of Māra make their presence known—is precisely that point where the aspirant nears the first definitive break with manifest forms of ego attachment and entering into stillness. Setting aside one's inclinations and attachments for a short period of meditation or prayer is difficult enough. The thought of dispensing with them *for good* is core-shakingly threatening, because these inclinations and attachments are those things that, up to this point, have served as the root definers of self. Now one begins to see quite clearly the stark choice at hand: cling to the self and give up the path, or surrender attachment to self and press steadily on. The logismoi and the nīvaraṇas may be based on a kind of stupidity, but it is a safe, comfortable, familiar, and, above all, *self-satisfying*

47 Nāgārjuna, *Nāgārjuna on the Six Perfections: An Ārya Bodhisattva Explains the Heart of the Bodhisattva Path: Exegesis on the Great Perfection of Wisdom Sutra Chapters 17–30*, trans. Dharmamitra (Seattle: Kalavinka, 2009), 405.

48 For a comprehensive account of the role and function of teacher in early Christian practice, see Irénée Hausherr, SJ, *Spiritual Direction in the Early Christian East*, trans. Anthony P. Gythiel (Kalamazoo, MI: Cistercian, 1990).

49 For an account of Evagrius's demonology, see David Brakke, *Demons and the Making of the Monk: Spiritual Combat in Early Christianity* (Cambridge: Harvard University Press, 2006), 48–77. On the psychologically symbolic and literal understandings of Māra and his armies in the Pāli texts, see Rupert Gethin, "Cosmology and Meditation: From the Aggañña-Sutta to the Mahāyāna," *HR* 36 (1997): 189–91.

stupidity that only the deepest resolve and the most concerted effort can overcome.

Moreover, because much of what the obstacles conjure up is rather normal and unproblematic to the everyday person (at least within socially acceptable bounds), they offer the aspirant an easy excuse for abandoning the renunciant-contemplative path itself, the very vehicle by which they might be seen into and overcome. To lead a fine life by most reckonings—even most religious ones—the aspirant does not *have to* set aside attachment to kith and kin, manage on adequate but meager food, or pass up the everyday pleasures of entertainment or the satisfactions of social standing. And because so much of social life is based on mutually tempered delusions, the fact that one is fundamentally deluded by the obstacles never necessarily presents itself as a problem, either. So if Evagrius's and the Buddha's depictions of renunciant-contemplative practice come across as overly exacting at times,[50] it is because they both reject the happy accommodation of delusion provided by the common understanding of virtue either as the mean between extremes or as that which the majority is willing to abide. Even a moderately tempered delusion is still a delusion, and one who would attain to stillness will derive no lasting peace from the concessions accorded to nonaspirants, or rest content with only a partial completion of the task at hand. To do so would mean surrendering the noble aim of his or her striving at the same time. Evagrius and the other Desert Elders "staked everything on the effort to destroy delusion and deception,"[51] and the same can be said for the Buddha and his noble disciples as well. As we will soon see, this *everything* is not the stuff of hyperbole but a straight-up, unvarnished description of the ante involved.

In short, the obstacles emerge at a crucial juncture on the prodigal's journey home. The everyday life is in the process of being abandoned, but one is still far from realizing the aim of one's striving. One has developed an initial dispassion with regard to one's usual self-centered way of doing things, but one is still not firmly established in the conviction that an alternative is possible or, even if it is, that it is all worth the cost involved. One may have caught the vaguest intimation of the liberation and peace to be attained, but one is still afraid to leave everything else behind and live that liberation in its fullness.

---

50 One researcher has gone so far as to raise the question whether Evagrius had obsessive-compulsive disorder. See Jonathan Hill, "Did Evagrius Ponticus (AD 346–99) Have Obsessive-Compulsive Disorder?," *Journal of Medical Biography* 18 (2010): 49–56.

51 Stewart, "Desert Fathers on Radical Self-Honesty," 7.

Without overcoming the obstacles, one will either remain stuck in one's tracks or—much more likely—simply return to one's former ways. This was true for the earliest renunciant-contemplatives in each tradition, and it is true for present-day aspirants as well. Far from being historical relics of a bygone age, the logismoi and the nīvaraṇas are obstacles that confront the dedicated practitioner even now, no matter which tradition one happens to call home.

When we focus on the obstacles in each tradition this way, today's renunciant-contemplative brothers and sisters of the Crucified-Risen One and the noble sons and daughters of the Awakened One can find themselves on very common ground—our shared frail and fraught humanity held under the sway of our dogged attachment to self. Here is the field on which both parties begin their spiritual labors, and it should come as no surprise that both have much the same initial work to do and that both will encounter many of the same obstacles, no matter how each tries to express the ultimate aim of practice. Moreover, by drawing attention to those things that bind us all, as the logismoi and nīvaraṇas most assuredly do, both parties can begin to form a better appreciation of the one perduring quality of renunciant-contemplative practice that alone makes a robust and selfless compassion for others at all possible: in coming to realize how difficult it is to get past my own obstructive states and delusions, my heart can begin to open up to the plight of those who, like me, even now remain deeply inured to their own. All the talk of love and compassion and loving-kindness in the world will ring hollow—and misfire in its exercise, one might add[52]—as long as one has not squarely confronted and abandoned, down to every last one of their manifestations, one's own delusions, unskillfulness, and self-centered arrogance.

Now, the caveats. First, although the words *monk* or *bhikkhu* will appear on almost every page, I would ask the reader not to resort to contrasting these with *layperson*, as if what is discussed here applies only to the one and not to the other.[53] It is easier to avoid this move from the perspective of the Dharma,

52 The Buddhist tradition has gone to some lengths to distinguish compassion and loving-kindness from what are called their "near enemies," states that bear a family resemblance to these but are still overlaid with the conceit of the self. Suffice it to say, the distinction between the two rests precisely in whether one has overcome the nīvaraṇas.

53 Still less should they be read as referring only to *males*. Peter Brown makes the interesting observation that such monks, in leaving aside the procreative duties of fatherhood so cherished in the ancient world, were, in a sense, no longer gendered but, like the denizen of heaven they sought to emulate, angelically *genderless*. See Brown, "The

since the path to liberation laid out by the Buddha was only ever understood as one to be taken up by anyone willing to commit to the practice, whether as a householder or as a homeleaver:

> Householders, you have presented robes, almsfood, lodgings and medicines and provisions for the sick to the Saṅgha of bhikkhus. You should not be content with merely this much, [thinking]: "We have presented robes, almsfood, lodgings and medicines and provisions for the sick to the Saṅgha of bhikkhus." Therefore, householders, you should train yourselves thus: "How can we from time to time enter and dwell in the rapture of solitude?" In such a way you should train yourselves.[54]

For present purposes it should not be overlooked that this training will, of course, include confronting and overcoming the nīvaraṇas, and in an interchange with a householder on accomplishment in wisdom, the Buddha pointed out that the noble householder no less than the homeleaver will know the five hindrances to be the defilements of mind that they are and therefore seek to abandon them.[55] Moreover, there is in principle nothing keeping both the noble householder and the noble homeleaver from realizing the liberation toward which this practice conduces:

> If [a lay follower] says, "My mind has been withdrawn from the brahmā world and I have directed my mind to the cessation of identity," then, Mahānāma, I say there is no difference between a lay follower who is thus liberated in mind and a bhikkhu what has been liberated in mind for a hundred years, that is, between one liberation and the other.[56]

Rise and Function of the Holy Man in Late Antiquity 1971–1997," *JECS* 6 (1998): 371. That aside, in what follows, where there is discussion of a textual source that refers to a monk or a bhikkhu, I will use the pronoun *he*. Where the discussion opens up to broader reflections on the obstacles, practice, and the like, I will generally use the pronoun *one* or, where fitting, *he* and *she* together. Examples will alternate between those dealing with a woman or with a man.

54 Bodhi, *Numerical Discourses*, 789.

55 Bodhi, *Numerical Discourses*, 450.

56 Bodhi, *Connected Discourses*, 1836. As Robert Bluck points out: "The difference between monastics and lay Buddhists in the Pāli Canon is more quantitative than qualitative. . . . The essential distinction, both then and now, is not between the monastic and the lay-follower, but between the 'ordinary disciple' (who may still be a devout Buddhist rather than a merely nominal one), and the 'noble disciple' who has glimpsed Nibbāna and who is genuinely committed to the understanding and practice of the Dhamma." Bluck, "The Path of the Householder: Buddhist Lay Disciples in the Pali Canon," *Buddhist Studies Review* 19 (2002): 18.

Without in any way denying the training benefits of homeleaver practice, ordaining as a bhikkhu or bhikkhunī is not a necessary condition for realizing the soteriological aim of the Dharma, and an overemphasis on—or, I would suggest instead, a misapplication of—the householder-versus-homeleaver distinction can have the effect of mistakenly underwriting a lay practitioner's exemption from the work the path entails. That such exemption also runs the risk of keeping one from realizing the promise of the Dharma simply follows as a matter of course.

The case is more nuanced from the Christian side. Of the three Abrahamic faiths, Christianity stands out as having developed a strong renunciant-contemplative current.[57] Even so, such practice has continued to arouse suspicion—if not outright condemnation—in most every era of its history, particularly in the Christian West. There are any number of reasons for this, but here I would simply highlight two. First, the overwhelmingly corporate nature of much of Christian religious expression tends to render suspect those who would devote themselves to living a life of quiet contemplative prayer, whether on their own or in the company of a small group of other like-minded persons. The sacramental life of the church requires all of the structure and oversight of a communal assembly or *ecclesia*, and deviations from that model can be tolerated only within certain margins. When the renunciant-contemplative life has not been condemned outright, it has been sanctioned more often than not as a grudging and carefully circumscribed concession for a select few rather than being commended as a fitting form of practice generally.

Second, since the Reformation, there has been such an insistence on leveling distinctions in spiritual attainment among individuals that anything that even hints at the slightest suggestion of some purported spiritual elitism is suspect from the start.[58] The abolition of the monasteries in many Reformation

57 The key difference here is that, while Judaism and Islam both denounce voluntary celibacy, Christianity has extolled it as a virtue, albeit a supererogatory one. Without acknowledging a value in voluntary celibacy, monasticism as an ongoing form of religious expression cannot get off the ground. See Glenn Holland, "Celibacy in the Early Christian Church," in *Celibacy and Religious Traditions*, ed. Carl Olson (New York: Oxford University Press, 2008), 65–84.

58 Martin Luther's critique of monasticism, for instance, was aimed more at the presumed spiritual superiority of the monk over the layperson than at the nature of the practice itself. See Dorothea Wendebourg, "Luther on Monasticism," in *The Pastoral Luther*, ed. Timothy J. Wingert (Minneapolis: Fortress, 2017), 335.

lands had the side effect of casting into disuse many of the renunciant-contemplative practices that had been developed in and around them—living the evangelical counsels of poverty, chastity, and obedience; direct personal guidance by those more advanced in the practice; and conformity to a rule of life that offers scant concessions to individuality and personal preference—as just so many bald attempts to somehow curry greater favor with God or esteem from one's neighbors. The resultant universalizing and equalizing attitudes, whether negative ("We are all sinners") or positive ("All spiritual paths are valid"), as vacuous and as vapid as they are, have had the effect of reducing spiritual practice either to a form of breezy self-actualization or, should it extend beyond the self—without, however, *surrendering* the self, it must be said—to social work and activism aimed at social transformation.

Still, it remains the case that each person is ultimately responsible for his or her own spiritual life, no one is exempt from the consequences of one's own actions and states of mind, and there is no shelter from facing those consequences in the observation that one is "just as good" or "just as bad" as everyone else. John Chrysostom, for one, is quite clear on this point:

> You greatly delude yourself and err, if you think that one thing is demanded from the layman and another from the monk; since the difference between them is in that whether one is married or not, while in everything else they have the same responsibilities . . . because all must rise to the same height; and what has turned the world upside down is that we think only the monk must live rigorously, while the rest are allowed to live a life of indolence.[59]

So, as is the case with all noble disciples in the Dharma, it can be argued that the Christian monastic and the dedicated Christian layperson have the same task given to them as well, irrespective of their station in life. That most everyday Christians (or even most everyday Buddhists, to be honest) elect not to pursue it does not invalidate or diminish the importance of its exercise in the least.

The second caveat is that, because of the limited focus of this study, some readers may notice certain things missing. Those familiar with the Evagrian corpus, for instance, will find only limited engagement with Evagrius's more speculative philosophical and theological work. This certainly saves us from having to wade too deeply into the rather murky waters of Evagrius's purported "Origenism," if nothing else, but it also frees us from the need to settle

59 John Chrysostom, *Pros piston patera* (To the Faithful Father) 3, 14; in PG 47:372–74.

on just how "Stoic," "Platonic, or "Aristotelian" Evagrius was.[60] The Evagrius we encounter in conjunction with his discussion of the logismoi is more the articulate monk and spiritual father, and less the speculative philosopher-theologian. Without taking time here to explain how I would align the two in any detail, suffice it to say that I view Evagrius's use of philosophical and theological concepts as being in service to his understanding and practice of the life of renunciation and prayer, rather than the other way around.[61]

Scholars and practitioners of the Mahāyāna might be rather curious as regards the overwhelming focus here on the *Nikāyas*. To this I can only respond that the practice of the Mahāyāna begins where the practice of any school of the Dharma begins. While the path of the bodhisattva may well extend beyond that of the arhat, there is no bodhisattva who does not first practice—and come to perfect—the threefold discipline of morality (*sīla*), contemplation (samādhi), and wisdom (paññā/prajñā), and this necessarily includes confronting and overcoming the nīvaraṇas.

Some of the brightest lights of the Mahāyāna were quite clear on this point. Nāgārjuna, for one, knew the dangers the nīvaraṇas posed for bodhisattvic aspiration:

> Ill-will, excitedness-and-regretfulness,
> Lethargy-and-drowsiness, desire, and doubtfulness—

---

60 Ample work has been done on this already. For rather comprehensive accounts of the relationship between Evagrius's writings on the logismoi and his theological-philosophical intellectual horizon, see Antoine Guillaumont, *Un philosophe au désert: Évagre le Pontique* (Paris: Vrin, 2004); Kevin Corrigan, *Evagrius and Gregory: Mind, Soul and Body in the 4th Century* (New York: Routledge, 2009); and Leszek Misiarczyk, *Eight* Logismoi *in the Writings of Evagrius Ponticus* (Turnhout: Brepols, 2021).

61 Guy Strousma puts this understanding of Evagrius particularly aptly: "We do not see in Evagrius simply 'a philosopher in the desert,' as Antoine Guillaumont has called him. For Evagrius, the gnostic has only one goal in his teaching (a goal ignored by the philosopher): he must teach salvation. Even as deep a thinker and independent a mind as Evagrius, then, remains first of all a spiritual master." See Strousma, "From Master of Wisdom to Spiritual Master in Late Antiquity," in *Religion and the Self in Antiquity*, ed. David Brakke, Michael L. Satlow, and Steven Weitzman (Bloomington: Indiana University Press, 2006), 192. This stands counter to a view, such as Linge's, that "the great unifying theme at work throughout Evagrius's thought is to be found in the Platonic ideas of the 'coming forth' of an original, spiritual cosmos from God, its fall into the plurality and becoming of the material-visible world, and its ultimate return to its original harmony with the transcendent Source" (Linge, "Leading the Life of Angels," 543). Evagrius no more needs Plato to account for the journey of the prodigal back home than Jesus does in Luke's Gospel.

Insurgent thieves such as these five hindrances
Constantly steal away all benefits of goodness.[62]

In the *Mahāprajñāpāramitā Upadeśa*, or *Instruction on the Great Perfection of Wisdom,* he addressed each of the hindrances in turn while expounding the perfection of contemplation (*dhyāna pāramitā*), and went on to conclude:

> It is just as with the sun and moon which may be obscured by five things: When they are blocked by smoke, clouds, dust, fog, or the hand of Rāhu the *asura*, they are unable to shine brightly. So too it is with a person's mind. When it is covered over by the five hindrances, one remains unable to benefit oneself and also unable to be of help to others.[63]

Indeed, the *Aṣṭasāhasrikā Prajñāpāramitā,* or *Perfection of Wisdom in Eight Thousand Lines*, lists the five hindrances among those things the mind will need to abandon to ever come to the fullness of the perfections (*pāramitās*).[64] So if Asaṅga could write, "[A bodhisattva] is a person in whom the mental afflictions are naturally weak, the hindrances [to meditative composure] are [naturally] weak, and [the states of] indisposition are [naturally] weak,"[65] one can only assume that where the bodhisattva is not "naturally" unswayed by the nīvaraṇas, he or she will be all too eager to do the work of overcoming them. In fact, the *Ugraparipṛcchā*, one of the most influential of the early Mahāyāna texts, lists the nīvaraṇas among those things an aspiring lay bodhisattva dreads so much that he takes to the wilderness and engages in added austerities better to confront and abandon them.[66] That Mahāyāna writers did

62 Nāgārjuna, *Letter from a Friend: A Bodhisattva's Advice to an Indian King on Right Living and the Buddhist Path,* The Suhṛllekha, *An Epistle Composed for King Śatakarṇī by Ārya Nāgārjuna (circa 200 CE)*, trans. Bhikshu Dharmamitra (Seattle: Kalavinka, 2009), 133. Evagrius, it is worth noting here, also referred to the logismoi as "thieves" (Evagrius, *Eulogios* 13.12; Sinkewicz, 38.)

63 Nāgārjuna, *Nāgārjuna on the Six Perfections*, 633. Rāhu is a titan (*asura*) whose body, according to the mythology, is as large as the great mountain Sumeru of Buddhist cosmology; from a human perspective, his hand would therefore be large enough to eclipse the sun and moon.

64 Edward Conze, trans., *The Perfection of Wisdom in Eight Thousand Lines and Its Verse Summary* (San Francisco: City Lights, 2006), 276.

65 Asaṅga, *The Bodhisattva Path to Unsurpassed Enlightenment. A Complete Translation of the* Bodhisattvabhūmi, trans. Artemus B. Engle (Boulder, CO: Snow Lion, 2016), 14–15.

66 Jan Nattier, *A Few Good Men: The Bodhisattva Path according to* The Inquiry of Ugra (Ugraparipṛcchā) (Honolulu: University of Hawai'i Press, 2003), 296–97.

not spill much ink on the hindrances overall (hence offering scant material to work with here) should in no way be taken to imply that they are irrelevant, or that the task of overcoming them on a personal level runs in any way counter to the bodhisattvic vow to liberate all beings.

Finally, the reader will find in these pages no extended discussion of the nature of the ultimate ends of practice in either tradition—nirvāṇa, theōsis, Buddhahood, prajñā, the kingdom of heaven, gnōsis, enlightenment, and the like. Still less will one find any attempt to equate, compare, or contrast them. Such exercises carried out by persons who have not come to know them directly for themselves—this author first among them—can produce little that is of much value. More importantly, however, if, as both Evagrius and the Buddha unequivocally maintain, the end of the path lies beyond thoughts, beyond words, beyond signs, beyond images, and beyond forms, we can do no better service than to maintain a noble silence with respect to them, particularly in a context such as this where thoughts, words, signs, images, and forms are the order of the day. If such must be used, best they be used where they can be most skillfully and fruitfully deployed for the benefit and ease of many.

PART ONE

The Renunciant Horizon

CHAPTER ONE

The Practical Life

Athanasius may have noted that the desert had been "made a city" by the large number of monks who settled there, but he singled out one, Antony, for particular mention. His *Life of Antony* enjoyed a vast readership, and before long his depiction of Antony's experiences in the desert came to stand as a model for the renunciant life itself.[1] Athanasius offers this account of Antony's homeleaving:

> He was left alone, after his parents' death, with one quite young sister. He was about eighteen or even twenty years old, and he was responsible both for the home and his sister. Six months had not passed since the death of his parents when, going to the Lord's house as usual and gathering his thoughts, he considered while he walked how the apostles, forsaking everything, followed the Savior, and how in Acts some sold what they possessed and took the proceeds and placed them at the feet of the apostles for distribution among those in need, and what great hope is stored up for such people in heaven. He went into the church pondering these things, and just then it happened that the Gospel was being read, and he heard the Lord saying to the rich man, *If you would be perfect, go, sell what you possess and give it to the poor, and you will have treasure in heaven.*

So, Antony did just that. He handed over his land, some two hundred acres, to the townsfolk, sold off his movable property, and gave most of the proceeds to the poor, keeping some money and goods in reserve for his sister. Soon enough, he found himself back in the church:

> When, entering the Lord's house once more, he heard in the Gospel the Lord saying, *Do not be anxious about tomorrow*, he could not remain any

1 Antony (251–356) is often called "Father of All Monks," though this is misleading, since there were others ahead of him.

> longer, but going out he gave those remaining possessions also to the needy. Placing his sister in the charge of respected and trusted virgins, and giving her over to the convent for rearing, he devoted himself from then on to the discipline rather than the household, giving heed to himself and patiently training himself.[2]

Antony was certainly not the first to have heard these words, and he was also not the first to heed them. But many *had* heard these words without taking the decisive step that Antony did. In fact, if they had frequented the synaxis at all regularly, they would have heard not only these but many more similar words besides—words to the effect that the rich cannot enter the kingdom of God (Matt 19:24), that one must deny oneself and take up one's own cross (Matt 16:24), that one must turn away from one's kinfolk (Luke 14:26), and that clinging to one's life is a surefire way to lose it (Matt 16:25). Even still, they did not take that next step.

But as those around him watched what came to pass once Antony had taken that step, they began to see something that was all too rare in the social landscape. Here now was one who obediently learned graciousness, eagerness for prayer, freedom from anger, patience, and watchfulness from the example of others, incorporating them all into his own life. Soon enough "all those . . . who were from his village and those good people with whom he associated, seeing him living thus, [called] him 'God-loved,' and some hailed him as 'son,' and some as 'brother.'"[3] And if there were any in the church who had heard the same words that Antony had and were taken by what had transpired once he followed them, they might have begun to wonder whether they, too, might be capable of such a life. Surely not all were capable, for, as they would also have heard, "not everyone can accept this teaching, but only those to whom it is given" (Matt 19:11). But that faint stirring within them might have given them some confidence, however slight, that they might become worthy of joining the likes of Antony, both in the discipline and in the fruits of that discipline. The question, of course, was *how* to do that.

Evagrius's account of the renunciant-contemplative life begins by asking a variation on that very question: "What sort of state does the mind need so that it can reach out to its Lord without turning back and commune with him

2 Athanasius, *Life of Antony*, 31–32.

3 Athanasius, *Life of Antony*, 32–33.

without intermediary?"[4] To understand his answer requires first understanding the specific way he casts the question and, in particular, his understanding of *mind*, *communion*, and *intermediary*.

Evagrius made use of a philosophical-theological anthropology that, drawing on various sources in Plato, Aristotle, Origen, and the biblical tradition, viewed the person as a holistically indivisible body/soul/mind.[5] These are not three otherwise discrete, *independent substances* that are then somehow conjoined with one another: rather, they are three *distinctive modes* of the awareness and activity of one and the same person.

The body is the point of one's contact with the world, both in terms of receiving what the world has to offer and as the means through which one makes one's way in it. This is what Evagrius calls the "intelligible" or experiencing body, as distinct from the "sensible" or experienced body. The sensible body is the object viewed by an outside observer: a mass of skin, flesh, organs, and bones. The intelligible body, by contrast, is not an object among objects but rather "involves organized development between higher possibilities or their opposites . . . an *interplay of activities* in the drama of possibilities, potentialities, and privations, which provides the organic sub-text for the five senses."[6] It is the body considered from the perspective of the embodied person. The intelligible body is perceived as *alive* and *dynamic*—defined not so much by its material composition but by the range of its powers. Through those powers, there is ongoing interaction with the world, and that interaction defines both what one takes to be one's body and what one takes to be the world.[7]

The soul, which gives direction to the body beyond simple reactivity, is the complex seat of affective life, encompassing rational, appetitive, and irascible

---

4 Evagrius, *Prayer* 3; Sinkewicz, 193.

5 Here is not the place to rehearse the intricacies of Evagrius's rather unsystematic rendering of these aspects and their relation to one another; others have more than sufficiently undertaken that task. See Guillaumont, *Un philosophe au désert*, 205–34; Corrigan, *Evagrius and Gregory*, 39–44; Misiarczyk, *Eight Logismoi*, 50–63. That said, the core idea that mind, soul, and body are inseparable is one Evagrius would have certainly learned from his teacher, Gregory of Nyssa. See Ramelli, "Gregory and Evagrius," 179.

6 Corrigan, *Evagrius and Gregory*, 114–15.

7 On this dynamic conception of the body and its relation to the soul and the mind among Evagrius's contemporaries, see Lisa D. Maugans Driver, "Apophatic Theophanies: Incarnational Knowledge of God in Early Eastern Christianity," in *The Routledge Handbook of Religion and the Body*, ed. Yudit Kornberg Greenberg and George Pati (New York: Routledge, 2023), 52–68.

dimensions. It guides the body in terms of assessing what to desire, what to avoid, and how to maintain the proper balance between them. Through a kind of ongoing negotiation between the body and the mind, it seeks out what is beneficial and good, avoids what is harmful and evil, and through all of that acts in accordance with a vision of the whole created order: "The rational soul acts according to nature when its concupiscible part longs for virtue, and the irascible part struggles on its behalf, and the rational part perceives the contemplation of beings."[8] Properly attuned, the soul serves a person in engaging with the particulars of the world in light of a sound awareness of how those particulars fit within the larger framework of the whole of creation.

That awareness is the domain of the mind, the seat of direct, intuitive knowledge of God and of a comprehensive, God-given understanding of the created order. Although immaterial, the mind is able to engage with the body through the rational soul by means of a range of concepts and mental representations (*noēmata*), the afterimages or echoes of sensory and psychophysical experience. Evagrius identifies four ways that the mind grasps these mental representations: through the eyes, hearing, memory, and temperament.[9] Those grasped through the body (eyes, ears, etc.) are rather unproblematic, since they are simply what healthy, functioning sense capabilities bring forth. Those grasped through memory and temperament, however, can be unproblematic or problematic, depending on the state of the soul, and the state of the soul depends on the state of the mind's awareness of God.

When the soul follows a mind that is cleared of everything but God, it guides the individual properly, because such a mind, now free of any obstructions, reflects "the image of God within us, that which is most like unto its creator."[10] Memory and temperament are then ordered such that they accord with the whole of God's creation, even as they direct one's particular responses to discrete sensory phenomena. However, when a soul follows a mind that has been obstructed in its clear vision of God, it directs one's bodily activity inappropriately. In this case, the soul relies on the individual's own limited self-understanding in assessing and responding to the world around it, placing his own ends in the place of God's. The state of one's mind can be read from one's actions, and so little are the mind, soul, and body to be separated

8 Evagrius, *Praktikos* 86; Sinkewicz, 111.

9 Evagrius, *Reflections* 17; Sinkewicz, 212.

10 William Harmless, SJ, and Raymond R. Fitzgerald, SJ, "The Sapphire Light of the Mind: The *Skemmata* of Evagrius Ponticus," *TS* 62 (2001): 513.

from one another that "the body by its actions reveals what the soul which dwells in it is like, and the soul in its turn by its movements proclaims what the mind, which is its head, is like."[11]

The mind is that aspect of the human person that is of the same nature as God. As such, it finds its most natural expression in prayer, which Evagrius calls a "communion of the mind with God."[12] This communion involves more than *conversing* with God, as Clement of Alexandria, for one, suggests. Clement hewed quite closely to a communicative model of prayer, right down to an account of sender, receiver, and the message relayed: "So even if we speak to him silently in a whisper without moving the lips, we cry out interiorly. For God listens unceasingly to all our interior converse."[13] Conversation, even such quiet, interior conversation, still involves a separation between God and the one who prays; one "talks" while the other "listens," even if tongues and ears are not actually involved. Clement himself indicates as much when he suggests that, even though God does not have hearing and sight in the ordinary sense, "there is the malleability of the air and the very acute sensitive faculty common to angels, and also the power of the conscience which, by a slight contact with the soul, knows everything by means of an ineffable power and without the aid of sensitive hearing, by immediate intellection."[14] This is enough to account for how the messages are transmitted: "Is their transport," Clement writes, "not assured by (our) conscience?"[15]

Evagrius, on the other hand, envisions the communion of prayer in a way that does not involve such logistics; rather, it is "a communion of constant presence, free of words and forms."[16] It is an intimate and abiding communion that fulfills Paul's injunction to "pray without ceasing" (1 Thess 5:17) because it is not an action one *does*—hence starting and stopping like any other action—but expresses rather what one *is*, namely, one who, from the very beginning, has been abundantly infused with the spirit of God. It is prayer that fulfills, from the human side, Christ's own vision of union with God: "As you, Father, are in me and I am in you, may they also be in us" (John

---

11 Evagrius, *Letter to Melania* 4, in M. Parmentier, "Evagrius of Pontus, 'Letter to Melania,'" *Bijdr* 46 (1985): 10.

12 Evagrius, *Prayer* 3; Sinkewicz, 193.

13 Clement of Alexandria, *Stromateis* 7.7.39.6, in *Les Stromates. Stromate VII*, trans. Alain Le Boulleuc (Paris: Cerf, 1997), 141; translated in Sinkewicz, 275n7.

14 Clement, *Stromateis* 7.7.37.2, in Le Boulleuc, 135; translation mine.

15 Clement, *Stromateis* 7.7.37.5, in Le Boulleuc, 137; translation mine.

16 Sinkewicz, 275n7.

17:21). This communion, however, is only possible as long as nothing stands between the mind and God. Because there is nothing in the divine nature, or in the created order arising from that divine nature, that could possibly stand in the way of this union, any obstruction must come from the one who prays.

Evagrius identifies self-love (*philautia*) as the fundamental obstruction, the root cause of all the further obstructions that can separate a person from God.[17] Self-love is clinging to an image of oneself as the standard and measure of all things. Under the rubric of that self-image, an individual then creates images of the world, others, and even God, not as they truly are, but as he takes them to be—so many things that either help or hinder him in his own project of identity formation and maintenance. Communion with God is impossible as long as the individual approaches that communion loaded with such an array of self-created clutter; as long as it is in tow, he will never be able to know God as God is, but rather as he fancies God to be.

True prayer "is a state of mind destructive of every earthly mental representation,"[18] including the root representation one makes of oneself. It is *imageless* prayer, one that "[approaches] the immaterial immaterially."[19] But such prayer is fundamentally less about the mere presence or nonpresence of images (a philosophical point) and more about surrendering the *drive* to hold on to thoughts and images by which one defines oneself independently of God (a point of contemplative life). Any prayer that is still driven by images and thoughts, whether of the morrow, the world, others, or even God, can only ever lead one back to oneself, since the origin of those thoughts lies completely within oneself to begin with. "One who loves God," Evagrius writes, "is ever communing with him as with a father, while turning away any mental representations tied to the passions."[20] Contemplation of the divinity and the renunciation of self are two sides of the same coin.

"Those to whom it is given" to enter into communion with God, then, are those who, having cleared the mind of all that is not of God by having first brought the soul in its constituent aspects into proper relation, have made themselves open to receiving that divine light. Now we can return to that initial question, "What sort of state does the mind need so that it can reach out to its Lord without turning back and commune with him without

17 Evagrius, *Reflections* 53; Sinkewicz, 215.

18 Evagrius, *Reflections* 26; Sinkewicz, 213.

19 Evagrius, *Prayer* 66; Sinkewicz, 199.

20 Evagrius, *Prayer* 54; Sinkewicz, 198.

intermediary?" The answer is what Evagrius calls a state of "pure prayer," and purifying one's soul of self-love is the first and primary order of business on the path to its attainment.

"Pray first to receive tears," Evagrius counsels the novice, "so that through compunction you may be able to mollify the wildness that is in your soul."[21] For an individual who is wholly under the sway of self-love, everything that he encounters will be subject to his own standard and measure: pursuing or accepting something if it conforms to his liking, avoiding or rejecting it if it does not. One who is subject to self-love neither measures one's actions in accordance with the demands of others, whether people or God, nor does one act in accordance with the constraints of the lived environment. The commandments of God and the simple dictates of nature are overridden with a conception of selfhood that fancies itself to be beyond subjection to either of them. But rather than demonstrating the self's power, such self-love actually reveals itself to be a heart of stone that is unresponsive to anyone or anything other than oneself.

Compunction—the Greek is *katanyxis*; the Latin, *compunctio*—is a piercing or a puncturing that penetrates that hardened heart, rendering it pliable and, to follow the metaphor, *porous*. It opens an awareness within the individual, however faint at the start, of the plain truth that one has in fact been following one's own inclinations rather than heeding the commandments. Even more to the point, this puncturing allows one to see that there even *is* a distinction between the two to begin with. To be sure, one may have *heard* the commandments and may in some ways even have *acknowledged* them. But letting them do their transformative work of rendering one completely at God's disposal without holding anything back will have come across as a threat—not because there is anything intrinsically threatening about them, but simply because they call that self-hardening into question.

With one's heart punctured, one can begin to recognize oneself for what one is—a plain and equal member of God's creation subject to God's command. This recognition is the beginning of humility.[22] "Compunction inte-

---

21 Evagrius, *Prayer* 5; Sinkewicz, 193.

22 Jeremy Driscoll provides a particularly poignant reflection on Evagrius's understanding of humility. See Jeremy Driscoll, OSB, "Gentleness in the *Ad Monachos* of Evagrius Ponticus," *StMon* 32 (1990): 309.

grally opens up the heart to others and to the whole created world,"[23] not from a position of superiority but from a position of utter lowliness. "If you measure yourself by the lowest measure," Evagrius writes, "you will not compare your measure to another. The person who discloses the weakness of his soul by his lamentations will not hold a high opinion of the ascetic labours he undertakes for himself, nor will he even give his attention to the faults of others."[24] One gifted with the tears of compunction will, with eyes lowered, focus only on one's own failings and the work to be done to overcome them.

This lowliness is not a crass abasement, however. The humility wrought by compunction and its accompanying tears softens the heart in a second, perhaps unexpected way—namely, by making it come more fully *alive*, like a heart of flesh where there had only been one of stone, filling it with an "infinite longing for the divine and an immeasurable zeal for work."[25] Having now sensed the activity of God directly in one's person in a limited but deeply visceral way, and having had a small taste of the freedom and vitality that comes with it, one responds by reaching out even more energetically toward God. The renunciant-contemplative life is nothing but the ongoing expression of that reaching out, and Evagrius's outline of the structure of that life is one that is designed to take that first puncturing and expand it further and further until there is nothing left to hinder one from an abiding communion in the love of God.

For Evagrius, this is a thoroughly Christian undertaking: "Christianity is the doctrine of Christ our Saviour. It is comprised of the practical, the natural, and the theological."[26] The practical, *praktikē*, involves ascetic training aimed at curbing the passions. The contemplation of the created order, *theōria physikē*, develops the aspirant's sense of the right relation between the spiritual and material worlds. The theological, *theologikē*, is nothing other than the direct knowledge of God. While these are three successive levels, they are all of a piece on a continuum of practice. Evagrius understood prayer to be a "wordless, imageless mystical ascent to God"[27] across all three levels, and it is marked by renunciation from beginning to end: "If you long to practice prayer," he writes, "renounce absolutely all things, so that you may inherit the

23 Kevin Corrigan and Gregory Yuri Glazov, "Compunction and Compassion: Two Overlooked Virtues in Evagrius of Pontus," *JECS* 22 (2014): 69.

24 Evagrius, *Eulogios* 3.4; Sinkewicz, 31.

25 Evagrius, *Praktikos* 57; Sinkewicz, 107–8.

26 Evagrius, *Praktikos* 1; Sinkewicz, 97.

27 Harmless and Fitzgerald, "Sapphire Light," 506.

whole."[28] Evagrius describes a threefold renunciation that roughly corresponds to this tripartite philosophical-theological anthropology—the abandonment of worldly things in relation to the body, the abandonment of evilness in the soul, and abandonment of ignorance in the mind.

The first renunciation begins by removing oneself from the run of everyday life and taking up the life of practice through a "voluntary abandonment of the things of the world for the sake of the knowledge of God."[29] For Evagrius, things do not have value—positive or negative—in and of themselves; that value is derived from their place and function within a form of embodied life and its own internal standard of value. The abandonment of *worldly* things, then, involves first walking away from the very *world* that values them. Talk of leaving the world might strike one as outlandish, so when Evagrius writes that "the first of the illustrious contests is voluntary exile" (*xenetia*), he offers a simile that most anyone could easily understand: "like an athlete stripped of homeland, family, and possessions."[30] Elsewhere, he relies on a soldiering metaphor to make the same point: "He should be a soldier of Christ, freed from matter and from anxieties, uninvolved in any business concerns and activities: as the Apostle says, 'No one serving in the army gets entangled in everyday affairs, since his aim is to please the enlisting officer.'"[31]

The athlete and soldier value what most everyone else does not—hours and hours of drills, a diet, and an attire that conforms to the task at hand. Consequently, the athlete and soldier cannot value what most everyone else does—plenty of time for doing what one feels like, eating whatever strikes one's fancy, and wearing clothes and amassing things just because they are in some way pleasing. To continue to live and associate with everyone else would mean to risk falling in again with their values, losing sight of one's own aims, and thwarting one's ability to see them through to completion. The case is no different for the aspiring monk:

> Do you want therefore, beloved, to take up the solitary life for what it is, and to race after the trophies of stillness? Leave behind the concerns of the world, the

28 Evagrius, *Prayer* 36; Sinkewicz, 196.

29 Evagrius, *On Thoughts* 26; Sinkewicz, 172. See also Evagrius, *Kephalaia Gnostika* 1.78, in Kephalaia Gnostika: *A New Translation of the Unreformed Text from the Syriac*, trans. Ilaria L. E. Ramelli (Atlanta: SBL Press, 2015), 73. Further quotations from the *Kephalaia Gnostika* will be cited as Evagrius, *Kephalaia Gnostika* section number; Ramelli, page number.

30 Evagrius, *Eulogios* 2; Sinkewicz, 29.

31 Evagrius, *Foundations* 2; Sinkewicz, 5. The reference is to 2 Tim 2:4.

> principalities and powers set over them (Eph. 6:12); that is, stand free of material concerns and the passions, beyond all desire, so that as you become a stranger to the conditions deriving from these you may be able to cultivate stillness properly. For if one were not to extricate himself from these, he would not be able to live this life successfully.[32]

The monk's success, like the success of the soldier and the athlete, requires this separation from the distractions of the world as a matter of practical necessity.

It is important to note that, again just like the athlete and the soldier, the aspirant does not undertake this separation out of any sense of misanthropy—*people* themselves are not the problem; the *values of the world* they create are. The values of the world arise from the same kind of self-love that had guided the aspirant himself before his having been stirred in the life of God by compunction. "The person who lives with those who are material-minded and involved in business affairs shares completely in their circumstances and becomes enslaved to human impositions, idle conversations, and all sorts of other dangers—anger, sadness, madness over material things, fear and scandal," Evagrius writes.[33] Such folk may well play their flutes, to borrow the Gospel metaphor, but the monk no longer joins them in the dance; they may sing their dirges, but the monk no longer joins them in their wailing (Matt 11:17). Those people will do what they do; the monk simply has something else to do.

What does one do, then, when such social promptings are taken away? Evagrius wrote primarily for those intent on taking up the semi-anchoritic, and eventually the anchoritic, life.[34] While a monastic in a cenobitic community will have an established rule that stands in place of the ordering of the everyday world, the solitary or semisolitary had to figure this out more or less on one's own—that is, of course, unless one could find someone from whom to receive good counsel. Evagrius's *Foundations of the Monastic Life*[35] provides just such counsel in the absence of a close *abba* or *amma*. "Be like a very good businessman," Evagrius advises the monk, "evaluating everything

32 Evagrius, *Foundations* 3; Sinkewicz, 5.

33 Evagrius, *Foundations* 5; Sinkewicz, 7.

34 "Either live alone or with brothers who are free of material concerns and think as you do," he counsels (Evagrius, *Foundations* 5; Sinkewicz, 7).

35 The full title is *The Foundations of the Monastic Life: A Presentation of the Practice of Stillness.*

with regard to the cultivation of stillness and always retaining those things that are peaceful and useful in this regard (cf. I Thess 5:21)."[36]

Since everyone needs to eat, recommendations concerning food come first. One should not use those foods that are "pleasant" but those that are "beneficial,"[37] with benefit here understood not as an optimal proportion of macronutrients or the like but as being conducive to apatheia: "Adhere to a frugal and measly diet, without great quantities and the sorts that easily cause distractions."[38] These distractions can come in any number of forms. One might have to do with the frequency of meals. One meal a day keeps the body alive; any more than that leads to extravagance and "trouble[s] your thinking."[39] But the exhortation to eat but one meal a day should not itself turn into yet another source of vexation: "But if a visit from brothers should occur and there is need for you to eat a second and a third time, do not be sullen and downcast; rejoice rather that you are obedient to necessity and, eating a second or third meal, give thanks to God himself as the one who disposes for your life."[40] Sickness places similar demands on the monk: "There will also be times when sickness of the body comes along and makes it necessary for you to eat a second and third time or even more often: so do not let your thoughts be saddened by this."[41] In addition to concerns about *how frequently* to eat, fretting over *what* to eat raises yet another set of distractions. Evagrius counsels against being overly fastidious about particular foodstuffs, noting that nothing is inherently forbidden according to the Christian Scriptures (Matt 15:11). That said, he advises the monk not to "become a lover of fine foods or the deceits of an indulgent lifestyle," filling one's belly "with foods favored by worldly people lest you acquire a craving for these and that in turn instil within you a craving to eat at their tables."[42]

Concerning clothing, the monk should "entertain no desire for extra clothing" but instead "make provision for those sufficient to meet the needs of the body. . . . Having therefore what you need for the present time, do not worry

---

36 Evagrius, *Foundations* 6; Sinkewicz, 7.

37 Evagrius, *Maxims* 18; Sinkewicz, 230.

38 Evagrius, *Foundations* 3; Sinkewicz, 5.

39 Evagrius, *Foundations* 10; Sinkewicz, 10. One can easily imagine some of the kinds of distractions Evagrius might have had in mind: "Should I eat more now and less later?" "Should I eat again before or after work?"

40 Evagrius, *Foundations* 10; Sinkewicz, 10.

41 Evagrius, *Foundations* 10; Sinkewicz, 10.

42 Evagrius, *Foundations* 8; Sinkewicz, 8.

about the future, whether that be a day, a week, or some months."[43] Moreover, one should avoid adornment, since it carries with it mental representations that carry one from the simple covering of the body toward thoughts of display and attractiveness—meaning that distracting thoughts of sex are not far behind. Addressing a monk, Evagrius writes, "One who adorns his clothing and fills his stomach shepherds shameful thoughts and with the chaste he keeps no company"; addressing a virgin, the caution is much the same: "She who adorns her clothing will also be wanting in chastity."[44]

Sexual temptations notwithstanding, the most important thing with respect to clothing, just as with food, is becoming free of the excessive concern with it, as pointed out in the Scriptures (Matt 6:28–32):

> Therefore, after laying aside the thoughts of anxiety, let us cast our anxiety on the Lord (cf. Ps 54:23; 1 Pet. 5:7) and be satisfied with what we now have (cf. Heb. 13:5); and living in poverty of life and clothing, let us cast off by day the authors of vainglory. If anyone thinks it unseemly to be in poor clothing, let him look at St. Paul who awaited the crown of righteousness "in cold and nakedness" (2 Cor. 11:27; 2 Tim. 4:8).[45]

Such excessive concern even extends to any thought one might entertain about stocking up on food and clothing in order to be of benefit to others. Concerning food, for example, Evagrius cautions that one should not secure food "for reasons of hospitality"; concerning possessions, one should not seek to have riches "in order to make donations to the poor."[46] And if one were to consider taking on a serving boy in part to benefit the lad, Evagrius counsels, "Do not let yourself be persuaded. This is not our work; it is the work of others, of the holy fathers living in community."[47] All of those seemingly good reasons, he points out, are deceptions from the evil one. This does not mean that one should not practice charity: "If you possess a surplus of these things, give to one who needs them," Evagrius adds in his discussion of clothing.[48] It means that amassing food and provisions *in order to* engage in charitable

43 Evagrius, *Foundations* 4; Sinkewicz, 6.

44 Evagrius, *To Monks* 82; Sinkewicz, 127; Evagrius, *To a Virgin* 23; Sinkewicz, 133.

45 Evagrius, *On Thoughts* 6; Sinkewicz, 157.

46 Evagrius, *Foundations* 3–4; Sinkewicz, 5–6.

47 Evagrius, *Foundations* 5; Sinkewicz, 6. Here we find already at the outset a distinction between the more anchoritic practice of Evagrius and his brothers and the cenobitic practice of the proto-monasteries such as the one Pachomius had recently founded at Tabennisi further south.

48 Evagrius, *Foundations* 4; Sinkewicz, 6.

work runs counter to this first renunciation (and to the subsequence ones as well, it should be noted). Mary's portion is not Martha's; few things at all are needed in conjunction with it, and certainly not any *concern* about attending to the material conditions of others, even as one might *happen to* benefit those in need, should circumstances present themselves. *Responding* to the needs of others does not involve calculation or the deployment of an agenda the way that *planning to accommodate* the needs of others does.[49]

Evagrius's counsels are anything but extreme. There is no suggestion that one must limit oneself to a single crust of bread per day, or that one should shun all human contact or walk about naked. Instead, the point is to adjust one's inclinations to the real and present needs of the body, not subject the body to one's own conceptions, no matter how sensible or noble-minded they might first appear. Moreover, this first renunciation lies wholly within the power of the aspirant to set in motion once prompted with the sting of compunction. There is nothing at this level of training that lies outside the scope of human initiative and ability. Others, such as the soldier and the athlete, do this on their own as well. So, too, did others such as the Stoics.[50] What distinguishes the monk from the others is his aim: the soldier wants the approval of the commanding officer, the athlete wants the prize, the Stoic wants the well-lived life, but the monk desires "knowledge of God."[51] From here forward, any ready parallels between the monk and the athlete or soldier fall away, for the monk's is an aim wholly unlike any of theirs.

The ascetic practices of the first renunciation set the stage for those of the second, which require not only the resolve of the practitioner but the active presence of God: "The second [renunciation] is the rejection of evil which ensues by the grace of Christ our Saviour and by the zeal of the human individual."[52] Through the first renunciation, the monk has begun to curtail his interactions with his physical environment, so as to bring those interactions

49 This point will be taken up more fully below in Evagrius's discussion of gluttony and avarice.

50 David Linge points out that the discipline of the Evagrius and the other desert monastics went far beyond the "gentlemanly asceticism" of the Roman upper-class Stoics (Linge, "Leading the Life of Angels," 550–52). See also Albrecht Diem, "The Limitations of Asceticism," *Medieval Worlds: Comparati) ve & Interdisciplinary Studies* 9 (2019): 120.

51 Evagrius, *Kephalaia Gnostika* 1.78; Ramelli, 73.

52 Evagrius, *On Thoughts* 26; Sinkewicz, 172. See also Evagrius, *Kephalaia Gnostika* 1.79; Ramelli, 73.

into accord with the immediate material circumstances of embodied life. The point of this was to still the soul with respect to the body. Now, the monk begins to confront an even stronger adversary to the soul's stillness: the projections of his own mind.

> The demons war with seculars more through objects, but with monks they do so especially through thoughts, for they are deprived of objects because of the solitude. Further, to the extent that it is easier to sin in thought than in action, so is the warfare in thought more difficult than that which is conducted through objects. For the mind is a thing easily set in motion and difficult to check in its tendency towards unlawful fantasies.[53]

As David Linge notes, "It is the experience of ascetics that while physical austerities may quiet the body by weakening it, they actually *focus and intensify* [the] internal struggle with one's own imagination and inner dispositions."[54] This is certainly true in Evagrius's understanding:

> The more the soul progresses, the greater are the antagonists that follow in succession, for I am not convinced that it is always the same demons that persist against it. They know this best who perceive the temptations with greater precision and who see the impassability they have attained being dislodged by successive demons.[55]

These antagonists are the logismoi: broad, perduring mental projections that not directly tied to the senses but rather to the habitual framework of one's own thought processes arising from self-love.

Evagrius deploys the word *demons* in conjunction with the logismoi generally, almost interchangeably, and each *logismos* is spoken of as being its own particular demon. Before one starts importing fantastic imagery,[56] it is important to be clear about what Evagrius understands by the *demonic* in this context by relying on his own definition: "A demonic thought is the image of the sensible man, which is constituted in the intellect, in consort with which the mind, when moved passionately, says or does something unlawfully in secret and with respect to the image that has in turn crept in."[57] Or, again, "A demonic thought is a mental representation of a sensible

---

53 Evagrius, *Praktikos* 48; Sinkewicz, 106.

54 Linge, "Leading the Life of Angels," 552.

55 Evagrius, *Praktikos* 19; Sinkewicz, 108.

56 Hieronymus Bosch's *Triptych of the Temptation of St. Anthony* comes to mind.

57 Evagrius, *Reflections* 13; Sinkewicz, 212.

object, which moves the irascible or the concupiscible part in a manner contrary to nature."[58]

The demons are not external entities; still less are they ruses of some malevolent external agent. Blaming one's lot on the wiles of Satan, as people sometimes do, gives Satan more power than is his due. On this point, an episode from Athanasius's *Life of Antony* might shed some helpful light:

> Once someone knocked at the door of my cell. And when I went out, I saw someone who seemed massive and tall. When I asked, "Who are you?" he said, "I am Satan." I said, "What are you doing here?" And he asked, "Why do the monks and all the other Christians censure me without cause? Why do they curse me every hour?" When I replied, "Why do you torment them?" he said, "I am not the one tormenting them, but they disturb themselves, for I have become weak. . . . I no longer have a place—no weapon, no city. There are Christians everywhere, and even the desert has filled with monks. Let them watch after themselves and stop censuring me for no reason!"

Though Satan was a liar, Antony knew he was not lying now: "You have spoken truly. For Christ in his coming reduced you to weakness, and after throwing you down he left you defenseless."[59] It would be to deny the definitive triumph of the cross for a Christian to insist that Satan still has such power.

If the demonic logismoi do not have Satan as their source, still less are they banes sent by God. Evagrius appeals to Scripture to oppose "the thought that supposes that temptations come upon human beings from God: No one, when tempted, should say, 'I am being tempted by God'; for God cannot be tempted by evil and he himself tempts no one. But one is tempted by one's own desire (James 1:13–14)."[60] Evagrius need not have broken off there, for, as James continues, "one is tempted by one's own desire, being lured and enticed by it; then, when desire has conceived, it gives birth to sin, and that sin, when it is fully grown, gives birth to death" (Jas 1:14–15).[61] The aspirant

---

58 Evagrius, *Reflections*, supplementary chapter 2; Sinkewicz, 216.

59 Athanasius, *Life of Antony*, 62.

60 Evagrius, *Antirrhetikos* 2.61; in *Talking Back: A Monastic Handbook for Combating Demons. Antirrhêtikos*, trans. David Brakke (Collegeville, MN: Liturgical, 2009), 82.

61 Brouria Bitton-Ashkelony notes that in his understanding of prayer Evagrius "merged the ascetic and monastic impulses with the transcendent thought, but at the same time he disconnected his discourse from the Neoplatonic current of thought that was guided by the logic of theurgy a well as from the theological and exegetical context of the Lord's Prayer" Bitton-Ashkelony, "Theories of Prayer in Late Antiquity: Doubts and Practices from Maximos of Tyre to Isaac of Nineveh," in *Prayer and Worship in Eastern Christianities, 5th to 11th Centuries*, ed. Brouria Bitton-Ashkelony and Derek Krueger (New York: Routledge, 2016), 22.

is not some hapless bit player tossed about in a drama carried out on some grand stage by other, much more powerful, protagonists. One is the author of one's own troubles. The desires that set this whole business into motion are not a sin that needs redemption or forgiveness (sin, following James, is desire *unleashed*). Rather, they are a fact of the human condition: a fact that, once that human condition is understood in its completeness—as a desiring being, yes, but one who is also made in the image and likeness of God—can be seen for what it is, kept in its place, and cease stirring up troubles.

Even though such demonic thoughts are one's own creation, one needs to confront them *as if* they were externally generated in order to develop impassability toward them. The key to doing this is to fully engage with them—neither bypassing nor suppressing them, but observing in a disinterested, almost clinical way the conditions under which they arise, how they affect mental and bodily states, and what conditions are present when they subside. In short, one is invited to see them as having a life of their own:

> If one of the monks should wish to acquire experience with the cruel demons and become familiar with their skill, let him observe the thoughts and let him note their intensity and their relaxation, their interrelationships, their occasions, which of the demons do this or that particular thing, what sort of demon follows upon another and which does not follow another.

This, too, is to Evagrius's mind a thoroughly Christian undertaking, and he adds at the end of this counsel, "Let him seek from Christ the reasons for these things."[62]

Christ, too, was beset by such demons, and the account of his temptation in the wilderness provides the prototype of this kind of direct engagement. When confronted with the enticing thought of bodily satisfaction ("command these stones to become loaves of bread"), the assertion of a self that wants reality tailored to its liking ("throw yourself down . . . [and angels] will bear you up"), and the claim that the self should be honored above all else ("All these I will give you, if you fall down and worship me", Christ appealed to scriptural sources that bore witness to the ultimate primacy of God over each

---

Asking God to "lead us not into temptation" is a curious thing to do if one is indeed the source of one's own temptations, unless one has at one's disposal an understanding of prayer that can encompass both petitionary and contemplative elements, an understanding that, as she points out, Evagrius did not develop. In chapter 5, in conjunction with the logismos of sadness, we will see precisely why he did not feel the need to develop one, either.

62 Evagrius, *Praktikos* 50; Sinkewicz, 106.

(Matt 4:1–11). Supplanting one's own enticing thoughts with the testimony of Scripture serves to dislodge self-love in favor of the love of God. As the mind cannot hold two thoughts simultaneously,[63] where the thought of God is, there the thought of self cannot be.

This model—countering a demonic thought characterized by some particular aspect of self-love with a counterthought that focuses on God's unassailable place as the Lord of all—is one that Evagrius fully deployed in conjunction with each of the logismoi. His *Antirrhetikos* is a compendium of the correlative thoughts that accompany each of the logismoi, each one paired with a passage from Scripture that counters it.

In identifying the logismoi, Evagrius points to those things that anyone seeking stillness will find themselves confronting. They are, as he put it, *generic* types of thoughts, and while everyone is prone to them, not everyone will be prone to them in equal measure:

> All the generic types of thoughts fall into eight categories in which every sort of thought is included. First is that of gluttony, then fornication, third avarice, fourth sadness, fifth anger, sixth acedia, seventh vainglory, eighth pride. Whether or not all these thoughts trouble the soul is not within our power; but it is for us to decide if they are to linger within us or not and whether or not they stir up the passions.[64]

While each of these obstacles has its own distinctive form and flavor, they are all variations on the root thought of self-love, something that afflicts us all. No matter which one of them is most prominent at any point in time, all of them eventually will have to be seen into and set aside.[65]

Only when all the logismoi have been uprooted will the aspirant at last find oneself near the threshold of pure prayer:

> When your mind out of a great longing for God gradually withdraws, as it were, from the flesh and turns aside all mental representations deriving from the senses or from memory or from temperament, being filled with both reverence and joy, then consider yourself to be near the frontiers of prayer.[66]

---

63 Evagrius, *On Thoughts* 7; Sinkewicz, 157–58. Thoughts, as Evagrius puts it, "cut off" one another.

64 Evagrius, *Praktikos* 6; Sinkewicz, 97–98.

65 Evagrius, *Prayer* 4; Sinkewicz, 193.

66 Evagrius, *Prayer* 61; Sinkewicz, 199.

Communion with God becomes possible, then, because the mind is no longer able to be swayed by self-love as it had been. Firmly fixed on God alone, the mind is essentially oblivious to anything else that the soul might throw up to obstruct it: "The mind that has completed the work of the practical life with the help of God and has approached knowledge possesses little or no awareness at all of the irrational part of the soul, for knowledge has carried it off to the heights and separated it from sensible things."[67] It is not that one has been, so to speak, broken into pieces—even here the soul is not somehow disjoined from the body or the mind. Rather, the mind is simply no longer so caught up with the soul's representations that it effectively "forgets" that those thoughts are even there. Imperfect apatheia allows one to enter into that state occasionally; perfect apatheia is the condition of one who continually abides in it.[68]

With perfect apatheia, the life of God, which at the beginning of this path was first perceived as a diremption of the self through the piercing of compunction, is now slowly becoming the very life of the aspirant: "The person who has established the virtues within himself and has become wholly mingled with them no longer remembers the law or the commandments or punishment, but says and does those things which this excellent state dictates to him."[69] All of one's thoughts are properly attuned, all of one's actions are properly oriented, and one lives and breathes as befits one's state—made in God's image and likeness, taught by Christ, and infused with the Spirit. Indeed, it was the Spirit that made one's victory over the logismoi possible in the first place:

> The Holy Spirit, out of compassion for our weaknesses, visits us even in our impurity; and if only he should find the mind praying to him in love for the truth, he enters it and annihilates the entire phalanx of thoughts and mental representations that surround it, while urging it on to love for spiritual prayer.[70]

Pure prayer, that state of mind that finds itself in communion with God, is "a state of the mind that arises under the influence of the unique light of the Holy Trinity,"[71] but only on the condition that one is willing to surrender

---

67 Evagrius, *Praktikos* 66; Sinkewicz, 109.

68 Evagrius, *Prayer* 52; Sinkewicz, 198.

69 Evagrius, *Praktikos* 70; Sinkewicz, 109.

70 Evagrius, *Prayer* 62; Sinkewicz, 199.

71 Evagrius, *Reflections* 27; Sinkewicz, 213.

everything else. The fullness of that surrender will only be attained with the third renunciation, the renunciation of ignorance in the mind. But that is yet to come. Any discussion of that final renunciation is premature until we have seen just how insidious each of the logismoi can be.

CHAPTER TWO

The Holy Life

Athanasius's account of Antony's homeleaving might have caused the stir that it did as much for its novelty as for its vivid portrayal of Antony's determination and resolve. The renunciant life was, after all, still something of an innovation in his environment. The same cannot be said for the first Buddhist monastics. By the time the Buddha began to teach, the presence of religious ascetics would have been a part of everyday life in the social landscape of the Indian subcontinent. Still, that did not make the account of a person leaving everything behind in pursuit of spiritual development any less compelling, and a rather formulaic version of such an account is repeated time and again in the *Nikāyas*:

> The Dhamma is heard by a householder or a householder's son, or one reborn in some family or other. Having heard this Dhamma, he gains faith in the Tathāgata.[1] Having gained faith, he reflects: "The household life is close and dusty, the homeless life is free as air. It is not easy, living the household life, to live the fully-perfected holy life, purified and polished like a conch-shell. Suppose I were to go forth from the household life into homelessness!" And after some time, he abandons his property, small or great, leaves his circle of relatives, small or great, shaves off his hair and beard, dons yellow robes, and goes forth into the homeless life.[2]

The Dharma he would have heard would have been some aspect or another of the one—indeed the only—thing the Buddha said he ever taught: suffering

1 *Tathāgata*, or "thus come One," is one of the traditional epithets of the Buddha.

2 Maurice Walshe, *The Long Discourses of the Buddha: A Translation of the Dīgha Nikāya* (Boston: Wisdom, 1995), 99.

and its end. This message was presented as the Four Noble Truths: suffering (dukkha), craving (tṛṣṇā), the cessation of craving (nirvāṇa), and the path to its cessation (*mārga*).[3] The householder would also have heard that everything is conditioned—including what he conceptualizes as himself, his life, his world, and everything within it—and that, because all is conditioned, it is all unsatisfactory and prone to disappoint. Further, he would have heard that the cause of this unsatisfactoriness lies not in conditioned things themselves, but in his own fundamental ignorance of their nature—an ignorance he perpetuates by filtering everything through the lens of his own drive to have things turn out one way rather than another in accordance with his self-conception.

But that householder would also have heard that it is indeed possible to put an end to the suffering that he has caused himself, not to mention that which he has caused others, through his ignorance-driven actions. To do so, however, would require a single-minded dedication to the path that conduces to that cessation of suffering—the Eightfold Path of the Noble Ones, a path marked out by right view (*sammādiṭṭhi*), and right aspiration (*sammāsankappa*), right speech (*sammavācā*), right effort (*sammāvāyāma*), right action (*sammākammanta*), right livelihood (*sammā-ājivo*), right mindfulness (*sammāsāti*), and right concentration (*sammāsamādhi*). Although he could not possibly comprehend what all of this means, he nevertheless would have discerned something fundamentally right about it. In response, he places his faith in the Three Jewels—in the One who teaches (the Buddha), in what that One has taught (the Dharma), and in those who have already gone some distance in realizing that teaching (the Saṅgha).

In taking refuge in the Three Jewels, he is not simply adding some new and interesting ideas to his mental repertoire. Rather, he is committing himself to a course of life in accordance with a teaching and practice directed toward one thing and one thing only: the "unshakable deliverance of mind that is the goal of this holy life, its heartwood, and its end."[4] That aim, no less than the course of life that conduces to it, cuts so deeply against the stream of his everyday understanding of himself and the world that he soon realizes that it will involve a rather complete break with life as he has lived it.[5] He then renounces everyday life in favor of a life lived in accordance with the Dharma.

3 To avoid confusion, the Sanskrit terms will be kept throughout.

4 Ñāṇamoli and Bodhi, *Middle Length Discourses*, 290.

5 Ñāṇamoli and Bodhi, *Middle Length Discourses*, 260.

Having faith in the Dharma and undertaking the path of renouncing that everyday stream are two sides of one and the same coin.[6]

This renunciation is not a one-and-done act, however, and the neophyte in the Dharma needs to be eased into the task at hand. This process is described in two different ways in the *Nikāyas*. On the one hand, it is described in broad strokes as a threefold process of sloughing off all those things that obscure the mind. This involves, first, the establishment of moral conduct (*śīla*); then the cultivation of mental concentration (samādhi); and finally, the realization of wisdom (prajñā/panna). Each of these three steps is developed according to the constituent elements of the Eightfold Path: moral conduct is developed through right speech, right action, and right livelihood; mental concentration is developed through right mindfulness and right concentration; and wisdom is reflected in right view and right intention.

On the other hand, this process is more frequently described in the *Nikāyas* in much smaller incremental steps.[7] The Buddha likens this gradual training to the kind of slow, step-by-step training a horse trainer uses to break and train a colt.[8] The simile is apt. The everyday mind is unwieldy, drawn now to this, now to that. It is also powerful and, left unbridled, tends to run roughshod over the terrain, oblivious to the damage it is causing. As only the most patient and exacting training will suffice to definitively break the colt, only the most painstaking attention to the least traces of attachment will suffice to free the aspirant definitively from his self-inflicted suffering. Because the nīvaraṇas are identified in the context of this gradual training, we here follow its steps to the point where the nīvaraṇas become the express point of focus.[9]

The very first step of this gradual training deals with corralling that unruly mind by first restraining its most obvious manifestations in behavior: "When

6 For an account of the intimate relation between faith and renunciation in the earliest sources, see Giuliano Giustarini, "Faith and Renunciation in Early Buddhism: Saddhā and Nekkhamma," *Rivista di Studi Sudasiatici* 1 (2006): 161–79.

7 For a discussion of these two differing descriptions of the Buddhist path, see Rupert Gethin, *The Foundations of Buddhism* (New York: Oxford University Press, 1998), 164–65.

8 Ñāṇamoli and Bodhi, *Middle Length Discourses*, 874. In other sutras, the gradual training is likened to taming a forest elephant (*Middle Length Discourses*, 990–96).

9 While this may seem overly technical at times, I have sought to highlight those aspects of the training that will be relied on again when confronting the individual nīvaraṇas. I beg the reader's patience while this foundation is being laid.

the Tathāgata obtains a person to be tamed he first disciplines him thus: 'Come, bhikkhu, be virtuous, restrained with the restraint of the Pāṭimokkha, be perfect in conduct and resort, and seeing fear in the slightest fault, train by undertaking the training precepts.'"[10] The Pāṭimokkha is the list of training rules (227 for male bhikkhus, 311 for female bhikkhunīs) that govern most every aspect of the homeleaving life and distinguish the actions of a home-leaver from those of an everyday householder. Householders, in turn, are similarly restrained by the five precepts (*pañca sīla/pañca śīla*)—not to kill, not to take what is not given, not to misuse sexuality, not to lie, and not to indulge in intoxicants.[11] Once a fortnight, on *uposatha* days,[12] a householder is also invited to approximate more closely the practice of the ordained by taking food only once in the course of the day, abstaining from all sexual activity, passing up all entertainment and adornment, and forgoing luxurious accommodations.[13]

The precepts and training rules are given to the aspirant, who receives them from a preceptor and abides by them without exception. At this point the aspirant is simply not in a position to decide what rules there should be. That one or the other rule might not make sense is rather irrelevant; that one might not have expressly or personally chosen some particular rule or another is also beside the point. Indeed, their efficacy lies precisely in their propensity to run up against one's self-directed, everyday way of doing things in order to demonstrate those points where, rather than surrendering the conceit of the self, one holds fast to it instead:

> There are certain misguided men here who, when told by me "Abandon this," say: "What, such a mere trifle, such a little thing as this? This recluse is much too exacting!" And they do not abandon that and they show discourtesy towards me as well as towards those bhikkhus desirous of training. For them that thing becomes a strong, stout, tough, unrotting tether and a thick yoke.

---

10 Ñāṇamoli and Bodhi, *Middle Length Discourses*, 874.

11 In later formulations, a roster of ten grave and forty-eight minor precepts for lay practitioners was drawn up that addressed more particularly the restraint that a householder pursuing the Dharma needs to maintain in the context of family and social life. See A. Charles Muller and Kenneth K. Tanaka, trans., *The Brahmā's Net Sutra* (Moraga, CA: BDK America, 2017), 44–73.

12 *Uposatha* days are kept in accordance with the lunar calendar and fall on the days of the new and full moons.

13 Bodhi, *Numerical Discourses*, 299–300.

By contrast, those who surrender their autonomy and submit to the rule find themselves less restrained through its observance:

> There are certain clansmen here who, when told by me "Abandon this," say: "What, such a mere trifle, such a little thing to be abandoned as this, the Blessed One tells us to abandon, the Sublime One tells us to relinquish." Yet they abandon that and do not show discourtesy towards me or towards those bhikkhus desirous of training. Having abandoned it, they live at ease, unruffled, subsisting on others' gifts, with mind [as aloof] as a wild deer's. For them that thing becomes a feeble, weak, rotting, coreless tether.[14]

The rule, no matter how great or trifling it might appear to utilitarian calculations, is only ever as confining as the amount of ego resistance thrown in its face.

The assembly of homeleavers gathers once a fortnight to recite the entire list of training rules and to confess openly any infractions made since the last recitation. The point is neither to obtain forgiveness nor even to express remorse, but to provide an occasion for setting into sharp relief the discrepancy between one's own behavior and that of one's fellow bhikkhus.[15] The idea is something like, "Here is the rule; I did not follow it; my fellow monks now also know I did not follow it. Moreover, I see that there are others who did, and if I am to be worthy of their company, I will resolve not to violate the rule going forward." This act of accountability provides the ground for the arising of moral shame (*hiri*) and moral dread (*ottappa*), which together make up "the first cause and condition that leads to obtaining the wisdom fundamental to the spiritual life when it has not been obtained and to its increase, maturation, and fulfillment by development after it has been obtained."[16] One follows the rule so as not to diminish one's own dignity as a pursuer of the Dharma, and one follows the rule out of fear of being known as one who does not measure up to the standards of the community.[17]

---

14 Ñāṇamoli and Bodhi, *Middle Length Discourses*, 553.

15 The issue of the need for divine mercy and forgiveness—so important to many other religious systems—does not arise here; one has simply taken a wrong turn away from the path, and the solution is simply to get back on course again without further ado. We will return to this point in the discussion of restlessness-remorse in chap. 6.

16 Bodhi, *Numerical Discourses*, 1112.

17 For a fuller account of hiri-ottappa, see Maria Heim, "Shame and Apprehension: Notes on the Moral Value of Hiri and Ottappa," in *Embedded Languages: Studies of Sri Lankan and Buddhist Cultures*, ed. Carol S. Anderson et al. (Colombo: Godage International, 2012), 237–60.

The cultivation of hiri-ottappa is the foundation for discernment: the ability to see clearly the difference between skillful and unskillful thought and action. The recognition that one had previously failed to see and follow skillful thought and action readies the aspirant for the next step of the gradual training:

> When, brahmin, the bhikkhu is virtuous . . . and seeing fear in the slightest fault, trains by undertaking the training precepts, then the Tathāgata disciplines him further: "Come, bhikkhu, guard the doors of your sense faculties. On seeing a form with the eye, do not grasp at its signs and features. Since, if you were to leave the eye unguarded, evil unwholesome states of covetous and grief might invade you, practice the way of its restraint, guard the eye faculty, undertake the restraint of the eye faculty."[18]

The same follows for the other sense faculties. Without hiri-ottappa, this step of guarding the doors of the sense faculties is said to lack its "proximate cause."[19] Without this step, there can be no further development on the path. Without the restraint of the senses, each of the subsequent levels of training will also lack its proximate cause, as each builds on the one previous to it.

To understand why it would be not simply ill-advised but *shameful* for the aspirant not to guard the senses, we need to look, however briefly, at the structure of individual experience.

In the Dharma of the Buddha the human person is not viewed as a changeable material body tethered somehow to an immaterial, immutable soul the way it was in the Brahmanic tradition of the time. On that account, the body and anything connected with it was to be eventually sloughed off in order that the true self, *ātman*, alone might remain. Instead, the Buddha taught that the person is best understood as something of a committee. The five *skandhas*, or "bundles" of experiential activity—embodiment (*rūpa*), sensations (*vedanā*), apperception (*saṃjñā/saññā*), volitional activities (*saṃskāra/saṅkhāra*), and consciousness (*vijñāna/viññāṇa*)—are the identifiable, mutually conditioning

18 Ñāṇamoli and Bodhi, *Middle Length Discourses*, 875.

19 Bodhi, *Numerical Discourses*, 1070. The Buddha taught that nothing arises ex nihilo and that every phenomenon (*dharma*) is caused by another. Each step of this gradual training, when mastered, provides the proximate cause for the successful mastering of the step that immediately follows it. Each stage we are looking at here is increasingly granular in focus. While one might get impatient with such an incremental account, it attests to the subtlety of the Buddha's analysis of the human condition.

moments in having any experience at all, and together they provide an exhaustive account of everyday personality.

Embodiment is the first conditioning moment. Without a living body there can be no experience at all. The body here is understood not as an object among other objects but as an opening for experience, an opening mediated in accordance with its sensory capabilities. A functioning body gives rise to the sensations of color and solidity and pain, pleasure, and neither-pain-nor-pleasure. As these sensations rise and fall and play off one another, the apperception of an object or state of affairs arises, and this business, say, of brown and hard and flat and pain-inducing-when-my-toes-run-into-it is identified as *table*. Because of that apperception, volitional activities such as placing a coffee cup on it or steering clear of it while walking can ensue. Finally, if someone asks what I am doing, I can report on these things because there is a conscious awareness of all of these goings-on. So seamless is the functioning of the skandhas that a remark such as "I just avoided that table!"—as if there were some point of merit in having done so—generally never even arises.

"Grasping at signs and features" by leaving the senses unguarded is the opposite of letting the experiential field simply rise and fall in this way. Instead, I take those experiences and turn them into a narrative about myself, insisting, as it were, that avoiding the table was indeed somehow about *me*. That grasping is nothing other than the craving (tṛṣṇā) that creates all of one's suffering (dukkha). The *Nikāyas* give a rather clear picture of the myriad ways I glom onto the ceaseless flow of conditioned states of affairs in service to my self-concept in my everyday life:

> And what, Bhikkhus, is craving—the ensnarer, streaming, widespread, and sticky—by which this world has been smothered and enveloped, and by which it has become a tangled skein, a knotted ball of thread, a mass of reeds and rushes, so that it does not pass beyond the plane of misery, the bad destination, the lower world, saṃsāra?
>
> There are, bhikkhus, these eighteen currents of craving related to the internal and eighteen currents of craving related to the external.
>
> And what are the eighteen currents of craving related to the internal? When there is [the notion] "I am," there are [the notions] "I am thus," "I am just so," "I am otherwise," "I am lasting," "I am evanescent," "I may be," "I may be thus," "I may be just so," "I may be otherwise," "May I be," "May I be thus," "May I be just so," "May I be otherwise," "I shall be," "I shall be thus,"

> "I shall be just so," "I shall be otherwise." These are the eighteen currents of craving related to the internal.
>
> And what are the eighteen currents of craving related to the external? When there is [the notion], "I am because of this," there are [the notions]: "I am thus because of this," "I am just so because of this," "I am otherwise because of this," "I am lasting because of this," "I am evanescent because of this," "I may be because of this," "I may be just so because of this," "I may be otherwise because of this," "May I be because of this," "May I be thus because of this," "May I be just so because of this," "May I be otherwise because of this," "I shall be because of this," "I shall be thus because of this," "I shall be just so because of this," "I shall be otherwise because of this," These are the eighteen currents of craving related to the external.[20]

As we can see here, there is *nothing* that is immune from being taken as an exercise in self-definition; every circumstance encountered and every action taken is evaluated in terms of its relation to what I take myself to be.

Far from revealing a self that can stand firm in the midst of all of these goings-on, however, the currents of craving instead reveal its utter ephemerality. When all I know of myself is given in conjunction with circumstances, and when those circumstances rise and fall as circumstances do, I begin to see that my self-definition never quite stays put. No matter what I try, no matter what I do, that *I* is always losing its support structure. One way to mitigate that, one might think, is to order circumstances so as to conform to my self-image, eliminating those elements that threaten it and advancing those that promote it. Parceling out the givenness of things as they are in this way, I thus create a world of my own choosing. *Saṃsāra* is the name given to this continuous process of world formation and dissolution in conjunction with the exercise of tṛṣṇā, and it is no more substantial than the self-concept I rely on in constructing it. Try as I might, things never stay put as I would like them.

Revulsion and dispassion arise from the growing realization that these *samsaric* worlds are not—and never were—anything that could add up to support for a self:

> Therefore, bhikkhus, any kind of form [feeling, perception, volitional formations, or consciousness] whatever, whether past, future, or present,

---

20 Bodhi, *Numerical Discourses*, 586–87. I cite this passage in full because its detail highlights just how *neurotic* tṛṣṇā is. We will also recognize many of these various expressions in the account of the nīvaraṇas below.

> internal or external, gross or subtle, inferior or superior, far or near, all [these] should be seen as [they] really [are] with correct wisdom thus: "This is not mine, this I am not, this is not my self."
>
> Seeing thus, bhikkhus, the instructed noble disciple experiences revulsion towards form, revulsion towards feeling, revulsion towards perception, revulsion towards volitional formations, revulsion towards consciousness.[21]

The cultivation of revulsion and dispassion toward conditioned states is an outgrowth of the desire not to be duped yet again.

Much like apatheia was for some of Evagrius's contemporaries, revulsion and dispassion are frequently misunderstood and all too quickly dismissed. They are often appealed to as evidence that the Dharma is "world-denying," and, in a sense, of course, it is, but not as is usually meant by the accusation. The Dharma is no more world-denying than it is self-denying:

> The Buddha did not deny self. What he denied was that self has any permanent, imperishable essence. The Buddha realized that self is essentially a constantly changing process, artificially created through the interaction of craving and ignorance. And, since it is "made-up" by activities which we have some influence over, craving and ignorance can also be "unmade" so that the deleterious effects of grasping self as permanent can come to cessation.[22]

The same is true of the world. Since what I take to be *the world* is only ever a product of my tṛṣṇā-laden projections in light of my ignorance, and because those projections are conditioned and impermanent, no world-formation can be said to last, nothing about it is ever satisfactory, and there is nothing that can be appealed to as a sure foundation outside it. What I take to be the world is just as ephemeral as what I take to be my self.

Revulsion, then, is "not a reaction of emotional disgust, accompanied by horror and aversion, but a calm inward turning away from all conditioned existence. . . . [It] arises from knowledge and vision of things as they really are (*yathābhūtañaṇadassana*), and naturally leads to dispassion (*virāga*)

21 Bodhi, *Connected Discourses*, 902–3.

22 Ajahn Thiradhammo, *Beyond I-Making. A Contemplative Investigation of the Concept of* Anattā *and the Path to Its Realization* (Hertfordshire, UK: Amaravati, 2022), 1.

and liberation (*vimutti*)."[23] I simply tire of the pointless exercises of self- and world creation and come to see in them nothing that is particularly worthy of my time and attention. I should be ashamed to keep pretending otherwise, and this is why hiri and ottappa are called "the bright guardians of the world" (*sukkka lokapāla*);[24] they guard the world, just as it is, from *me* and the impositions I would bring to bear on it out of the conceit that there is a self, independent of everything else, whose responsibility it is to commandeer reality into a world tailored to nothing quite so much as its own satisfaction.

Moral shame and moral dread also serve to guard me from myself, and the next step in the gradual training focuses on the ways in which grasping at signs and features manifests in conjunction with the maintenance of the body:

> When, brahmin, the bhikkhu guards the doors of his sense faculties, then the Tathāgata disciplines him further: "Come, bhikkhu, be moderate in eating. Reflecting wisely you should take food neither for amusement nor for intoxication nor for the sake of physical beauty and attractiveness, but only for the endurance and continuance of this body, for ending discomfort, and for assisting the holy life, considering: 'Thus I shall terminate old feelings without arousing new feelings, and I shall be healthy and blameless and shall live in comfort.'"[25]

Although only food is generally mentioned in the stock formulation of the gradual training, it is understood that at issue here is not simply food but all of the other things a body needs as well: clothing, shelter, and medicinals. Taken together, these are called *the four requisites*, and the wise attitude we have just seen with respect to food applies to them as well: clothes are for protection and modesty; shelter is for protection from cold, heat, and insects, and for enjoying seclusion; medicinals are used for the benefits of health.[26] Here, too, there is a blamelessness in keeping such bodily support in line with bodily needs. Protecting one's feet from damage by wearing shoes requires no explanation; it is simply a matter of what it means to have feet in a world where the ground is littered with things that might damage them. Using shoes as a display of wealth, taste, style, or status creates a situation where the justification of one's choice leads sooner or later to a reinforcement of one's self-conception and an affirmation of one's likes and dislikes. At that point

---

23 Bodhi, *Connected Discourses*, 53.

24 Bhikkhu Bodhi, *Dhamma Reflections: Collected Essays of Bhikkhu Bodhi*, ed. Buddhist Publication Society (Onalaska, WA: BPS Pariyatti Editions, 2016), 101.

25 Ñāṇamoli and Bodhi, *Middle Length Discourses*, 875.

26 Ñāṇamoli and Bodhi, *Middle Length Discourses*, 94.

one moves from simply being a human with feet to being a certain *kind* of person, now decked out with the trappings of a tṛṣṇā-induced identity.

Here, no less than in conjunction with the training precepts, the company one keeps will either help or hinder one's efforts. If I associate with others who value such trappings of identity, I will find myself playing along; if I associate with those who are not taken in by such pretenses, I will find myself investing a lot less in their maintenance. Dukkha may love company, but the cessation of dukkha requires company, too—just of a rather different sort. In leaving home, the bhikkhu sets aside the pressures and constraints of everyday life that demand he act as yet another saṃsāra-wandering being. In taking refuge in the saṅgha of the noble ones, he accepts the pressures and constraints of the holy life that guide him toward the cessation of his dukkha.

These three components—observing the precepts, guarding the senses, and making fitting use of the necessities of life—constitute the proximate causes for the establishment of mindfulness. Once the precepts are no longer felt to be constricting, once one competently guards the sense doors, and once one is content and satisfied with the necessities of life, one is now in a position to view not only food, clothing, shelter, and medicinals with dispassion, but to begin to view every last action with the same degree of dispassionate awareness:

> When, brahmin, the bhikkhu is moderate in eating [and the rest], then the Tathāgata disciplines him further: "Come, bhikkhu, be devoted to wakefulness. During the day, while walking back and forth and sitting, purify your mind of obstructive states. In the first watch of the night, while walking back and forth and sitting, purify your mind of obstructive states. In the middle watch of the night you should lie down on the right side in the lion's pose with one foot overlapping the other, mindful and fully aware, after noting in your mind the time for rising. After rising, in the third watch of the night, while walking back and forth and sitting, purify your mind of obstructive states."[27]

This awareness is then refined to an even more granular level:

> When, brahmin, the bhikkhu is devoted to wakefulness, then the Tathāgata disciplines him further: "Come, bhikkhu, be possessed of mindfulness and full awareness. Act in full awareness when going forward and returning; act in full awareness when looking ahead and looking away; act in full awareness when flexing and extending your limbs; act in full awareness when wearing your robes and carrying your outer robe and bowl; act in full awareness when eating, drinking, consuming food, and tasting; act in full awareness when defecating

27 Ñāṇamoli and Bodhi, *Middle Length Discourses*, 875.

> and urinating; act in full awareness when walking, standing, sitting, falling asleep, waking up, talking, and keeping silent."[28]

The *Kāyagatāsati Sutra* describes any number of such mindfulness practices related to the body, including the exercises mentioned here. As it describes each of them in turn, it indicates what is at stake in the given practice, and each of the descriptions concludes with the same refrain: "As he abides thus diligent, ardent, and resolute, his memories and intentions based on the household life are abandoned; with their abandoning his mind becomes steadied internally, quieted, brought to singleness, and concentrated. That is how a bhikkhu develops mindfulness of the body."[29]

"Memories and intentions based on the household life" refers to those connected with the ties of sensual pleasure and displeasure—in other words, those based on the utilitarian calculus by which everyday persons conduct their lives. These stand contrasted to those memories and intentions "based on renunciation," those connected with the development of stillness and insight. So when one acts in full awareness of the gross and subtle movements in the processes related to the body, one is not simply *monitoring* the ups and downs of physical and affective states with a view to noting gains and losses, improvements or deteriorations; instead one is focused on seeing all of them as just so many conditioned moments, *no matter how they happen to turn out*, free of grasping or rejecting them, and thus gradually abandoning any thought of how much more pleasurable and how less painful they might be if they were otherwise.

Mindfulness practice properly undertaken thus functions as a tool that facilitates the transition between everyday life and the noble life. In becoming increasingly aware of the exercise of tṛṣṇā in every movement and thought, I can begin to take dead aim at the points where I overlay the direct experience of those movements and thoughts with a narrative about myself and, in the process, come to be free of the drive to engage in that narrative at all.

So far in the training sequence, there has been little discussion of anything expressly connected with the practice of what we would today call *meditation*. This is not at all an oversight. Up to this step, one will have had

28 Ñāṇamoli and Bodhi, *Middle Length Discourses*, 875–76.

29 Ñāṇamoli and Bodhi, *Middle Length Discourses*, 950–51.

no shortage of material to work with—the training rules, everyday sense objects, the diet and wardrobe and dwelling, the various manifest states of mind and body, along with the memories and intentions of the household life connected with them. At each step along the way, one will have been presented with an occasion to look at a discrete everyday circumstance, to assess the degree to which one is either attracted to or repelled by it, and to abandon any lingering attachment or aversion connected with it. Now the aspirant, in seclusion from all of that, can turn toward a direct examination of his own mind:

> When, brahmin, the bhikkhu possesses mindfulness and full awareness, then the Tathāgata disciplines him further: "Come, bhikkhu, resort to a secluded resting place: the forest, the root of a tree, a mountain, a ravine, a hillside cave, a charnel ground, a jungle thicket, an open space, a heap of straw."
>
> He resorts to a secluded resting place: the forest . . . a heap of straw. On returning from his almsround, after his meal he sits down, folding his legs crosswise, setting his body erect, and establishing mindfulness before him.[30]

Having taken his seat, he now asks himself, "Is there any obsession unabandoned in myself that might so obsess my mind that I cannot know or see things are they actually are?"[31] If he is uncertain as to what such an obsession might be, he will have heard what to look for: "If a bhikkhu is obsessed by sensual lust, then his mind is obsessed. If he is obsessed by ill will . . . sloth and torpor . . . restlessness and remorse . . . doubt, then his mind is obsessed."[32] The five nīvaraṇas—sensory desire, ill will, sloth-torpor, restlessness-remorse, and doubt—are those very obsessions.

The nīvaraṇas are a particular group within a much larger inventory of obstructive mind states that have their roots in the basic defilements (*kilesas/ kleśas*), often called the three "unwholesome roots"[33] of attachment (*rāga*),

---

30 Ñāṇamoli and Bodhi, *Middle Length Discourses*, 876. It is worth noting that this is the first mention of the practice of seated meditation in the training sequence.

31 Ñāṇamoli and Bodhi, *Middle Length Discourses*, 421.

32 Ñāṇamoli and Bodhi, *Middle Length Discourses*, 421. Here, in the *Kosambiya Sutra*, speculation about this world, speculation about the other world, and being given to quarreling, brawling, and disputatiousness ("stabbing others with verbal daggers") are added to the list of obsessions. As we will see in chap. 5, these are subsumed under the nīvaraṇa of doubt.

33 In the Mahāyāna, these are often referred to as the "Three Poisons."

aversion (*dvesha/dveṣa*), and ignorance (*moha*). All of them have their origin in a fundamental ignorance (*avidyā*) of one's true nature, all of them are manifestations of tṛṣṇā, and all of them conduce without fail to dukkha. There is some overlap between the nīvaraṇas and the *saṃyojanas*, or the ten fetters.[34] As with the "eight" logismoi in Evagrius, one should not read too much into the exact number of nīvaraṇas; it is enough that these five are consistently found grouped together in the canon and in the tradition.

However they are categorized, the nīvaraṇas are particularly troublesome, and the Buddha does not mince words when it comes to describing their perniciousness: "Bhikkhus, saying 'a heap of the unwholesome,' it is about these five hindrances that one could rightly say this. For these five hindrances are a complete heap of the unwholesome."[35] They are such a mess of unwholesomeness that, without having abandoned them, "it is impossible that a bhikkhu, with his powerless and feeble wisdom, might know his own good, the good of others, or the good of both, or realize superhuman distinction in knowledge and vision worthy of the noble ones."[36] As long as they are present, one will continue to lose one's bearings in the practice, for the hindrances are "makers of blindness, causing lack of vision, causing lack of knowledge, detrimental to wisdom, tending to vexation, leading away from Nibbāna."[37] They are the nutritive ground for the ongoing arising of ignorance, "wildernesses in the heart," and they are so much trouble that one who finds oneself given to them should put the same effort into abandoning them that one would if one's clothes or head had caught fire.[38] The nīvaraṇas

---

34 The ten fetters are the view of personal existence (*sakkāya-diṭṭhi*), doubt (*vicikicchā*), attachment to rules and rituals (*sīlabbata-parāmāsa*), sensual lust (*kāma-rāga*), ill will (*vyāpadā*), passion for what has form (*rūpa-rāga*), passion for what is without form (*arūpa-rāga*), conceit (*māna*), restlessness (*uddhacca*), and ignorance (*avijjā*). The *Nikāyas* and subsequent Theravādin commentary tradition are nothing if not encyclopedic in their listings of all the various kinds of mental defilements. Owing to the vagaries of textual traditions, some of the listings seem to overlap.

35 Bodhi, *Numerical Discourses*, 681.

36 Bodhi, *Numerical Discourses*, 680.

37 Bodhi, *Connected Discourses*, 1593.

38 Ñāṇamoli and Bodhi, *Middle Length Discourses*, 194–95; Bodhi, *Numerical Discourses*, 1402. While there is no first point of ignorance in the broadest sense, the five hindrances keep it going. See Bodhi, *Numerical Discourses*, 1415.

Things do not arise from nowhere, and in the teaching of the Buddha, every phenomenon is understood in conjunction with some cause. Frequently in the *Nikāyas* he speaks in terms of *nutrition* to capture that causal relationship. Just as plants need nutrition to grow, thoughts, defilements, and, as we will see, the nīvaraṇas have their nutritive ground,

are clearly meant to be taken seriously, so much so that the Buddha declares that "this Noble Eightfold Path is to be developed for direct knowledge of these five hindrances, for the full understanding of them, for their utter destruction, for their abandoning."[39]

As troublesome as the nīvaraṇas are, they are only seen as such in light of the individual's aspiration, and thus their placement at this point in the gradual training is not at all incidental. The aspirant may well have incorporated the discipline into one's life, may have come to some measure of guardianship over the sense faculties, and may have even developed a keen faculty of mindfulness. Even with all of this accomplished, however, one has still not come even close to any first and fleeting abandonment of the self (*sotāpanna*) and certainly no definitive liberation. It is wholly possible that one will follow the training rules and precepts for any number of reasons—for show, perhaps, or to spite one's family, or even, as we might say today, to make oneself a better person. This is why the Buddha thought there was no particular merit in simply observing the rules, and anyone who would praise him (or anyone else) for following them would be focusing on "inferior matters."[40]

Working with the nīvaraṇas places one in very new territory or, perhaps more accurately, it leads one to abandon any *familiar* territory and to surrender any preconceived notions of where all of this is heading:

> "It is just as if this River Aciravatī were brimful of water so that a crow could drink out of it, and a man should come along wishing to cross over . . . and were to lie down on this bank, covering his head with a shawl. What do you think, Vāseṭṭha? Would that man be able to get to the other side?" "No, Reverend Gotama."
>
> In the same way, Vāseṭṭha, in the Ariyan discipline these five hindrances are called obstacles, hindrances, coverings-up, envelopings. Which five? The hindrance of sensuality, of ill-will, of sloth-and-torpor, of worry-and-flurry,

---

the causal context out of which they arise. In contemporary language, we speak of *feeding* our desires or our addictions; the stuff we feed them with would be their nutritive ground. The point of practice is not just to *get rid* of defilements but to *cut off their food supply* so they never arise again. See Ñāṇamoli and Bodhi, *Middle Length Discourses*, 134.

39 Bodhi, *Connected Discourses*, 1565. The paucity of any discussion of the nīvaraṇas in the scholarly and popular literature is curiously disproportionate to their apparent weight.

40 Walshe, *Long Discourses*, 68–73.

> of doubt. These five are called obstacles, hindrances, coverings-up, envelopings.[41]

Without confronting—and overcoming—the five hindrances, there is no crossing to the other, still unknown, shore, the unshakable deliverance of mind and the cessation of tṛṣṇā.

The hindrances are labeled as such because of their capacity for "obstructing and hindering and concealing [reality] from consciousness" (hence the shawl metaphor in the passage above).[42] They conceal the aspirant from reality by casting a veneer of independence and solidity and worthiness over the plain and sober truth that all conditioned things are marked by impermanence and nonself. They are particularly vexing and difficult to work through, since they are the last strong attempts of the mind to remain with what is familiar and comforting—the samsaric worlds of one's own making and the conceit of the self that they support, as ephemeral and unsatisfying as they ever are. They are hindrances "because they hinder the mind, or because they hinder beneficial practice. The meaning is that they conceal."[43] They conceal the reality of "things as they really are"—in other words, the Noble Truths.

The hindrances all have an element of fear about them (hence *hiding under* the shawl) that keeps the practitioner from pressing on. They function as a kind of security blanket for the self, interwoven with all of those conceptions and reasonings that sustain one's identity. In confronting them, one exposes the conceit of the self to the prospect of its undoing. The overcoming of the nīvaraṇas is therefore essential to any meditative practice that would accord with the overall aim of the Dharma:

> The Blessed One, brahmin, did not praise every type of meditation, nor did he condemn every type of meditation. What kind of meditation did the Blessed One not praise? Here, brahmin, someone abides with his mind obsessed by sensual lust, a prey to sensual lust, and he does not understand as it actually is the escape from sensual lust. While he harbours sensual lust within, he meditates, premeditates, out-meditates, and mismeditates. He abides with his mind obsessed by ill will, a prey to ill will . . . with his mind obsessed by sloth and torpor, a prey to sloth and torpor . . . with his mind obsessed by restlessness and remorse, a prey to restlessness and remorse . . . with his mind obsessed by doubt, a prey to doubt

---

41 Walshe, *Long Discourses*, 191–92.

42 Buddhaghoṣa, *The Path of Purification: Visuddhimagga*, trans. Bhikkhu Ñāṇamoli (Kandy, Sri Lanka: Buddhist Publication Society, 1999), 714.

43 Bodhi, *Suttanipāta*, 379.

> and he does not understand as it actually is the escape from arisen doubt. . . . The Blessed One did not praise this kind of meditation.[44]

In the *Māratajjaniya Sutra*, that word string "meditates, premeditates, outmeditates, and mismeditates" is used pejoratively to describe a kind of "meditation" in which one just sits silently and intently—like a jackal by the side of the stream waiting for a fish, or a cat in an alley waiting for a mouse.[45] One is certainly quite immobile, focused, and rather impervious to whatever else is going on, but missing in all of that is the penetrating investigation of one's own mind and the ever clearer awareness of one's own obstructive states—not to mention the requisite effort needed to abandon them altogether.

And abandon them one must if one is to attain even the first level of meditative concentration, or *jhāna*. Jhāna, or meditative absorption, is achieved "through the attainment of full . . . concentration (*appanā*, samādhi), during which there is a complete, though temporary, suspension of five-fold sense-activity and of the five hindrances, . . . a state of full alertness and lucidity."[46] Buddhaghoṣa glosses on this point: "No jhāna arises until these [five] have been abandoned, and so they are called the factors of abandoning. For although other unprofitable things too are abandoned at the moment of jhāna, still only these are specifically obstructive to jhāna."[47] Whatever meditation one imagines oneself doing while still under the sway of the nīvaraṇas, it can only be considered at best but the very dimmest form of meditation:

> Suppose an oil-lamp is burning with impure oil and an impure wick; because of the impurity of its oil and its wick it burns dimly. So too, here a bhikkhu abides resolved upon and pervading [an area with] a defiled radiance. His bodily inertia has not fully subsided, his sloth and torpor have not been fully eliminated, his restlessness and remorse have not been fully removed; because of this, he meditates, as it were, dimly.[48]

Those who have set themselves to realizing the Dharma will simply not be content with such an inadequate form of practice.

---

44 Ñāṇamoli and Bodhi, *Middle Length Discourses*, 885.

45 Ñāṇamoli and Bodhi, *Middle Length Discourses*, 433.

46 Nyanatiloka, *Buddhist Dictionary: Manual of Buddhist Terms and Doctrines* (Onalaska, WA: Pariyatti, 2019), 73.

47 Buddhaghoṣa, *Path of Purification*, 140. Buddhaghoṣa (fifth century CE) synthesized and commented on the extensive teachings of the Pāli canon. His *Path of Purification* is considered a masterpiece of Theravada exegesis.

48 Ñāṇamoli and Bodhi, *Middle Length Discourses*, 1006.

Suffice it to say that this is not the time for "just sitting" or simply "being aware." This is the time for carefully examining the rising of obstructive thoughts, noting the conditions and antecedent thoughts that give them rise, and uprooting as much as one is able the greed, anger, and delusion that underlie them all. In the tradition, this process is described as "application of thought" (*vittara/vitakka*) and "examining" (*vicāra*): "When these two aspects of thinking are developed in the context of a particular skill we are trying to learn [in this case, meditation], a certain kind of quickening occurs; suddenly the mind is enlivened by its facility in the task at hand and begins to take pleasure in it; in consequence, it begins to feel more at ease and content."[49] In short, the mind develops an ever keener facility for distinguishing between wholesome and unwholesome, unobstructed and obstructed mind states. Without that facility, one will be continually mired in the hindrances, if for no other reason than one will not even be aware of their presence and how dim one's meditation is as a result:

> When a bhikkhu enters upon a jhāna without [first] completely suppressing lust . . . completely tranquilizing bodily irritability . . . completely removing stiffness and torpor . . . and without [first] completely abolishing agitation and worry . . . then that bhikkhu soon comes out of that jhāna again, like a bee that has gone into an unpurified hive, like a king who has gone into an unclean park.[50]

Such momentary abidings in jhāna are not, however, in vain. As one becomes gradually free of the hindrances, one's ability to dwell in jhāna increases, furthering the abandonment of whatever of the hindrances still remain until the mind is "concentrated . . . purified, cleansed, unblemished, rid of defilement, malleable, wieldy, steady, and attained to imperturbability."[51] Whatever seeming ease and tranquility one might have in such an instance runs the risk of being quite short-lived indeed if one is not vigilant in seeing the arising of the nīvaraṇas at every turn.

Until they are definitively overcome, the nīvaraṇas will continue to thwart any meditative efforts, and they are so tenacious that they seem to have a life of their own. In the tradition this persistence is cast as the wiles of Māra, who continually entices the practitioner to abandon the path. Māra can only

---

49 Gethin, *Foundations of Buddhism*, 181.

50 Buddhaghoṣa, *Path of Purification*, 144; brackets in original.

51 Bodhi, *Numerical Discourses*, 585; further on, *luminous* is added to this list (*Numerical Discourses*, 641).

do this, however, as long as the practitioner gives him something to work with—the root conceit of the self that desires nothing so much as its own continued existence. Without that, Māra can throw up any obstacle, but it will not be able to land. As ego abates with the attainment of each of the jhānas, one further throws Māra off the pursuit: "A bhikkhu enters upon and abides in the first [second, third, and fourth] jhāna. . . . This bhikkhu is said to have blindfolded Māra, to have become invisible to the Evil One by depriving Māra's eye of its opportunity."[52] Try as Māra might, there will be no self poised and ready to take the bait.

Any practice of meditative awareness that accords with the Dharma thus requires all of the resources the holy life offers. As Nyanaponika Thera points out,

> This widespread harmful influence of the five hindrances shows the urgent necessity of breaking down their power by constant effort. One should not believe it sufficient to turn one's attention to the hindrances only at the moment when one sits down for meditation. Such last-minute effort . . . will rarely be successful unless helped by previous endeavor during one's ordinary life.[53]

From the initial corralling of the unruly mind to one's first confrontation with the nīvaraṇas, each step in the process has provided an invitation to note the discrepancy between what one imagines oneself to be doing and what one is actually doing. Now that the aspirant has come to a clearer awareness of the hindrances and their obstructive capabilities, all of that can now be pressed into service in overcoming them. The practice of renunciation that set the noble disciple apart from the everyday person is the very practice that makes the fruits of insight at all possible.

---

52 Ñāṇamoli and Bodhi, *Middle Length Discourses*, 267.

53 Nyanaponika Thera, trans., *The Five Mental Hindrances and Their Conquest: Texts from the Pali Canon and the Commentaries* (Kandy, Sri Lanka: Buddhist Publication Society, 2018), 6–7. Mahāsi Sayadaw in *Manual of Insight*, for instance, mentions them almost in passing and, in the short space he does devote to them, gives the impression that they go away rather quickly: "These mental hindrances may disappear when you note them once, twice, or several times." Sayadaw, *Manual of Insight*, trans. Vipassanā Mettā Foundation Translation Committee (Boston: Wisdom, 2016), 209. Quite frankly, that seems too good to be true, at least if the domain of practice is not simply a particularly tranquil and insightful *meditation session* but a *life lived in the unshakable deliverance of mind*, and Nyanaponika's observation is well-taken on this point.

Once stilled in samādhi, the noble disciple will now be in a position to proceed unhindered toward the cultivation of the seven factors of enlightenment (*bojjhaṅgas*) that conduce to final liberation: "When, bhikkhus, a noble disciple listens to the Dhamma with eager ears, attending to it as a matter of vital concern, directing his whole mind to it, on that occasion the five hindrances are not present in him; on that occasion the seven factors of enlightenment go to fulfillment by development."[54] These are the enlightenment factors of mindfulness, discrimination, energy, rapture, tranquility, concentration, and equanimity,[55] all of which are indispensable for attaining realization: "Just as all the rafters of a peaked house slant, slope, and incline towards the roof peak, so too, when a bhikkhu develops and cultivates the seven factors of enlightenment, he slants, slopes, and inclines towards Nibbāna."[56]

There is not much detail in the tradition concerning nirvāṇa; it is pointed to but not described.[57] One thing that is known is that where the nīvaraṇas are, no enlightenment is to be found:

> For those bhikkhus who are arahants, whose taints are destroyed, who have lived the holy life, done what had to be done, laid down the burden, reached their own goal, utterly destroyed the fetters of existence, become completely liberated though final knowledge, these five hindrances have been abandoned, cut off at the root, made like palm stumps, obliterated so that they are no more subject to future arising.[58]

Thus, when the nīvaraṇas continue to be experienced, this only indicates how far one has yet to go.

---

54 Bodhi, *Connected Discourses*, 1592.

55 Bodhi, *Connected Discourses*, 1571–72.

56 Bodhi, *Connected Discourses*, 1577.

57 Nirvāṇa is a cessation of conditioned states arising from tṛṣṇā—an "extinguishing" or "going out"—not a new set of conditioned states. Any *description* of nirvāṇa would presuppose that it is *something* to talk about. Language concerning nirvāṇa, when it is used, is therefore necessarily apophatic (not this, not that). See Peter Harvey, *An Introduction to Buddhism: Teachings, History and Practices* (New York: Cambridge University Press, 2013), 74–75.

58 Bodhi, *Connected Discourses*, 1779. Arahants are those who have attained enlightenment and for whom there is no further rebirth.

PART TWO

Confronting the Obstacles

CHAPTER THREE

The Varied Allures of Sensory Desire

The training sequences up to this point have brought the aspirant, whether Christian or Buddhist, to the threshold of confronting the deeply rooted mental states that bolster one's sense of self. Like a person who has made it to the edge of a stream, the time has now come to throw off any lingering attachment to dry land and cross to the other shore. As fear inducing as this prospect may be, it would be even more intimidating if the aspirant had not first passed through the preliminary training of the body and its comportment. The impetus that led one to submit to the constraints of renunciant life in the first place is the same impetus that now can be pressed into service in order to face one's own obstructive states of mind. Both are moments of one and the same process, a process of "radical risk, in a continual opening of the self without prejudice or constraint to everything emerging from within and without, in particular the anomalous and chaotic and fearful, all those elements of reality that are most difficult to face and absorb."[1] Leaving the everyday world behind and aligning one's comportment with the dictates of the body were only the very beginning of a much protracted process. One who would aspire to communion in God or to the unshakable deliverance of mind must therefore be nothing short of intrepid in confronting everything else that gets thrown in the way of that aspiration or otherwise obstructs its

1 Douglas Burton-Christie, "Simplicity, or the Terror of Belief: The Making and Unmaking of the Self in Early Christian Monasticism," *Cistercian Studies Quarterly* 40 (2005): 357–58.

attainability. This means even letting go of what seem to be patently obvious truths about oneself and the world—truths that, until now, will have appeared incontrovertible and just as defining of oneself as the nose on one's face.

One of the most obvious of such truths is that there is nothing quite so important as maintaining oneself in a pleasurable and comfortable state for as long as possible. To many, this is simply a natural imperative that issues forth from our bodily constitution itself—we are drawn to pleasure, and we recoil from pain. On the whole, this is a good thing, for without paying attention to the cues that pain and pleasure provide we would hardly be able to distinguish healthy from unhealthy activities and things. Since the senses are instrumental in navigating bodily activity in the world, it might seem that nature intends us to seek out sensory pleasures for their own sake and that anything that compromises that aim is therefore suspect. According to this notion, everything pleasurable is taken to be good, and anything that diminishes the fullest extent of pleasure is considered bad.

The Christian would have heard this apparent dictate of nature called into question already in the Gospels: "If your right eye causes you to sin, tear it out and throw it away; it is better for you to lose one of your members than for your whole body to be thrown into hell" (Matt 5:29). The follower of the Dharma would have heard a strikingly similar message:

> It would be better, bhikkhus, for the eye faculty to be lacerated by a red-hot iron pin burning, blazing, and glowing, than for one to grasp the sign through the features in a form cognizable by the eye. For if consciousness should stand tied to gratification in the sign or in the features, and if one should die on that occasion, it is possible that one will go to one of two destinations: hell or the animal realm. Having seen this danger, I speak thus.[2]

The straightforwardness of unquestioningly following sense pleasure is, perhaps, not so straightforward after all, and keeping the body satisfied might not be the most important thing in the world.

Happily, there is no need to destroy body parts in order to avoid trouble; what is claimed here is that it is *better* to lose one's eye or render it blind than to end up in a hellish state, not that one *has to* lose one's eye or eyesight to avoid such a fate. As the Buddha points out with respect to the functioning of the skandhas, and as Evagrius maintains in his understanding of the body, our embodied state is simply a given that need not to be dispensed with

2 Ñāṇamoli and Bodhi, *Middle Length Discourses*, 1234.

outright. What is required instead is a clear understanding of the distinction between sensory *experience* (that is, the unproblematic everyday functioning of a living body in its environment when appropriately guided by sensory feelings) and sensory *desire* (the attempt to steer that functioning in light of one's self-conception). Sensory desire involves a misapprehension of sensory experience that turns that experience from a mere fact of the matter into a narrative about oneself. Rather than simply *experiencing*, sensory desire drives one to *seek out experiences*, not because they are necessarily helpful but simply because one longs for the pleasure they bring.

The first three logismoi that Evagrius addresses—gluttony, fornication, and avarice—are all forms of sensory desire that reflect sensory experience misunderstood and mistakenly pursued. To borrow a modern turn of phrase, they are the "gateway" logismoi. They are the logismoi most directly experienced in everyday engagement with the world, and all subsequent logismoi follow from them. Moreover, unless they are overcome, it will be close to impossible to overcome the rest: "Among the demons who set themselves in opposition to the practical life, those ranged first in battle are the ones entrusted with the appetites of gluttony, those who make to us suggestions of avarice, and those who entice us to seek human esteem. . . . No one can fall into a demon's power, unless he has first been wounded by those in the front line."[3]

Sensory desire is also the first of the nīvaraṇas, and it, too, serves as a gateway for the others. Left unattended, sensory desire renders one particularly vulnerable to Māra's further wiles, because one will have placed oneself under Māra's dominion by having freely ambled right across his doorstep:

> Bhikkhus, there are forms cognizable by the eye that are desirable, lovely, agreeable, pleasing, sensually enticing, tantalizing. If a bhikkhu seeks delight in them, welcomes them, and remains holding on to them, then he is called a bhikkhu who has entered Māra's lair, who has come under Māra's control; Māra's snare has been fastened to him so he is bound by the bondage of Māra and the Evil One can do with him as he wishes.[4]

As with the eye, so too with the other senses. There are good grounds, then, for taking up the first three Evagrian logismoi in conjunction with the nīvaraṇa of sense desire as described in the teaching of the Buddha. Taken together, they address the first and foundational obstacle in the renunciant-contemplative

---

3 Evagrius, *On Thoughts* 1; Sinkewicz, 153.

4 Bodhi, *Connected Discourses*, 1187.

life—the conceit of the self as manifest in thoughts and ideas related to bodily form and activity.[5]

In Evagrius's ordering of the logismoi, gluttony is always the first of those obstacles related to sense desire. The image commonly associated with gluttony is that of a person who cannot resist making yet another pass along the all-you-can-eat buffet, a person who always wants more. But Evagrius's description of gluttony tacks in the opposite direction—instead of dwelling on getting *more*, the glutton dwells on the prospect of *not having enough* or, at the limit, *any at all*.

Recall that already in the earliest stage of the practical life, the aspiring monk was counseled to take his leave of the tables of worldly people so as not to be caught up in their values. At his own table, he was to keep to a plain diet and restrict his food intake to one scant meal a day unless he were ill or if the demands of hospitality required otherwise. No doubt the monk often found himself hungry as a result, and whereas an everyday person might just have a little nosh to tide herself over, the monk was simply left with a rumbling stomach. But rather than just letting it rumble on until the next meal, the monk's mind would start rumbling along with it as well, giving rise to thoughts not only about his noisy stomach but what that noise might portend for the rest of his innards as well:

> The thought of gluttony suggests to the monk the rapid demise of his asceticism. It describes for him his stomach, his liver and spleen, dropsy and lengthy illness, the scarcity of necessities and the absence of doctors. Frequently it brings him to recall certain of the brethren who have fallen prey to these sufferings.[6]

Hypochondria, from the least concern over one's physical state to the full-fledged fear of disease and the prospect of death, is the core manifestation of the logismos of gluttony.[7] It involves creating an image of some projected bodily state and then concocting thoughts related to one's food intake

5 Because gluttony, fornication, and avarice will all be placed in relation to the nīvaraṇa of sense desire here, this chapter is necessarily on the long side, and I beg the reader's indulgence in following through to the end.

6 Evagrius, *Praktikos* 7; Sinkewicz, 98.

7 Evagrius, *Antirrhetikos* 1.56, 1.57, 1.59; Brakke, 65. In a modern context, orthorexia, the persistent concern about eating the *right* foods, rather than what is simply obtainable and nourishing enough, would have to be included here as well.

accordingly. The monk, thinking that the discipline of fasting is going to cut him off from any prospect of managing his body in this way, and fearful of what such a lack of management might lead to, now considers abandoning the renunciant path.

There are any number of correlative thoughts that would seem to justify this mindset, and these, too, will seem rather obvious to the everyday person. Perhaps the most basic is that nothing of harm comes to the soul from eating and drinking at will.[8] Whatever the soul is, a monk might think, it is not affected by foodstuffs one way or another in the way that the body is. If that is the case, there is certainly no reason to engage in fasting as a *spiritual* discipline, even as one might do it for health or performance benefits, but neither is there any need to restrain oneself at table if one chooses to eat as much as one likes. Both cases would fall under the rubric of *bodily management* rather than anything connected to the conduct of one's prayer life.

This thought is beguiling, because it attests to something that is true enough as far as it goes: the soul is not simply to be *equated* with the body.[9] But obsession with the body's nutrition and the stock in the larder most assuredly does affect the vision and resolve of one who would attain to stillness. The degree of gluttony's grip is not measured by the bathroom scale or even one's triglyceride levels, but rather by the degree of one's preoccupation with food and its attendant impact on the body. Because the mind cannot hold two mental representations at the same time, it follows that where thoughts of bodily states are, there thoughts of freeing the mind for God cannot arise. It is not that the monk should be neglectful of his food intake, but there is a proper measure here, and Evagrius passes on the counsel he himself received on this point:

> The monk must ever hold himself ready as though he were to die tomorrow, and in turn must treat the body as though he would have to live with it for many years. The first practice . . . cuts off the thoughts of acedia and makes the

8 Evagrius, *Antirrhetikos* 1.6; Brakke, 54.

9 The tempting nature of such a thought relies on its appeal to the everyday assumption that body and soul are different in kind—one material, one not. Under such a dualistic view, food (as more material stuff) cannot affect the soul, so whatever one eats or does not eat is irrelevant as far as one's spiritual practice goes. Evagrius, as we saw above, does not hold such a dualistic view. Body, soul, and mind may be on a continuum as aspects of one and the same *person*, but that does not mean that body, soul, and mind are *themselves* the same.

> monk more zealous; the latter keeps the body healthy and always maintains its abstinence in balance.[10]

There is nothing problematic about eating as long as one eats in accordance with the natural order of things: being content with what one does have, not worrying about the morrow, and leaving it at that.

As long as he is guided by fear of the loss of food in the future,[11] the monk will likely begin to lay up a store of whatever he does have. Not wishing to appear a selfish hoarder, he reaches for some seemingly defensible pretext for keeping that extra food on hand. A ready one is the idea that one should stockpile food on the pretext of hospitality.[12] Since hospitality in the desert could indeed mean the difference between life and death, then surely it just makes sense to keep provisions on hand so that anyone who finds themselves needing food might find solace from hunger in my larder. As we saw already with food in the initial stages of practice, however, skirting one's ascesis on the pretext of providing assistance to others is best viewed as yet another ploy of the demons trying to break one's ascesis by any means necessary.

Even though one should not amass food in expectation of some need to offer hospitality, one should not instead turn around and be stingy with what one does have, either. One of the manifestations of gluttony is not giving to the needy from one's own food and clothing, either because of presumed lack of resources ("the provisions we have gathered are not sufficient both for us and for the brothers who come to us") or lack of worthiness on the part of the other ("there is someone weaker or in greater need than this person, and we should give to that person rather than this one, for this one is lazy and wants to eat and be clothed without working").[13]

Whether it is the prospect of illness, hospitality, or future scarcity that is troubling, the Gospel injunction—"Do not worry about your life, what you will eat or what you will drink, or about your body, what you will wear. Is not life more than food, and the body more than clothing?" (Matt 6:25)[14]—flies in the face of all of them. A rumbling stomach is simply a rumbling stomach. It is a condition, not a pathology. It is information, not an imperative. The monk who lets his concern for food override his concern to live according to

---

10 Evagrius, *Praktikos* 29; Sinkewicz, 103.

11 Evagrius, *Antirrhetikos* 1.21; Brakke, 57.

12 Evagrius, *Antirrhetikos* 1.12; Brakke, 56.

13 Evagrius, *Antirrhetikos* 1.10, 1.49; Brakke, 55, 63.

14 Evagrius, *Antirrhetikos* 1.47; Brakke, 63.

the commandments has declared his allegiance to his stomach rather than to God. But allegiance to God should not itself turn into yet another kind of self-serving preoccupation that overshoots the mark by treating his body poorly, and it is telling that Evagrius includes in his inventory of thoughts related to gluttony

> the vain thought that persuades us to extend our discipline beyond what is appropriate by putting sackcloth on our loins, setting out for the desert, living continuously under the sky, and tending wild plants; and that advises us as well to flee from the sight of human beings who comfort us and who are comforted by us.[15]

Being a "glutton for punishment," too, would seem to be an instance of this logismos, and there are variations on this thought connected with some of the other obstacles as well.[16]

Following closely on the heels of gluttony is the logismos of sexual desire, or fornication:

> There is gluttony, then, the mother of fornication, nourishing the thoughts with words, the relaxation of fasting, the muzzling of ascesis, terror over one's moral purpose, imagining of foods, picturer of condiments, a dissolute fawn, an unbridled madness, a receptacle of disease, envy of health, an obstruction of the throat, a groaning of the innards, the extremity of insults, a fellow initiate in fornication, pollution of the intellect, weakness of the body, wearisome sleep, gloomy death.[17]

Or again,

> Fornication is a conception of gluttony, that which softens the heart in advance, a furnace of lustful burning, an arranger of marriages with idols, unnatural activity, a form covered in shadows, an (sexual) intertwining wrought in the imagination, a bed of dreams, unfeeling sexual congress, bait for the eyes, immodesty of sight, dishonouring of prayer, shame of the heart, guide to ignorance.[18]

The close connection Evagrius sees between gluttony and fornication might seem forced if one simply considers their respective areas of concern: everyone needs to eat, but it is not a matter of life and death whether one has sex.

---

15 Evagrius, *Antirrhetikos* 1.37; Brakke, 60.

16 We will see this particularly in conjunction with the logismos of acedia and the nīvaraṇa of restlessness-remorse.

17 Evagrius, *Vices* 1.2; Sinkewicz, 62.

18 Evagrius, *Vices* 2; Sinkewicz, 62–63.

But here, again, the issue is not about food or sex per se, but about whether one will be thrown off from the single-hearted pursuit of the renunciant-contemplative life:

> The demon of fornication compels one to desire various bodies. It attacks more violently those who practice abstinence in order that they give it up, convinced that they are accomplishing nothing. In defiling the soul, the demon inclines it to shameful deeds, has it speak and hear certain things, almost as if the object were visible and present.[19]

The first aim of any demon is to lure the monk *away from* his practice, not to lure him *toward* particular objects or bodies and the pleasure they provide. At most that may be a secondary consequence—troubling, to be sure, but still only secondary.[20]

Even though the monk is now living in a situation where the opportunity for sexual encounters has been almost thoroughly eliminated, this does not curtail the lure of fornication in the least: in fact, it only strengthens its hold. As food relates to gluttony, so sex to fornication—it is the prospect of its ongoing absence rather than the momentary inability to satisfy some urge that so occupies the mind and clouds one's vision. Evagrius identifies one of the correlative thoughts of fornication in "the thought of sadness that arises in us due to the many temptations of fornication that come upon us and cut off our hope by saying to us, 'What beautiful thing do you expect after all this labor?'"[21] Sex is more than simple sensory stimulation; it is also a reward, a way of celebrating, a way to console or be consoled, and a way to relax, and all of that is taken away by the monk's discipline of celibacy. Whatever communion with God offers, the monk is tempted to think, it certainly does not offer any of *that*. Perhaps most telling is the series of thoughts associated with fornication that would lead one to think that it can never be overcome,[22] since the thoughts of those pleasures never seem to go away.

On the other hand, Evagrius thought that it was the young monk, much more so than the elder one, who was most prone to thoughts of fornication. A young monk might find himself thinking, "Youth can never cease from

---

19 Evagrius, *Praktikos* 8; Sinkewicz, 98.

20 Here we see one of the reasons why the logismoi are not the deadly sins. The logismoi are particular to cultivating the practice of pure prayer; the deadly sins are simply violations of the moral law.

21 Evagrius, *Antirrhetikos* 2.2; Brakke, 69.

22 Evagrius, *Antirrhetikos* 2.18, 2.31; Brakke, 73, 76.

the desires of fornication and offer to God thoughts purified of it" or "Youth is neither guilty nor culpable if it fornicates or if it gladly receives unclean thoughts."[23] This may have had as much to do with the young monk's marriageability as with his youthful hormonal profile, since the range of sexual desire covers not only pleasing oneself and one's partner but manifesting the fruit of that desire in starting a family. That being the case, fornication suggests to the young monk that he should "marry a woman and become the father of sons."[24] For the everyday Christian, this would be a noble enough thought; for the monk, it spelled the end of his monastic career and all that it held in store.

All close connections between gluttony and fornication notwithstanding, it remains that food needs to be procured from elsewhere, while sexual satisfaction is something one can always indulge in on one's own. The account of fornication's wiles would therefore not be complete without Evagrius's mention of "the demon of fornication that, whenever its thoughts ceased, began to explore and touch the body's members—those who have been tempted by this demon will understand what I am saying."[25]

Like its kindred logismoi, gluttony and fornication, avarice has less to do with thoughts of unbridled acquisition and more to do with the prospect of utter indigence. The demon of avarice, Evagrius writes, "suggests a lengthy old age, inability to perform manual labor, famines that will come along, diseases that will arise, the bitter realities of poverty, and the shame here is in accepting goods from others to meet one's needs."[26] It is

> the parsimony of idols, the prophecy of the crowd, a vote for stinginess, a hoarding mentality, a wealth of captivity, a race of injustice, an abundance of illnesses, a diviner of many years, an enchanter for industriousness, a counsellor of sleeplessness, poverty of the belly, meagreness of foods, insatiable madness, a wickedness of many cares.[27]

It is "the thought that shows me bitter poverty and the evils that arise from it and suggests to me that on the day of need I will not find a helper."[28] Avarice

23 Evagrius, *Antirrhetikos* 2.4–5; Brakke, 70. "Boys will be boys" would be a clear contemporary version of this thought.

24 Evagrius, *Antirrhetikos* 2.49; Brakke, 79.

25 Evagrius, *Antirrhetikos* 2.55; Brakke, 81.

26 Evagrius, *Praktikos* 9; Sinkewicz, 98.

27 Evagrius, *Vices* 3; Sinkewicz, 63.

28 Evagrius, *Antirrhetikos* 3.2; Brakke, 85.

is but another name for the attempt to insure oneself against the vicissitudes of life and the prospect of an early demise.

Evagrius lists any number of thoughts that involve withholding one's wealth or goods from others.[29] The reason for the other's need does not seem to matter—perhaps a brother just asks, perhaps he has been sick, or perhaps he is simply suffering from hunger. One beset by avarice does not even need to think the reason is a particularly good one, and Evagrius draws attention to "the thought of love of money that did not want to give alms to the brothers on the pretext that 'they are not in need' and so in action renounced God's love."[30] So attached am I to the control of my resources that I now set myself up as the arbiter of others' needs and wants, as if my possessions endowed me with some *power* or *authority* over them. So deep is the connection between power and the respect it commands that the "thought that I lose esteem in the eyes of others, since no one respects the poor person but the rich are ever the subject of honors and riches"[31] seems to capture an obvious consequence of abandoning wealth altogether.

One has one not freed oneself from thoughts associated with avarice by simply transferring the acquisition of money for one's own benefit to acquiring money for religious purposes, however. Thinking that one's wealth might prove useful for God's purposes generally, or for the success of the church in particular,[32] are also deceptions. If it is not an individual's job to pick and choose among worthy recipients of their liberality, it is also not their job to ripen God's harvest as they see fit. In fact, it is one of the most cunning aspects of avarice that it does not differentiate among the seemingly contradictory ways it manifests, but instead embraces all of them:

> It appears to me that the demon of avarice is the most varied and ingenious in deceit. Often constrained by the most severe renunciation, he immediately pretends to be the administrator and friend of the poor; he generously receives guests who are not yet there; he sends assistance to others who are in need; he visits the city's prisons and he buys those who are being sold; he associates himself with wealthy women and indicates to them who should be treated well; and those who have acquired an ample purse he advises to renounce it.[33]

---

29 Evagrius, *Antirrhetikos* 3.5, 3.10, 3.37; Brakke, 86, 87, 93.

30 Evagrius, *Antirrhetikos* 3.57; Brakke, 98.

31 Evagrius, *Antirrhetikos* 3.18; Brakke, 89.

32 Evagrius, *Antirrhetikos* 3.42, 3.50; Brakke, 94, 96.

33 Evagrius, *On Thoughts* 21; Sinkewicz, 167.

Even when one owns next to nothing, one can pretend to magnanimity in thought, imagining just how generous one might be if only one had the resources.

Like all the obstacles, avarice is tempting because it is based on a misunderstanding of the nature of the self. Avarice relies on the assumption that one can direct one's own fate while ignoring the plain and incontrovertible fact that one "entered the world bare and it will leave it naked."[34] In the end, all of one's wealth and possessions cannot undo the basic fact of existence—that all, rich *and* poor, are ultimately destined for death. Evagrius calls avarice "the mother of idolatry"[35] because it allows the self to see itself as the lord and master of its own destiny, and thus subverts the relationship between God and the created order. While all Christians will have heard of the man who built bigger granaries to secure his harvest as a safeguard against the future only to die that very night (Luke 12:15–21), only those who have confronted and overcome every least trace of avarice in their hearts will be free of such foolishness and live according to their station in relation to God.

In facing the first three logismoi, the aspirant is schooled in each of them individually, but also in the nature of all the logismoi together. "It is due to the desires," Evagrius writes, "that every kind of temptation from the demons comes upon it."[36] What makes the temptations thrown up by the demons so tempting is that they are so *appealing*: one would be hard-pressed to imagine a temptation that does not involve some picture of a life more comfortable, more respected, more beautiful, or more satiating. Anger, sadness, acedia, vainglory, and pride will all have their attendant appeals, but gluttony, fornication, and avarice wear on their sleeves their unbridled confidence in the ability of pleasure to guide one's actions appropriately. Since these first three present themselves most straightforwardly to the monk, by learning to identify, see into, and combat them, he is honing his technique for dealing with the other five, which, as we will see, are not always as obvious in the way they operate.

The monk's initial training in the practical life had been intended to set the foundations for combating the logismoi effectively. His exile from the world, his restraint at the table, and the abandoning of the possessions of everyday life—intended at the outset just to tame the wildness in his soul—can now be developed as virtues that bring forth counterthoughts to those thoughts

---

34 Evagrius, *Antirrhetikos* 3.53; Brakke, 97.

35 Evagrius, *Exhortations* 1.2; Sinkewicz, 218.

36 Evagrius, *Antirrhetikos* 2.62; Brakke, 83.

that the demons prompt in the monk. Fortifying the monk against gluttony is abstinence:

> Abstinence is a bridle for the stomach, a scourge of immoderation, a balance of due proportion, a muzzle for gourmandise, renunciation of rest, the undertaking of austerity, a place of chastisement for thoughts, an eye for vigilance, deliverance from lustful burning, pedagogue of the body, a tower of ascetic works and a wall for our ways, reserve in morals and repression of the passions, mortification of one's (bodily) members, revivification of souls, imitation of resurrection, a life of sanctification.[37]

Chastity is the disposition that counters fornication:

> Chastity is a robe of truth, an axe for wantonness, a charioteer for the eyes, an overseer for one's thinking, a circumcision of thoughts, excision of licentiousness, a planting opposed to nature and a counter to lustful burning, an assistant to our works and a collaborator with abstinence, a lantern for the heart and an inclination for prayer.[38]

And finally, voluntary poverty, both material poverty as well as poverty of the spirit, bring the monk back from the temptations of avarice:

> Freedom from possessions is the uprooting of avarice and the rooting of freedom from it, a fruit of love and a cross of life, a life free of suffering, a treasure free of envy, a heaven free of care, a sun without distraction, immeasurable matter, incomprehensible wealth, a scythe for cares, the practice of the Gospels, the world readily abandoned, a fast-running contestant.[39]

Through each of them, the monk surrenders his confidence in his own assessment of these various bodily states and places his trust more and more in God. Whatever he had hoped to gain from gluttony, fornication, and avarice is set aside in favor of "hope in God [which] circumscribes corporeal concerns."[40]

The Buddha may have suggested that it would be better to lose one's sight than fall into a lower realm of existence: but he consistently challenged the

---

37 Evagrius, *Vices* 1; Sinkewicz, 62.

38 Evagrius, *Vices* 2; Sinkewicz, 63.

39 Evagrius, *Vices* 3; Sinkewicz, 63.

40 Evagrius, *Exhortations* 1.3; Sinkewicz, 218.

idea that simply obliterating one's sense capabilities or otherwise denying them is a precondition for the cultivation of the mind. Such an idea is as misguided as it is common among ascetics in every age. Indeed, it was clearly advocated among some of the Buddha's contemporaries, as we see in this dialogue between the Buddha and a disciple of an ascetic teacher at the time:

> "Uttara, does the brahmin Pārāsariya teach his disciples the development of the faculties?"
>
> "He does, Master Gotama."
>
> "But, Uttara, how does he teach his disciples the development of the faculties?"
>
> "Here, Master Gotama, one does not see forms with the eye, one does not hear sounds with the ear. That is how the brahmin Pārāsariya teaches his disciples the development of the faculties."
>
> "If that is so, Uttara, then a blind man and a deaf man will have developed faculties, according to what the brahmin Pārāsariya says. For a blind man does not see forms with the eye, and a deaf man does not hear sounds with the ear."[41]

The root mistake of *denying* sensory function is that its aim is off.

Just because one happens to see something does not imply anything concerning one's action toward it. Phenomena (*dharmas*) have no power to *make one* subject to them.[42] In response to the question "How is it, friend Sāriputta, is the eye the fetter of forms or are forms the fetter of the eye? Is the ear the fetter of sounds or are sounds the fetter of the ear? . . . Is the mind the fetter of mental phenomena or are mental phenomena the fetter of the mind?"[43] the Buddha's answer is *neither*:

> "Suppose, friend, a black ox and a white ox were yoked together by a single harness or yoke. Would one be speaking rightly if one were to say: 'The black ox is the fetter of the white ox; the white ox is the fetter of the black ox'?"
>
> "No, friend. The black ox is not the fetter of the white ox nor is the white ox the fetter of the black ox, but rather the single harness or yoke by which the two are yoked together: that is the fetter there.

41 Ñāṇamoli and Bodhi, *Middle Length Discourses*, 1147.

42 When lowercase, *dhamma/dharma* refers to a phenomenon; when uppercase, *Dhamma/Dharma* refers to the teaching of the Buddha.

43 Bodhi, *Connected Discourses*, 1230.

> "So too, friend, the eye is not the fetter of forms . . . nor are mental phenomena the fetter of the mind, but rather the desire and lust that arise there in dependence on both: that is the fetter there.
>
> "If, friend, the eye were the fetter of forms or if forms were the fetter of the eye, this living of the holy life could not be discerned for the complete destruction of suffering."[44]

Simply rendering oneself blind makes the practice of the holy life itself impossible, since it cuts off any way to pursue it. The liberation of the mind involves clearly seeing the mutual conditioning of sensibility and sense object, not in avoiding this or that situation or thing. One cannot clearly see into that conditioning if either of the moments of that conditioning are not able to give rise to it. This is why, in conjunction with sensory desire, the Buddha speaks of *abandoning* the eye, the ear, and the rest by becoming dispassionate with respect to them.[45] When one sees that neither what one experiences nor that which does the experiencing has any abiding nature, but rather they rise and fall with each other, one can see that there is nothing about a self in all that. One can stop hoping that there is by simply let the rising and falling of sense experience play itself out without *identifying* with it.[46]

While tṛṣṇā is the root cause of one's suffering, it is often hard to see just how, exactly, it functions that way in the course of everyday life. So automatic are our responses to phenomena that their straightforward ability to affect our thoughts, choices, and activity is taken as a given. Crude behaviorism is just part and parcel of the naive realism by which most everyone conducts their affairs. But the Buddha discovered that between stimulus and response any number of factors are operative, each of which must be in place for our samsaric state to arise. These are the twelve *nidānas* or *causal links* in the process of dependent origination (*paṭiccasamuppāda*): out of ignorance (*avijjā/avidyā*) arise volitional formations (*saṅkhāra/saṃskāra*), then consciousness (*viññāṇa/vijñāna*), name-and-form (*nāmarūpa*), the six sense bases (*saḷāyatana/ṣaḍāyatana*), contact (*phassa/sparśa*), feeling (*vedanā*), craving (*tanha/tṛṣṇā*), clinging (*upādāna*), existence (*bhava*), and

44 Bodhi, *Connected Discourses*, 1230.

45 Bodhi, *Connected Discourses*, 1141.

46 Here we see why guarding the senses as part of the gradual training is instrumental in combating this nīvaraṇa.

birth (*jāti*), in that order through to aging-and-death (*jarāmaraṇa*).[47] The links up through feeling are the operation of the skandhas in conjunction with some intentional act. I am hungry and want a snack. My body registers the object in front of me as an apple, as good for nourishment, as something palatable. So far, so good, and I can, without further ado, eat the apple. But, taking delight in its taste, I soon enough find that I want to taste another apple whether I am particularly hungry or not. Tṛṣṇā has now entered the sequence, and the rest, which is just a mass of trouble and suffering, follows.

Now each of the nīvaraṇas has its nutritive ground, the causes and conditions that give it rise. Like any other dependently arising dharma, cutting off its food supply is the key to cutting off the dharma in question. As we saw above, it is not the eye that is the problem, nor is it the object seen. The nutritive ground is instead a mental fabrication, a sign or mark (*nimitta*)[48] that is introduced, as it were, by the seer with respect to the seen that then fuels the seer's craving. In the case of apples, such a nutritive ground might be their good taste: "Apples are yummy, and I could really go for an apple right now." The apple's yumminess is one variation on what the Buddha identified as the sign or mark of the beautiful (*subhanimitta*):

> And what, bhikkhus, is the nutriment for the arising of unarisen sensual desire and for the increase and expansion of arisen sensual desire? There is, bhikkhus, the sign of the beautiful: frequently giving careless attention to it is the nutriment for the arising of unarisen sensual desire and for the increase and expansion of arisen sensual desire.[49]

Or again:

> Bhikkhus, I do not see even one other thing on account of which unarisen sensual desire arises and arisen sensual desire increases and expands so much as the mark of the attractive. For one who attends carelessly to the mark of the attractive, unarisen sensual desire arises and arisen sensual desire increases and expands.[50]

---

47 Bodhi, *Connected Discourses*, 537–39.

48 *Nimitta* is rendered into English as both "sign" and "mark." Both terms will be found in what follows, in accordance with the translation of a particular passage.

49 Bodhi, *Connected Discourses*, 1568.

50 Bodhi, *Numerical Discourses*, 90.

The apple is no longer just an apple but has become, as we say today, eye candy. But finding myself now voraciously eating an apple at every opportunity, I might begin to think that it is the apple that is making me overconsume: "The apple was calling to me, and I just *had* to eat it," one might say. Coming to think better of my now established apple habit, I entertain the thought that I should cut apples out of my life altogether, freeing myself from their spell. I might succeed in no longer eating apples, but I will not have uprooted the nīvaraṇa that had me going for them in the first place. For that, another tactic is required.

Rather than eliminating the objects of desire, one can cut to the root of that desire by counteracting the sign that gave rise to my compulsion:

> Bhikkhus, when a bhikkhu is giving attention to some sign, and owing to that sign there arise in him evil unwholesome thoughts connected with desire, with hate, and with delusion, then he gives attention to some other sign connected with what is wholesome, any such evil unwholesome thoughts are abandoned in him and subside, and with the abandoning of them his mind becomes steadied internally, quieted, brought to singleness, and concentrated.[51]

By introducing a wholesome countersign, the first sign is rendered impotent. Here, in the case of the sign of the beautiful, the way to undercut its hold is to introduce the sign of the unattractive:

> Bhikkhus, I do not see even one other thing on account of which unarisen sensual desire does not arise and arisen sensual desire is abandoned so much as the mark of the unattractive. For one who attends carefully to the mark of the unattractive, unarisen sensual desire does not arise and arisen sensual desire is abandoned.[52]

The sign of the beautiful was ascribed to the apple's appealing characteristics; the sign of the unattractive is now ascribed to its unappealing ones: its having bruises, being subject to decay, and the rest. An honest accounting of sense objects includes both their appealing and their unappealing characteristics, and, in the end, leads one to see the apple as it is without any selectivity on one's part.

The cultivation of dispassion in the gradual training comes to the aspirant's assistance here in conjunction with taking on the nīvaraṇa of sense desire. The first place to exercise that dispassion is with an unvarnished consideration

51 Ñāṇamoli and Bodhi, *Middle Length Discourses*, 213.

52 Bodhi, *Numerical Discourses*, 91.

of bodily form. When I focus on something that is pleasurable, I am in fact carrying out a cherry-picking exercise in reality by disregarding the full range of sensory dharmas, which include not only pleasurable ones but unpleasurable or neutral ones as well. An honest accounting of the body, taking note of what being a body entails, cuts against that selectivity and opens one up to the nature of all conditioned dharmas:

> A bhikkhu reviews this same body up from the soles of the feet and down from the top of the hair, bounded by skin, as full of many kinds of impurity thus: "In this body there are head-hairs, body-hairs, nails, teeth, skin, flesh, sinews, bones, bone-marrow, kidneys, heart, liver, diaphragm, spleen, lungs, intestines, mesentery, contents of the stomach, feces, bile, phlegm, pus, blood, sweat, fat, tears, grease, spittle, snot, oil of the joints, and urine."[53]

And that is just a description of *living* bodies. Paying close attention to *dead* ones further underscores the ultimate unattractiveness of bodily forms:

> Again, bhikkhus, as though he were to see a corpse thrown aside in a charnel ground, one, two, or three days dead, bloated, livid, and oozing matter, a bhikkhu compares this same with it thus: "This body too is of the same nature, it will be like that, it is not exempt from that fate."

The Buddha then goes through all of the stages of decomposition until there is nothing but a crumbling heap of bones bleached by the sun, and the bhikkhu at each stage reflects: "This body too is of the same nature, it will be like that, it is not exempt from that fate."[54] And, of course, it is not just bodies but every possible dharma that is like this:

> Bhikkhus, these seven perceptions, when developed and cultivated, are of great fruit and benefit, culminating in the deathless, having the deathless as their consummation. What seven? The perception of unattractiveness, the perception of death, the perception of the repulsiveness of food, the perception of non-delight in the entire world, the perception of impermanence, the perception of suffering in the impermanent, and the perception of non-self in which is suffering.[55]

If one were in need of a model of a way of life that stands at the opposite end of the spectrum from that lived by the noble disciple who developed such perceptions, it would be that of an aesthete. An aesthete measures everything

53 Ñāṇamoli and Bodhi, *Middle Length Discourses*, 147.
54 Ñāṇamoli and Bodhi, *Middle Length Discourses*, 148–49.
55 Bodhi, *Numerical Discourses*, 1031–32.

by the standard to beauty. Countering the sign of the beautiful with the sign of the unattractive does not mean preferring that everything be ugly. It simply means that a focus on beauty to the exclusion of the unattractive results in an unbalanced, hence obstructed, view of oneself and the world.

Gluttony, avarice, and fornication are all addressed in the *Nikāyas*, not as nīvaraṇas in their own right but as variations on one and the same obstacle: sensory desire. Whereas Evagrius draws a clear causal line from gluttony through fornication to avarice, the Buddha demurs when asked to rank the various forms of sensual desire:

> What is chief among the five cords of sensual pleasure is determined by whatever is most agreeable. Those same forms that are agreeable to one person . . . are disagreeable to another. When one is pleased and completely satisfied with certain forms, then one does not yearn for any other form higher or more sublime than those forms. For him those forms are supreme; for him those forms are unsurpassed.[56]

Ultimately the particular object domain in question is not as important as the disposition to see in anything—visual forms, pleasant feelings, the security of money and possessions, delicious foods—a bolster for the self, which then turns around and arranges circumstances to its advantage. Keeping that in mind, taking gluttony, fornication, and avarice individually can shed some further light on just how it is that this nīvaraṇa is as pernicious as it is.

Few indeed are the places in the *Nikāyas* where something like gluttony is taken up expressly. The *Pāṭimokkha* contains any number of training precepts related to food, and the number of meals was limited, as we already saw. Even though meals were begged, however, it would not take long for a bhikkhu to figure out which households offered the tastier food and raise hopes that they might still have some to offer by the time he passed their door. Once back from the alms round, a bhikkhu might poke around in his bowl for the tastier morsels to eat first or raise his nose at the things he did not particularly care for.[57] Thus, even if he was not filling his cupboard, the bhikkhu might still display a misguided view of the nature of food in thinking that his palate

56 Bodhi, *Connected Discourses*, 175.

57 The training rules required that a monk beg from everyone equally and that he eat everything that was placed in his begging bowl in order to undercut these kinds of thoughts.

had any bearing on the matter, and the same would hold true for the noble lay disciple as well.

To illustrate a fitting view of food, the Buddha offers the following (admittedly somewhat disturbing) parable:

> "And how, bhikkhus, should the nutriment edible food be seen? Suppose a couple, husband and wife, had taken limited provisions and were travelling through a desert. They have with them their only son, dear and beloved. Then, in the middle of the desert, their limited provisions would be used up and exhausted, while the rest of the desert remains to be crossed. The husband and wife think, 'Our limited provisions have been used up and exhausted, while the rest of the desert remains to be crossed. Let us kill our only son, dear and beloved, and prepare dried and spiced meat. By eating our son's flesh we can cross the rest of this desert. Let not all three of us perish!' . . .
>
> "What do you think, bhikkhus? Would they eat that food for amusement or for enjoyment or for the sake of physical beauty and attractiveness?"
>
> "No, venerable sir."
>
> "Wouldn't they eat that food only for the sake of crossing the desert?"
>
> "Yes, venerable sir."
>
> "It is in such a way, bhikkhus, that I say the nutriment edible food should be seen."[58]

We take food to sustain our bodies for the work that needs to be done, and taking delight in flavors and aromas, rather than simply filling the belly, transforms the fulfillment of necessity into a way to bolster the conceit of a self whose tastes and preferences are the measure of what is appropriate.

As one might expect in the training of celibate bhikkhus, the issue of sexual desire received markedly more attention than gluttony. There were the training rules and precepts to be followed, of course, and the *Pāṭimokkha* is nothing if not encyclopedic in listing any number of sexual acts—and even intimations of sexual acts—that are prohibited for the homeleavers.[59] For the

58 Bodhi, *Connected Discourses*, 597–98.

59 So thorough is the *Pāṭimokkha* on these matters that Isabel Blew Horner, one of the first translators of the Pāli textual sources, left a whole section on masturbation out of her English translation of the monastic rules on the grounds that "the outspokenness and crudeness which it contains . . . appears unsuitable for incorporation in a translation designed principally for Western readers." Isabel Blew Horner, ed. and trans., *The Book of the Discipline* (Oxford: Pali Text Society, 1938), 1:197; cited in J. Duncan M. Derrett, "Monastic Masturbation in Pāli Buddhist Texts," *Journal of the History of Sexuality* 15

householders, the precept not to misuse sexuality, while not specific in terms of enumerating specific acts, still reflected the need for a measured dispassion, even among the lay disciples. As with all of the other manifestations of sense desire, at issue is not simply nonengagement in particular acts but the disposition of mind that would give rise to the pursuit of such pleasure in the first place.

The Buddha illustrates this with the distinction between living a "complete and pure celibate life—unbroken, flawless, unblemished, unblotched" and living one that is not. When pressed to explain the difference between the two, the Buddha responds that if there were someone claiming to be perfectly celibate who did not actually engage in intercourse with women but consented to being "rubbed, massaged, bathed and kneaded by them," then by relishing, desiring, and finding satisfaction in it, he would not be living an unblemished celibate life. Moreover, he continues, even if one were not to engage in such activity but instead were to joke around and play with women and amuse himself by that, then he would not be living an unblemished celibate life, either. Failing that, even if he were to gaze at them and stare them in the eyes, or, further still, delight in listening to their voices from behind a wall, or, still further yet, enjoy recollecting having cavorted with them in the past, then here, too, it could not be said of him that he lived an unblemished celibate life.

But the Buddha is still not finished, and, as if to emphasize the continuity of this kind of blotched celibacy with every other form of sense desire, he continues that even if the ascetic did not engage in any of the above but instead "looks at a householder or a householder's son enjoying himself furnished and endowed with the five objects of sensual pleasure," or, failing that, if he "lives the spiritual life aspiring for [rebirth in] a certain order of devas,[60] [thinking]: 'By this virtuous behavior, observance, austerity, or spiritual life I will be a deva or one [in the retinue] of the devas,'" then he, too, would live an impure celibate life.[61] One is not "freed from birth, from old age and death, from sorrow, lamentation, pain, dejection, and anguish,"

(2006): 2. It would seem that the *Pāṭimokkha* was a bit *too* encyclopedic for polite society in Horner's time.

60 Bodhi, *Numerical Discourses*, 1137–39.

61 The Buddha made frequent use of the religious imagination of his time. Devas are a kind of celestial being in the Brahmanic religious pantheon.

nor is one "freed from suffering,"[62] as long as one holds on to *any* prospect of fulfilling sense desire—even in the next life. Directing one's thoughts and actions to achieve some pleasurable heavenly state is just as much an obstacle on the path as inappropriately indulging one's sexual appetites.

We see this last exemplified in the case of a certain bhikkhu, Nanda. As the story goes, Nanda was finding it harder and harder to live the holy life. When the Buddha asked him why, Nanda replied:

> On departing from home, revered sir, a Sakyan girl, the loveliest in the land, with her hair half-combed, looked up at me and said, "May you return soon, master." Recollecting that, revered sir, I am discontented with leading the holy life. . . . I am unable to endure the holy life. I will give up the training and return to the low life.

So the Buddha took Nanda by the arm, and together they found themselves among the devas of the Tāvatiṃsa heaven,[63] where they saw five hundred pink-footed nymphs. When the Buddha asked Nanda which was more alluring, his Sakyan girl or all of those nymphs, Nanda said that, compared to the nymphs, the Sakyan girl, lovely as she was, looked like a "mutilated she-monkey that has had its ears and nose chopped off."[64] So the Buddha assured him he would obtain those five hundred pink-footed nymphs if only he were to live the holy life, and Nanda said that if that was the case then he would certainly live the holy life in all contentment.

Nanda's fellow bhikkhus caught wind of what had transpired, and they were not at all impressed:

> Then the bhikkhu-friends of the Venerable Nanda went about calling him "hireling" and "menial," saying: "The Venerable Nanda is a hireling! The Venerable Nanda is menial! He is living the holy life for the sake of nymphs! It is said that the Lord has guaranteed that he will obtain five hundred pink-footed nymphs!"[65]

One can practically hear them falling all over themselves laughing. Nanda, of course, was humiliated. He then set himself resolutely to the path, surrendered

62 Bodhi, *Numerical Discourses*, 1138.

63 The Tāvatiṃsa heaven is, in Buddhist cosmology, the realm of thirty-three devas or gods, and is ruled by Śakra, who is considered one of the *dharmapālas*, or protectors, of the Dharma in Mahāyāna tradition.

64 John D. Ireland, trans., *The Udāna and the Itivuttaka* (Onalaska, WA: Pariyatti, 2018), 32.

65 Ireland, *Udāna and the Itivuttaka*, 33.

all thoughts of gain, and soon came to realization. Then, knowing directly for himself the real fruits of the holy life, he told the Buddha he need not bother with any promises of nymphs—but of course the Buddha had known all along that this was how the ruse would play out.

We can suppose that a bhikkhu who had contemplated quitting due to lack of food, money, or comfort of any kind would have been jeered as a sellout in much the same way were he promised an ample supply of food, wealth, or bliss in the next life for hewing to the demands of the holy life in this one. That being the case, we can profitably read the issue of sexuality here as a placeholder for all forms of sense desire and their attendant pleasures. Indeed, as the Buddha elsewhere says: "So long, brahmin, as I saw that I had not abandoned one or another of these seven bonds of sexuality, I did not claim to have awakened to the unsurpassed perfect enlightenment in the world with its devas, Māra, and Brahmā, in this population with its ascetics and brahmins, its devas and humans."[66]

As concerns avarice, a bhikkhu was not even to touch money, let alone amass it. Simply having coin on one's person gave one the means to pursue any pleasure that could be procured through it:

> Gold and silver are not allowable for the ascetics following the Sakyan son; the ascetics following the Sakyan son do not accept gold or silver. They have renounced jewellery and gold; they have given up the use of gold and silver. If gold and silver are allowable for anyone, the five cords of sensual pleasure are allowable for him. If the five cords of sensual pleasure are allowable for anyone, you can definitely consider him to be one who does not have the character of an ascetic or of a follower of the Sakyan son.[67]

The ability to secure goods at will reinforces the idea that one has power over conditioned dharmas.

To be sure, money makes things happen, and one can use it for better or worse ends. The classic example in the Buddhist world is the foremost patron of the Buddha himself, Anāthapiṇḍika. Anāthapiṇḍika was perhaps the wealthiest merchant in Sāvatthī, the area where the Buddha spent most of his teaching career. Upon encountering the Buddha and becoming a lay follower, he purchased at great expense a forested glade where the Buddha and his bhikkhus could dwell, naming it Jetavana after its owner, Prince Jeta. But

66 Bodhi, *Numerical Discourses*, 1039.

67 Bodhi, *Connected Discourses*, 1347.

Anāthapiṇḍika lives on in the recollection of the saṅgha not because of his largesse, but because he set himself to realizing as far as he could the Noble Truths, attaining stream-entry, and serving as a model for nonattachment to wealth on the part of the lay disciples.[68] Through his wholehearted practice, he understood the true nature of money—in the end it buys nothing worth adhering to:

> For one who has taken birth . . . there is nothing other [to expect] than aging and death. Even in the case of those affluent khattiyas—rich, with great wealth and property, with abundant gold and silver, abundant treasures and commodities, abundant wealth and grain—because they have taken birth, there is nothing other [to expect] than aging and death.[69]

All the riches of the world will not put a stop to the inevitable, and the bhikkhu, in renouncing all use of money and all that it promises to secure, simply demonstrates that fact day in and day out.

Everyday people might praise the Buddha or the renunciant who does not engage in gluttony, sexual desire, avarice, or any other manifestation of sense desire. Merely refraining from engaging in them is, on the Buddha's account, an "elementary, inferior" matter,[70] for the fact that one is merely doing without does not reveal one's intentions. Perhaps it is only for show, or perhaps it just happens to be the case that circumstances are not right for engaging in that activity at that time. Everyday persons might even laud fasting, voluntary poverty, or celibacy as a strategy for obtaining some future heavenly reward, but this, too, is to miss the point of the exercise. As long as one is abandoning one form of sensory desire for the sake of another—whether obtained in this life or the next does not matter[71]—one is still not free of the obstacle, and further development on the path is impossible.

---

68 Stream-entry (*sotāpanna*) is the first level of realization. For key texts on Anāthapiṇḍika's life and practice, see Nyanaponika Thera and Hellmuth Hecker, trans., *Great Disciples of the Buddha: Their Lives, Their Works, Their Legacy*, ed. Bhikkhu Bodhi (Somerville, MA: Wisdom, 2003), 335–62.

69 Bodhi, *Connected Discourses*, 167.

70 Walshe, *Long Discourses*, 69–73. Here we find a parallel to the distinction between overcoming the logismoi versus not committing the deadly sins noted above. Not committing sinful acts is, by comparison to putting an end to obstructive thoughts, also an inferior matter.

71 One of the common impressions of the Dharma is that it is nihilistic since it does not address the prospect of life after death. Here we can see why there is simply no need to talk about it. If one is still on the lookout for pleasurable states, even after death, one

The Buddha employed metaphors to describe each nīvaraṇa and to capture something of what it means to be free of it. One metaphor that runs through the description of each is a bowl of water in a condition that corresponds to the nature of the nīvaraṇa. The nīvaraṇa of sense desire is likened to "a bowl of water mixed with lac, turmeric, blue dye, or crimson dye. If a man with good sight were to examine his own facial reflection in it, he would neither know nor see it as it really is. So too, brahmin, when one dwells with a mind obsessed by sensual lust."[72] Colored by sense desire, one can never know oneself; the dye is not the water. Moreover, anything that might be put in the dyed water would take on, like a piece of cloth, the color of the dye. When I take in sense experience through the dyes of my sense desire, I never quite get the object in question as it is but only as it conforms to my criteria of agreeableness and beauty. And not only objects but people, too, are seen not as they are but only in the colors I paint them. I persist in ignorance as long as I continue to parcel out reality in accordance with my personal color scheme. Persisting in ignorance, I also persist in dukkha. Things are never quite as I make them out to be, and as I fail to take people and things as they are, my actions are bound to be unskillful, and everyone and everything around me will sooner or later disappoint my expectations. To continue with the metaphor, they are not really blue, and they are not really red. When the colors I have painted them in fade or wear off, I am bound to be disappointed indeed.

Overcoming sense desire is also likened to being freed from debt: "Just as a man who had taken a loan to develop his business, and whose business had prospered, might pay off his old debts, and with what was left over could support a wife, might think: 'Before this I developed my business by borrowing, but now it has prospered . . . ,' and he would rejoice and be glad about that."[73] Any sense satisfaction is never possessed outright but is only a kind of borrowing, taking one's pleasure in some sign attached to conditioned dharmas that must be paid back:

> "Householder, suppose a man borrowed goods on loan—a fancy carriage and fine-jewelled earrings—and preceded and surrounded by those

has still not abandoned tṛṣṇā; for one who has come to the cessation of tṛṣṇā, any hankering for future pleasurable states—or even any ideas or discussion about them—will not even arise.

72 Bodhi, *Connected Discourses*, 1611.

73 Walshe, *Long Discourses*, 101.

> borrowed goods he went to the marketplace. Then people, seeing him, would say: 'Sirs, that is a rich man! That is how the rich enjoy their wealth!' Then the owners, whenever they saw him, would take back their things. What do you think, householder? Would that be enough for that man to become dejected?"
>
> "Yes, venerable sir. Why is that? Because the owners took back their things."[74]

Sense pleasure is "a filthy pleasure, a coarse pleasure, an ignoble pleasure"[75] because it is still caught up in the stickiness of tṛṣṇā and attachment to self and its desires.

There is, however, another kind of pleasure to be had outright, incurring no such debt: the pleasure "born of seclusion." This is a nonsensuous pleasure that arises in the conjunction with the stillness attained through the jhānas and what that stillness will bring to fruition through further cultivation—"the bliss of renunciation, the bliss of seclusion, the bliss of peace, and bliss of enlightenment."[76] This is an uncolored bliss, an untinged pleasure. Prior to setting himself on the path, the Buddha had asked himself, "Why am I afraid of that pleasure that has nothing to do with sensuality, nothing to do with unskillful qualities?"[77] His analysis of the nīvaraṇa of sense desire gives the clear answer: one is likely to feel as if one has been shortchanged by that pleasure unless one has given up the prospect of a life marked through and through with the sign of the beautiful.

Counteracting the sign of the beautiful with the sign of the unattractive is a training exercise, not an invitation to see everything as disgusting, for unattractiveness is no more a quality of dharmas than beauty is. But when beauty's hold is neutralized, things can be seen as they really are—nothing but the rising and falling of conditioned phenomena without any trace of self:

> Herein, Bāhiya, you should train yourself thus: "In the seen will be merely what is seen; in the heard will be merely what is heard; in the sensed will be merely what is sensed; in the cognized will be merely what is cognized." In this way you should train yourself, Bāhiya.

---

74 Ñāṇamoli and Bodhi, *Middle Length Discourses*, 471.
75 Ñāṇamoli and Bodhi, *Middle Length Discourses*, 1083.
76 Ñāṇamoli and Bodhi, *Middle Length Discourses*, 1083.
77 Ñāṇamoli and Bodhi, *Middle Length Discourses*, 340.

> When, Bāhiya, for you in the seen is merely what is seen . . . in the cognized is merely what is cognized, then, Bāhiya, you will not be "with that." When, Bāhiya, you are not "with that," then, Bāhiya, you will not be "in that." When, Bāhiya, you are not "in that," then, Bāhiya, you will be neither here nor beyond nor in between the two. Just this is the end of suffering.[78]

Everything will be just as it is, no self will be found in the picture, and nothing will be tinged with the colors with which the self paints its world.

Māra cannot ply his temptations where there is just the seen in the seen, the heard in the heard, and the rest. Māra's only tools are those that one provides him, and sense desires fill his toolbox abundantly:

> Bhikkhus, sensual pleasures are impermanent, hollow, false, deceptive; they are illusory, the prattle of fools. Sensual pleasures here and now and sensual pleasures in lives to come, sensual perceptions here and now and sensual perceptions in lives to come—both alike are Māra's realm, Māra's domain, Māra's bait, Māra's hunting ground. On account of them, these evil unwholesome mental states such as covetousness, ill will and presumption arise, and they constitute an obstruction to a noble disciple in training here.[79]

The demons of gluttony, fornication, and avarice, too, can only operate with the materiél one supplies them with: "The demons do not know our hearts," Evagrius writes. "Rather, they recognize the many mental representations that are in the heart on the basis of a word that is expressed and movements of the body."[80] When my body stops blindly reacting and when my thoughts are stilled, the demons are powerless, since I have nothing left with which they might assail me. Neither the bhikkhu nor the monk needs to fight against the obstacles; they simply need to stop supplying them with weapons.

---

78 Ireland, *Udāna and the Itivuttaka*, 18.

79 Ñāṇamoli and Bodhi, *Middle Length Discourses*, 869.

80 Evagrius, *On Thoughts* 37; Sinkewicz, 179.

CHAPTER FOUR

The Sheer Madness of Anger and Ill Will

The logismoi related to sensory desire and the nīvaraṇa of sense desire are, on the whole, the easiest of the obstacles to overcome. It is a matter of sound everyday understanding that those things, circumstances, and people I hold dear—myself included—only last so long. My favorite coffee cup will soon enough start to chip and crack and will, if dropped to a hard floor, most likely break. My job is at all times contingent on the demand for my skills in the economy, the fate of the company or institution that cuts my paycheck, and my ongoing ability even to be able to show up for work hale and hardy. My body and the bodies of those around me are so constituted that, absent favorable circumstances or just given enough time, we all die. Overcoming sense desire is surrendering the pointless hope that there is any exception to any of this, and fearlessly facing the plain truth of the limitations of embodied forms and action in the world.

But it is one thing for me in my klutziness to drop my coffee cup to the ground; it is another for someone to pick it up and throw it against the wall. It is one thing if I am a flip-phone designer and flip phones fall out of market demand; it is another for the CEO to fire me and many of my colleagues to cut labor costs just so the stock value of the company rises and shareholders get richer. And it is one thing to die when one is ninety-five or has contracted stage-four pancreatic cancer, but quite another to die in a mass shooting. Or so it would seem to the everyday mind, at least, despite the fact that the net results are *exactly the same.*

It is a generally accepted commonplace that these situations and others like them are not to be tolerated at all but should be fought against, stopped, and, as far as humanly possible, prevented from ever happening again. Because these are all situations that come to pass through the agency of some person or persons, preventing or stopping the situation means focusing one's attention on *them*, making sure *they* desist, and ensuring as far as possible that *they* do not do it again. But it is in conjunction with this commonplace, in this seemingly natural desire to bring such situations to an end, that one who would aspire to stillness encounters an adversary even more formidable than sense desire—the logismos of anger or, as it is cast in the Dharma, the nīvaraṇa of ill will.

Evagrius and the Buddha were of one voice on maintaining that anger or ill will toward another is *never* a fit state of mind, that there is *nothing* noble in it, and that anyone who would seek to live in the life of God or to attain the unshakable deliverance of mind will make *no* progress as long as one continues to insist otherwise. This cuts so deeply against the grain of our everyday understanding that it is hard to imagine that they could possibly be right. If nothing else, the prerogative of self-defense would seem to command otherwise, and one can scarcely find an ethics or philosophy that does not take that prerogative as axiomatic. The concept of self-defense is the foundation for any discussion of rights and provides the bedrock for determining the scope of social and political authority. Whatever else good government does, it protects the lives of those under its rule from those who do them harm. Should the state somehow fall short in its charge to protect life and limb, any number of philosophical and theological systems are all too ready to step up and point out that, when positive law is silent or ineffective in such matters, a moral law as set in place by God or by the natural order of the world is always there as the ultimate sanction for a fitting and justified corrective anger to be exercised by any who are able.

While wanton violence against another is never appropriate by most everyone's reckoning, many will be eager to make a concession for the exercise of righteous anger, particularly in the face of injustice and harm to self and others. The demands of morality seem positively to require it. No sooner had Christianity become the state religion of the Roman Empire than some of its most illustrious spokespersons felt compelled to develop a set of criteria for the legitimate use of force on the part of the faithful to maintain the moral order of society. While the Dharma was never pressed into service in quite the same way in the course of its history, many present-day advocates of a socially engaged Buddhism are putting a good deal of effort into developing a theory of "right anger" or "loving anger" in an attempt to render such social service on the basis of what they take to be the teaching of the Buddha.[1] To fail to exercise such moral indignation, so the arguments go, would be implicitly to sanction or at least condone those harmful acts, impugning one's own moral uprightness in the process.

In ranking anger among the logismoi and the nīvaraṇas, however, both Evagrius and the Buddha indicate that even such seemingly noble considerations, no matter how sound their justifications may at first appear, are always deceptive obstacles to the attainment of stillness. The obstacles connected with sensory desire may have sent me chasing after things to keep me satisfied, but the obstacles of anger and ill will set me on the path to eliminating anything that might stand in my way or in the way of others I cherish. Sense desire may keep my vision distracted, but anger renders me nothing short of blind to the true nature of things, as both Evagrius and the Buddha are swift to point out.[2] If I persist in my blindness, I will never know the clarity and vision the renunciant-contemplative path opens up.

Columba Stewart has noted that Evagrius's writings "fairly crackle with the problem of anger."[3] Robert Sinkewicz puts a fine point on Evagrius's concern with anger by noting that "ascetic practice without control of irascibility is worthless."[4] While all of the logismoi are troublesome, Evagrius certainly minces no words in describing the perverse character of this logismos: "No evil makes the intellect into a demon as much as anger through the troubling of wrath."[5] By definition it is the very antithesis of stillness: "Anger is a

1 See, for example, Kristin Johnston Largen, "Introduction to Liberation Theology and Engaged Buddhism," *Buddhist-Christian Studies* 36 (2016): 51–53; John Daido Loori, *Invoking Reality: Moral and Ethical Teaching of Zen* (Boston: Shambhala, 1998), 55; and Hozan Alan Senauke, "Right Anger and the Path to the End of Caste," Clear View Project, November 4, 2014, https://www.clearviewproject.org/2014/11/right-anger-and-the-path-to-the-end-of-caste/.

2 See Andrew Louth, "Evagrios on Anger," *StPatr* 47 (2010): 183; Bodhi, *Numerical Discourses*, 1068.

3 Columba Stewart, OSB, "Evagrius Ponticus on Prayer and Anger," in *Religions of Late Antiquity in Practice*, ed. Richard Valantasis (Princeton: Princeton University Press, 2000), 66.

4 Sinkewicz, *Evagrius of Pontus*, 140.

5 Evagrius, *Letter* 56; cited in Ramelli, Kephalaia Gnostica, 188.

plundering of prudence, a destruction of one's state, a confusion of nature, a form turned savage, a furnace for the heart, an eruption of flames, a law of irascibility, a wrath of insults, a mother of wild beasts, a silent battle, an impediment to prayer."[6] Whatever wildness of the soul the practical life was meant to tame runs the risk of being all too quickly reignited and stoked into an inferno by the least spark of the fiery savagery of anger. While sensory desire tends to come and go, anger only intensifies, and it is so gripping that "it renders the soul furious all day long."[7]

More often than not, when one considers anger's perniciousness, it is anger's harmful effects on others that one is most concerned about. It is OK to *be* angry, one might think, as long as one does not impulsively *act* on it and cause pointless damage. For the renunciant-contemplative, however, anger is not to be managed but eliminated, because the first person harmed by the least thought of anger is none other than oneself: "No one with a love for true prayer who entertains anger or harbours resentment escapes madness, for that is like one who wants acuity of vision but does harm to his own eyes."[8] That anger is a form of self-inflicted blindness was already attested in the Scriptures:

> Whoever says, "I am in the light," while hating a brother or sister, is still in the darkness. Whoever loves a brother or sister lives in the light, and in such a person there is no cause for stumbling. But whoever hates another believer is in the darkness, walks in the darkness, and does not know the way to go, because the darkness has brought on blindness. (1 John 2:9–11)

Presumably no one *wants* to be blind, so how is it that one can fall so quickly under anger's sway?

Evagrius's answer is that anger is a particularly cunning demon because the justifications it musters are so self-satisfyingly compelling. The first, which we already have had occasion to mention, has to do with the idea that there is such a thing as righteous anger: "When you are praying as you should, such things will come over you that you may think it utterly just to resort to anger, but there is absolutely no such thing as just anger against your neighbour."[9] In any case of perceived injustice, from the slightest verbal affront to outright

6 Evagrius, *Vices* 5; Sinkewicz, 64.
7 Evagrius, *Praktikos* 11; Sinkewicz, 99.
8 Evagrius, *Prayer* 64; Sinkewicz, 199.
9 Evagrius, *Prayer* 24; Sinkewicz, 195.

persecution, I become angry when the behavior of another person does not measure up to the standard of how I would like to be treated. But whether bodily injury or a wounded sensibility is the result of that person's actions, anger misapprehends reality by imagining it to be the case that the other person is *causing* me harm when, in point of fact, I am the one *taking offense* at their actions. For Evagrius, as Leszek Misiarczyk notes, "other people are not hurting us but our own excessive and exaggerated expectations towards them."[10]

People are, well, *people*. Guided by self-love, as everyday people are, their actions are sooner or later going to impinge on others, and one would be hard-pressed to find someone who never, whether wittingly or unwittingly, caused difficulty for or harm to another person. This is why Evagrius suggested that the first prayer of a budding renunciant-contemplative should be for the gift of compunction: the ability to see, as if for the first time, that I am that kind of person, too. What I know of myself I can also know of others. That they persist in acting in accordance with their self-love is nothing for me to be offended by in the least, since they can no more act differently that I could have while also in the grips of self-love. For me now to be angry at them is to pretend that they are not the kind of beings they are. In fact, the more I hold to some kind of *right* to be angry, making as if I *of course* should be offended by them, the more I will find that I cannot bear other people much *at all*, since every last one of them is liable to fail to live up to my expectations sooner or later. "Anger," Evagrius writes, "is a passion that leads to madness and easily drives those who possess it out of their senses; it makes the soul wild and moves it to shun all (human) encounter."[11] Blind to their nature, assuming that I am not what they are, I want nothing more than to have them and their actions out of my sight.

Anger is so self-satisfying that I might not even care that it distances me from others, since that distance only reinforces my specialness and their otherness. One of the thoughts associated with anger is one that "wants to repay evil for evil or abuse for abuse and does not want, through blessings,

10 Misiarczyk, *Eight Logismoi*, 204. This was a position Evagrius shared with the Stoics. Epictetus, for instance, put it rather starkly: "What upsets people is not things themselves but their judgments about the things. . . . So when we are thwarted or upset or distressed, let us never blame someone else but rather ourselves, that is our own judgments." Epictetus, *The Handbook (The Encheiridion)*, trans. Nicholas P. White (Indianapolis: Hackett, 1983), 13.

11 Evagrius, *Eight Thoughts* 4.1; Sinkewicz, 80.

to forget abusive and slanderous thoughts."[12] To bless those who harm me or even to wish them well would be to concede my ground, let them have the upper hand, and surrender myself to their abusive ways—and I cannot have *that*. Better to imagine myself in the right and alone than to not be angry with them and abide their company. Moreover, if I overlook an affront, it would seem that I am condoning that person's actions, particularly if it is not the first time that this person has caused offense. An isolated misstep might be tolerable, but for me to remain silent while the person persists in such an action almost seems like a dereliction of duty.

Evagrius suggests that such a presumed duty, however, is nothing other than a pretext for self-love to show itself yet again, and he indicates the need for the monk to resist

> the thoughts of anger that do not permit us to be reconciled to the brothers because they depict before our eyes pretexts that are "suitable" yet actually are shame, fear, and pride—"Did he not fall into the very same offenses as earlier, he who transgressed in this matter?"—this is an indication of the craftiness of the demon, which does not want to let the intellect become free of resentment.[13]

It may well be true that the brother has once again committed the very same act he has many times before, but whether *he* has done it seven or seventy times changes nothing as far as *my* actions with respect to him are concerned. Having now built up quite a track record, and seeing him fall yet again, it might seem perfectly reasonable to think, "I should do what I can to stop him from doing this again." But why, exactly? "So he doesn't hurt me in the future"—but that is an exercise in fear. "So people don't think I condone his action"—that is shame speaking. "So he does no further harm to others"—there is pride, thinking oneself capable of effectively managing other people and directing the future course of events and their impact on others.

As these examples indicate, it is not really the perpetrator—actual, potential, or recidivist—I am actually concerned with when I seek to curb or prevent his or her harmful behavior. It is myself. I might tell myself otherwise, and I can certainly spin a yarn about harm, its effects, and how much better it would be if harm did not occur, and all of that may well be true enough as far as those things go. None of that, however, adds up to anything the committed renunciant-contemplative need concern himself with, and Evagrius throws all

12 Evagrius, *Antirrhetikos* 5.61; Brakke, 132.

13 Evagrius, *Antirrhetikos* 5.49; Brakke, 129.

of these justifications back into the monk's court: "Over what, pray tell me," Evagrius asks, "'do you fall to fighting so quickly' (cf. Prov. 25:8), if indeed you have scorned food, riches, and esteem? And why do you feed this dog, if you claim to own nothing? If it barks and attacks people, it is obvious that it has possessions inside and wants to guard them."[14] Those interior possessions are, of course, nothing but the trappings of selfhood. When property, limb, and life are no longer viewed as external extensions of self-love, what matter if others damage or deprive me of them? For one who has renounced everything, there is absolutely nothing left to defend.

Still, one might object that even if one is not concerned with the harm caused by another, it is altogether fitting to be solicitous for the state of his soul all the same. "Hate the sin, but love the sinner," one might think, and the way to show that love is to help him abandon his sin and try to change him for the better. But trying to change others, like any other exercise of anger, takes its toll on the practitioner more so than it impinges on those others: "Be careful lest in thinking you can heal another person you become incurable and set an obstacle to your prayer," Evagrius warns.[15] This is particularly true for those who would instruct others: "May the gnostic, when he teaches, be free from anger, resentment, sadness, bodily pain, and worries!" Evagrius writes in *Gnostikos*.[16] Elsewhere he expands on that point:

> Let the gnostic examine himself to know whether it is possible for him, in thought, first not to do or say anything shameful, second not to resent whomever has hurt or saddened him, third not to hold a grudge against those who have spoken ill of us, and fourth whether he prays without concepts or representations.[17]

Resentment and grudge holding cannot exist without mental representations, in this case representations of the other as *offender* and myself as *moral judge*.

If I am to commune with God as a father, I need to admit that God is the father of all, before whom everyone stands. It is not given to me to stand in the place of God with respect to others who are but my brothers and sisters, nor is it proper for me to keep my focus on those others when my sole focus should be on God. Thomas Cattoi notes that, for Evagrius, "anger actually

14 Evagrius, *On Thoughts* 5; Sinkewicz, 156.

15 Evagrius, *Prayer* 25; Sinkewicz, 195.

16 Evagrius, *Le Gnostique* 10; Guillaumont, 103; my translation.

17 Evagrius, *Chapitres des Disciples d'Évagre* 6, in *Chapitres des Disciples d'Évagre*, trans. Paul Géhin (Paris: Cerf, 2007), 109; my translation.

leads to a sort of idolatry, since whatever the *nous* [mind] visualizes when attempting to pray is the object of our worship and if we visualize anything but God, we are effectively turning the object of our resentment into the center of our inner lives."[18]

In light of what we have seen, one could press this observation a bit further yet. The idolatry here is not the object of our anger, since one can be angry about just about anything with respect to just about anyone. We love our anger primarily because it is, as it turns out, *ours*. It is the self that creates the desire for the object or situation in question, and it is the self that feels it necessary to be *able* to be angry and to feel justified in its exercise. It is the self, more than anything else, that stands center on the altar of one's adoration in surrendering to the logismos of anger, and in reserving some claimed right to anger, it claims lordship over all it surveys. Where the self and all of its representations stand, God cannot be present.

The antidote to anger is gentleness and the patient forbearance of harm—precisely those dispositions and states of mind that anger, by its very nature, refuses to recognize as appropriate. Patience, following Evagrius, is

> a shield for prudence, a tribunal for anger, a surgery for the heart, admonition of the over-confident, calm for the troubled, a harbour from storms, beneficence towards those in sorrow, gentleness towards all; it blesses when slandered, rejoices when insulted; a consolation for those in difficult circumstances, a mirror of things hoped for, a prize of those mistreated.[19]

Patient endurance of difficulties caused by others can do all of this because it reflects a sound understanding of myself, the nature of things, and God: I am the lowest of all, others are no different than myself, and God alone is Father and sovereign. By maintaining patience and freedom from resentment the agitated soul is calmed,[20] and the obstructive thoughts that arise from its churning can abate.

---

18 Thomas Cattoi, "Holy Anger, Holy Wrath: The Role of Anger and the Emotions in Early Christian Spirituality and the Mahayana Buddhist Tradition," *Buddhist-Christian Studies* 39 (2019): 57. Gabriel Bunge makes a similar point. Bunge, *Dragon's Wine and Angel's Bread: The Teaching of Evagrius Ponticus on Anger and Meekness*, trans. Anthony P. Gythiel (Crestwood, NY: St. Vladimir's Seminary Press, 2009), 74.

19 Evagrius, *Vices* 5; Sinkewicz, 64.

20 Evagrius, *On Thoughts* 3; Sinkewicz, 154.

Patience also issues forth in a reorientation of one's temporal framework. Without that reorientation, Evagrius's claim, "If you search you will find . . . that it is possible even without anger for the matter to be settled properly,"[21] might ring hollow. Anger tends to demand swift recompense from harm. "Justice too long delayed is justice denied"—as Martin Luther King Jr. puts it in "Letter from Birmingham Jail"—might apply to matters of civil jurisdiction, but the jurisdiction here is God's. God's time frame is free of any representations of temporal measure—*sub specie aeternitatis*, as it is rendered philosophically. Far from rendering life meaningless, such a timeless perspective is an integral component of wisdom: "The person who nobly bears dishonours with humility is all the more impelled by them towards the height of philosophy."[22] Mere cleverness might indicate how one can evade pain and distress; wisdom allows one to see it as an inexorable fact of life as a finite created being within the infinite life of God. Such a perspective, for the Christian, is itself a gift of the Spirit to the practitioner, a more complete sharing in the divine life.

That gift, in turn, becomes the foundation of pure charity. The everyday understanding of charity involves any number of representations of giver, gift, and recipient. From the perspective of the divine life, however, charity is best understood as the patient acceptance of persons and circumstances just as they are. "It is not possible to love all the brothers equally," Evagrius writes, "but it is possible to conduct our relationships with all without passion and free from resentment and hatred."[23] One does not have to be everyone's bosom buddy; one just needs to be no one's rival. When no one is able to provoke me to anger and resentment, I can stop viewing them as adversaries. No one will be able to find a stumbling-block in one who has overcome anger because that stumbling-block, the self, will have no grounds for making an appearance.

Above all else, patience is the disposition of one who prays truly: "The prayer of the irascible person is an abominable incense offering; the psalmody of an angry person is an irritating noise. The gift of the resentful person is a blemished sacrifice and does not approach the consecrated altar."[24] It is not

---

21 Evagrius, *Prayer* 24; Sinkewicz, 195.

22 Evagrius, *Eulogios* 3; Sinkewicz, 31. *Philosophy* here is another name for what Evagrius calls "the gnostic life," a life lived in accordance with the truth, the embodiment of the love of wisdom. The gnostic life follows after the practical life of the first and second renunciations.

23 Evagrius, *Praktikos* 100; Sinkewicz, 113.

24 Evagrius, *Eight Thoughts* 4.18, 4.19; Sinkewicz, 81.

that God is refusing to accept the angry person's prayer; that would be to imagine God to be just as petty as the angry person. The prayer of the angry does not rise to the altar because it is weighed down by resentment, tied to the grievances one refuses to let go of. Now a victim of his self-inflicted blindness, the angry person cannot see what the patient person sees: "A patient person has visions of encounters with holy angels, and one free from resentment discourses on spiritual matters and receives in the night the answers to mysteries."[25] *Angry prayer* is a contradiction in terms.

Overcoming anger has the added benefit of keeping one from again falling under the sway of sense desire: "Armed against anger, you will never give in to desire, for desire provides material for anger, and the latter in turn troubles the intellectual eye, spoiling the state of prayer."[26] I get angry only in response to attacks on things I cherish; if I do not cherish something, I find that I am indifferent to its fate, and I will have a hard time mustering any kind of angry sentiment at all with respect to anything that might befall it. The fewer possessions, the fewer the bonds of human attachment, and the less the attachment to self, so much fewer the occasions for anger's beastliness to erupt.

In the Dharma, no less than for Evagrius, the first casualty of anger is oneself: "Getting angry with another person is like taking hold of a hot flameless coal or an iron stake smeared with excrement in order to strike someone."[27] Even if the object of my anger knows nothing about just how angry I am, I am the one with the seared or soiled hand. In fact, one can come across as rather meek and timid yet still have plenty of defiling anger at the ready, as we see illustrated in a story from the *Kakacūpama Sutra.*

It seems that a certain woman, Vedehikā, enjoyed quite the reputation around town: "Mistress Vedehikā is gentle, Mistress Vedehikā is meek, Mistress Vedehikā is peaceful," the neighbors would say. Her maid, Kāli, however, was not so convinced that her mistress lived up to her reputation, and she wondered whether Vedehikā was really that peaceful, or whether she had simply not yet had occasion to get particularly angry about anything. Since her work was otherwise good, Kāli decided to test Vedehikā by doing a bad job instead. The next day, she got up a little late, and Vedehikā scowled. The

25 Evagrius, *Eight Thoughts* 4.21; Sinkewicz, 81.

26 Evagrius, *Prayer* 27; Sinkewicz, 195.

27 Buddhaghoṣa, *Manorathapūraṇī* (*Aṅguttaranikāya-Aṭṭhakathā*), Pali ed. (N.p.: Theravada Tipitaka, 2010); cited in Bodhi, *Numerical Discourses*, 1595n32.

following day, she got up even later, and her mistress yelled at her. Then, on the third day, Kāli woke up still later, and this time Vedehikā took a rolling pin to her head: "Then the maid Kāli, with blood running from her cut head, denounced her mistress to the neighbours: 'See, ladies, the gentle lady's work! How can she become angry and displeased with her only maid for getting up late? How can she take a rolling-pin, give her a blow to the head, and cut her head?'" Kāli's suspicions had turned out to be true. Vedehikā was not at all free of anger; things had just been going so well for her that she had no occasion to show it. From then on Vedehikā found herself with a new reputation in the neighborhood: "Mistress Vedehikā is rough, Mistress Vedehikā is violent, Mistress Vedehikā is merciless."[28]

The nīvaraṇa of ill will is closely related to the defilement of anger (*dosa*) generally,[29] and it has ties to other forms of defilement such as resentment, antipathy, and grudge.[30] Strictly speaking, it is the desire to see another meet with ill fortune, captured in such thoughts as "May these beings be slain and slaughtered, may they be cut off, perish, or be annihilated!"[31] Wanting to see another deprived of life and limb lies at the furthest end of the spectrum of ill will, of course, and the Buddha lists many other such thoughts that arise from ill will: "May he be ugly!" "May he sleep badly!" "May he not succeed!" "May he not be healthy!" "May he not be famous!" "May he have no friends!" "With the breakup of the body, after death, may he be reborn in the plane of misery, in a bad destination, in the lower world, in hell!"[32] Like the Mistress Vedehikā, one may not actively be engaged in disfiguring another person's face or raising a ruckus outside their bedroom window in the middle of the night to spite them, but such thoughts come all too quickly to mind in any case.

And it is not just persons on the receiving end of ill will; *anything* perceived to be in one's way or posing a resistance of some kind can function as the object of ill will. If I find myself rather miffed that it rained on my backyard barbecue, that the puppy chewed up one of my favorite shoes, or that my alternator keeps conking out as I am trying to get home from work in a snowstorm, I have encountered yet another instance of ill will. In attachment,

28 Ñāṇamoli and Bodhi, *Middle Length Discourses*, 219–20.

29 See Piya Tan, "Nīvaraṇa: Mental Hindrances," The Minding Centre, https://www.themindingcentre.org/dharmafarer/sutta-discovery/sutta-discovery-vol-30-39, ms. 17.

30 Nyanatiloka, *Buddhist Dictionary*, 57.

31 Ñāṇamoli and Bodhi, *Middle Length Discourses*, 381.

32 Bodhi, *Numerical Discourses*, 1066–67.

another dharma is singled out for particular affection; in anger, it is the *self* that is singled out for protection against all comers. Attachment betrays a *misunderstanding* of the connection between myself and others, revealing a *deficiency* of insight. Anger, on the other hand, *seeks to abolish* the connection between myself and others, and so, far from a mere weakness or deficiency of insight, it reveals instead its thoroughgoing *absence*—a much graver matter.[33] For this reason, the Buddha could claim that for a person who is overcome with anger "there is just blindness and dense gloom,"[34] since no light is able to be seen with respect to anyone—or anything.

In confronting the nīvaraṇa of sense desire, the bhikkhu was counseled to look carefully at those things taken to be beautiful in order to see that there is nothing inherently beautiful and hence desire-worthy in dharmas of any kind. This involved cultivating disenchantment with respect to the things and beings around oneself, resolutely refusing to sugarcoat reality with a view to making it pleasing. In confronting the nīvaraṇa of ill will, a similar tactic is employed, but instead of attending to the sign of the beautiful, the bhikkhu is counseled to attend to the sign of the *repulsive*: "There is, bhikkhus, the sign of the repulsive: frequently giving careless attention to it is the nutriment for the arising of unarisen ill will and for the increase and expansion of arisen ill will."[35] Or again, "Bhikkhus, I do not see even one other thing on account of which unarisen ill will arises and arisen ill will increases and expands so much as the mark of the repulsive. For one who attends carelessly to the mark of the repulsive, unarisen ill will arises and arisen ill will increases and expands."[36]

Attending carefully to the sign of the repulsive involves a different line of approach from the one used in attending to the sign of the beautiful. Instead of being drawn to the beautiful, as we are with sense desire, ill will causes

33 This idea was developed further in Mahāyāna sources:

> [I]f a Bodhisattva continues to break precepts out of desire for kalpas as numerous as the sands of the Ganges, his offense is still minor. If a Bodhisattva breaks precepts out of hatred, even just once, his offense is very serious. Why? Because a Bodhisattva who breaks precepts out of desire [still] holds sentient beings in his embrace, whereas a Bodhisattva who breaks precepts out of hatred forsakes sentient beings altogether.

Garma C. C. Chang, ed., *A Treasury of Mahāyāna Sūtras: Selections from the Mahāratnakūta Sūtra* (University Park: Pennsylvania State University Press, 1984), 270.

34 Bodhi, *Numerical Discourses*, 1068.

35 Bodhi, *Connected Discourses*, 1568.

36 Bodhi, *Numerical Discourses*, 91.

us to recoil from the repulsive. If sense desire is a way to *inflate* the ego by feeding its desires, aversion and ill will are instead a way to *defend* the ego from a perceived threat. The sign of the beautiful may send me clamoring for more satisfaction in things and situations around me, but the mark of the repulsive has me throw up a defensive phalanx to distance myself from any harm that might come from things and situations and, most particularly, persons around me. Such harm can be made out in many instances:

> Bhikkhus, there are these ten grounds for resentment. What ten? (1) thinking: "They acted for my harm;" (2) thinking: "They are acting for my harm;" (3) thinking: "They will act for my harm;" (4) thinking: "They acted for the harm of one who is pleasing and agreeable to me;" (5) thinking: "They are acting for the harm of one who is pleasing and agreeable to me;" (6) thinking: "They will act for the harm of one who is pleasing and agreeable to me;" (7) thinking: "They acted for the benefit of one who is displeasing and disagreeable to me;" (8) thinking: "They are acting for the benefit of one who is displeasing and disagreeable to me;" (9) thinking: "They will act for the benefit of one who is displeasing and disagreeable to me;" (10) and one becomes angry without a reason. These, bhikkhus, are the ten grounds for resentment.[37]

Careful attention to the repulsive means noting the rising of such observations, but, instead of letting resentment rise in response to them, one simply recalls that this is the action of some person acting out in accordance with causes and conditions in light of his or her own tṛṣṇā. And because these causes and conditions do not arise ex nihilo but only from antecedent causes, in resenting this one person's actions, I am in effect resenting reality itself. That person could no more act differently than any other conditioned phenomenon.

One of the techniques set forth as a way to abandon the nīvaraṇa of ill will is called "reviewing ownership of karma,"[38] a systematic reflection on the fact of one's conditioned nature: "A woman or a man, a householder or one gone forth [should] often reflect thus: 'I am the owner of my kamma, the heir of my kamma; I have kamma as my origin, kamma as my relative, kamma as my resort; I will be the heir of whatever kamma, good or bad, that I do.'"[39] The teaching on the skandhas indicates that—in addition to offering no discrete phenomenon to which the idea of a self can be attached or ascribed—the

37 Bodhi, *Numerical Discourses*, 1439.

38 The Pāli equivalent of the Sanskrit *karma* is *kamma*. As with *nirvāṇa/nibbāna*, I use *karma* as is custom in English, while leaving it as *kamma* where it appears in a quoted translation.

39 Bodhi, *Numerical Discourses*, 687.

skandhas themselves are always undergoing change as one set of conditions gives rise to the next. What at any given time I take to be "me" is just the present moment in that causal chain. I am the heir, so to speak, of that causal chain, which is all that the word *karma* was ever meant to refer to. Some elements in that causal chain I had a direct intentional hand in bringing about, but even then I was intentionally responding just to the given conditions at hand. Had there been other conditions, I might have undertaken different actions with respect to them. Whether nature or nurture matters little here, because, no matter how I happen to think of the origination of the conditions I find myself in—something the Buddha suggests is impossible to discover in any case[40]—they are the only present circumstances and conditions for me to work with. There is no second reality to appeal to.

What I know of myself, I know of others as well: "This noble disciple reflects thus: 'I am not the only one who is the owner of one's kamma. . . . All beings that come and go, that pass away and undergo rebirth, are owners of their kamma, heirs of their kamma; all have kamma as their origin, kamma as their relative, kamma as their resort; all will be heirs of whatever kamma, good or bad, that they do.'"[41] The person who is doing me harm no more chose the conditions that make their life possible than I did, and they are no more freely autonomous than I was in making my choices. That they now undertake actions that are harmful to me or others is a not entirely unexpected consequence, in much the same way as the destruction of my home is a not entirely unexpected consequence when hit by a tornado. When certain causal conditions obtain, they give rise to a tornado, and it is the nature of tornados to tear apart houses. When certain causal conditions obtain, they give rise to a harm-causing person, and it is the nature of harm-causing persons to hurt others.

When I consider that the person I see before me is nothing but an assemblage of causal relations that give rise to one another without a single, autonomous center of agency commandeering it all, I am confronted with the fact that there is nowhere for my anger to land. Should I be angry with his third-grade teacher (or his econ professor)? His mom (or his dad)? His choice to go to college (or to drop out of school)? That he was born in Kansas (or the south side of Chicago)? That he recently got divorced (or married)? The act he undertook that now has me so incensed has all of these as conditions and

40 Bodhi, *Connected Discourses*, 651–61.
41 Bodhi, *Numerical Discourses*, 688.

more besides. I will never, given the beginninglessness of saṃsāra, come to discern an end of it.[42] As soon I am able to see this, the sooner my anger will dissipate: "As he often reflects on this theme, the path is generated. He pursues this path, develops it, and cultivates it. As he does so, the fetters are entirely abandoned and the underlying tendencies are uprooted."[43]

Those who are intent on pinning blame on the perpetrator all the same will no doubt find this review of the ownership of karma dissatisfying: "I don't care why he did it. He shouldn't have done it at all!" one might think. To this, one can counter that the very drive to pin blame is itself but a further manifestation of ill will. What is denied here is *guilt*, not *responsibility*. It is one thing to point out that the bundle of skandhas I call John is the cause of some action; it was not Meghan, and it was not Mohinder who threw the ball through my window. But *John* is not the proper object of my anger, since *anyone* who has the dispositions John has and who would have gone through the same life circumstances that he did could well now find herself, like him, throwing balls through windows. For me to wish ill on him is completely ancillary to the matter at hand and changes nothing. As long as I hold to that wish, I will continue to be unsettled after the incident has long since passed.

This being the case, I can come to see that there is—quite starkly put—*nothing* to be done as far as the perpetrator goes. The Buddha goes on to take up each of the ten grounds for resentment above and adds to each of them "What can be done about it?" as a way of underscoring the point ("Thinking: 'They acted for my harm, but what can be done about it?,'" etc.).[44] Peter J. Vernezze characterizes the approach to anger taken here as an "intellectualist" one, by which he means that "a defective moral state is understood as resulting from a failure to reason properly and that the correct ethical point of view can be achieved through a similarly rational process."[45] Yet as we will see below in the discussion of the nīvaraṇa of indecision, the Buddha questioned the ability of simple reasoning to come to definitive conclusions on any matter related to the Dharma, so something else besides a failure of

42 The Buddha taught that saṃsāra, this constant rising and falling of conditions, admits of no prime moment (something like an original fall as portrayed in Genesis) to which all subsequent moments in the causal chain are linked. See Bodhi, *Connected Discourses*, 651–53.

43 Bodhi, *Numerical Discourses*, 688–89.

44 Bodhi, *Numerical Discourses*, 1440.

45 Peter J. Vernezze, "Moderation or the Middle Way: Two Approaches to Anger," *Philosophy East and West* 58 (2008): 6.

reasoning must be at work here. Reviewing ownership of kamma is perhaps better understood not as a process of thinking from sound premises to a valid conclusion, but as an unfiltered *direct seeing* of what is right before one's eyes once tṛṣṇā no longer skews one's vision in accordance with the interests of the self. Here, too, there is "just the seen in the seen." It is the conceit of a karmically independent self, whether ascribed to me or to another, that sets the stage for succumbing to the nīvaraṇa of ill will, and it is a thoroughgoing settling into the truths of impermanence and nonself that leads to its overcoming.

Reviewing ownership of kamma is the third in a list of six strategies for overcoming ill will found in the *Nikāyas*. The others are learning the meditation on loving-kindness, cultivating meditation on loving-kindness, abundant reflection, good friendship, and suitable conversation.[46] Loving-kindness (*mettā*) is singled out in particular as the antidote to ill will: "Bhikkhus, I do not see even one other thing on account of which unarisen ill will does not arise and arisen ill will is abandoned so much as the liberation of the mind by loving-kindness."[47] Loving-kindness is one of the more popularized aspects of the Dharma, and some of its descriptions do sound quite lovely. The *Mettā Sutra* certainly contains language that might lead one to that conclusion—"Just as a mother would protect her son, her only son, with her own life, so one should develop toward all beings as state of mind without boundaries" is a pleasing image indeed.[48]

If loving-kindness strikes one as a rather ill-equipped counter to the nīvaraṇa of ill will, it is perhaps because one is not yet clear on just what a Dharmic understanding of loving-kindness entails.[49] Loving-kindness—along with compassion (*karuṇā*), sympathetic joy (*muditā*), and equanimity (*upekkhā*)—is one of the *brahmavihāras*, so named because they are the "abodes of Brahma" or "divine abodes." They are also called boundless

---

46 Bodhi, *Numerical Discourses*, 1595n32.

47 Bodhi, *Numerical Discourses*, 92.

48 Bodhi, *Suttanipāta*, 180.

49 Ajahn Thiradhammo cautions against understanding loving-kindness as something congenial even to the point of calling for a different rendering of *mettā* into English: "Personally, I think that the translation of 'loving-kindness' often imposes over-grand expectations upon the practice. . . . Relating with 'loving-kindness' is still on the idealistic side of reality." Thiradhammo, *Working with the Five Hindrances* (Northumberland, UK: Aruno, 2014), 97.

states (*appamañña*), since their exercise transcends every form of distinction between self and other, and they extend without limit, pervading all. As a whole, they are cultivated only with the attainment of the first jhāna:

> *A disciple goes forth, practices the moralities, attains the first jhāna.*
>
> Then, with his heart filled with loving-kindness, [compassion, etc.], he dwells suffusing one quarter, the second, the third, the fourth. Thus he dwells suffusing the whole world upwards, downwards, across, everywhere, always with a heart filled with loving-kindness, [compassion, etc.], abundant, unbounded, without hate or ill-will.
>
> Just as if a mighty trumpeter were with little difficulty to make a proclamation to the four quarters, so by this meditation, Vāseṭṭha, by this liberation of the heart through loving-kindness, [compassion, etc.], he leaves nothing untouched, nothing unaffected in the sensuous sphere.[50]

Unlike the other brahmavihāras, however, one can exercise loving-kindness in a limited way, even without having overcome the nīvaraṇas or having entered on the brahmavihāras. This is because loving-kindness does not rely on supramundane awareness for its cultivation. Compassion, sympathetic joy, and equanimity are universal states of mind that do not take into view particular individuals (doing so is an exercise in what the tradition calls the "near enemies" of the brahmavihāras),[51] and it is for this reason they are called supramundane, not caught up in particular dharmas. Loving-kindness, however, is cultivated in the first instance precisely with respect to individuals, and only then is it subsequently extended without limits. Specifically, it is cultivated in maintaining an absence of ill will in the face of harm—something that, most will agree, tends to occur one affront at a time.

Loving-kindness cannot coexist alongside ill will, and where there is ill will, there is no loving-kindness to be found:

> A monk might say: "I have developed the emancipation of the heart (*cetovimutti*) by loving-kindness (*mettā*), and expanded it, made it a vehicle and base, established, worked well on it, set it well in train. And yet ill will still

50 Walshe, *Long Discourses*, 194; italics original.

51 Buddhaghoṣa (*Path of Purification*, 313) distinguishes the brahmavihāras from their near enemies on the basis of the distinction between what is "based on the home life" and what is "based on renunciation." We will take this up in more detail in conjunction with Evagrius's treatment of the logismos of sadness.

> grips my heart." He should be told: "No! do not say that! Do not misrepresent the Blessed Lord, it is not right to slander him thus, for he would not have said such a thing! Your words are unfounded and impossible. If you develop the emancipation of the heart through loving-kindness, ill will has no chance to envelop your heart. This emancipation of the heart through loving-kindness is the cure for ill will."[52]

The notion of a *righteous* or *compassionate anger* is thus a contradiction in terms, since it assumes that ill will and loving-kindness can exist side by side, and that a thought, intention, or action can be characterized as having both of those qualities about it.

Kāli's strategy for testing Vedehikā's gentleness offers a sure technique for sussing out whether one has cultivated loving-kindness, because the test of *mettā* is patient forbearance (*khanti*/*kṣānti*) in the face of every adversity, from the smallest affront to the cost of one's own life. The Buddha does not sugarcoat what the practice of loving-kindness requires:

> Bhikkhus, even if bandits were to sever you savagely limb by limb with a two-handled saw, he who gave rise to a mind of hate towards them would not be carrying out my teaching. Herein, bhikkhus, you should train thus: "Our minds will remain unaffected, and we shall utter no evil words; we shall abide compassionate for their welfare, with a mind of loving-kindness, without inner hate. We shall abide pervading them with a mind imbued with loving-kindness; and starting with them, we shall abide pervading the all-encompassing world with a mind imbued with loving-kindness, abundant, exalted, immeasurable, without hostility, and without ill will." That is how you should train, bhikkhus.[53]

Loving-kindness is not at all a milquetoast sentiment. It calls for nothing less than the fullest exercise of resolve, strength, endurance, and selflessness. Even if one leaves to the side the delusions concerning others that give rise to ill will, this nīvaraṇa leaves one not even knowing oneself: "Suppose, brahmin, there is a bowl of water being heated over a fire, bubbling and boiling. If a man with good sight were to examine his own facial refection in it, he would neither know nor see it as it really is. So too, brahmin, when one dwells with a mind obsessed by ill will."[54] As long as one is boiling with anger—or even

---

52 Walshe, *Long Discourses*, 500.

53 Ñāṇamoli and Bodhi, *Middle Length Discourses*, 223.

54 Bodhi, *Connected Discourses*, 1612.

ready to boil with it[55]—one will never abide long in the stillness of samādhi, let alone come to realization.

The Dharmic teaching on ill will and its overcoming and Evagrius's depictions of anger and its overcoming cut against the grain of everyday ways of looking at oneself in one's relation to others. Patiently enduring harm, particularly when it would seem that something could be done about it, will strike many as one of the most foolish things one can do. There are some currents within contemporary culture that advocate restraint in the face of sense desire—the glutton, the rake, and the miser are often enough the butt of jokes, and their propensities to excess are easy fodder for caricaturists. By contrast, those who patiently endure insult and harm—particularly when it would appear that they could have done something about it—are called doormats, pushovers, simps, and much worse besides. To most, they invite not humorous taunts, but abject contempt.

Those who act in light of the Dharma and practice patient forbearance in the face of direct harm will no doubt be considered fools by the everyday person:

> He practices for the welfare of both—
> His own and the other's—
> When, knowing that his foe is angry,
> He mindfully maintains his peace. . . .
>
> When he achieves the cure of both—
> His own and the other's—
> The people who consider him a fool
> Are unskilled in the Dhamma.[56]

Everyday people are unskilled in the Dharma because they fail to grasp what "the cure of both" entails—insight into the emptiness of the self and the thoroughly conditioned nature of all dharmas, both of myself and of the other. They do not understand that, once that emptiness is grasped, it

55 Evagrius, it is worth noting here, thought of anger similarly as "a boiling over of the irascible part [of the soul]" (Evagrius, *Praktikos* 11; Sinkewicz, 99).

56 Bodhi, *Connected Discourses*, 256–57, 322–23.

is clear that there is nothing at which to take offense and certainly nothing to defend. Far from being pushovers, those who patiently endure insult and harm are strong beyond any everyday measure, for when nothing can incite the least anger or ill will in me, I am utterly invincible—nothing anyone does can harm *me* in the least.

In the same way, those Jews and gentiles who are stymied when confronted with "Christ crucified" (1 Cor 1:22–23) also do not understand that salvation lies precisely within such patient suffering. To them, no respectable God would suffer the insults of the world, and no sane human being would follow in the footsteps of a God who invites them to do the same. God's job, in such a view, is to commandeer forces to set things aright consistent with his name—*dominus deus sabbaoth*, the Lord God of army hosts.[57] But for those whom God has called, Paul counters, the Crucified is the perfect expression of "the power of God and the wisdom of God" (1 Cor 1:24). For the Christian who would aspire to communion with God, then, there is no surer path than the one set down by his or her Lord through his submission to the insults of the world in his suffering and death.

The noble disciple of the Buddha or the renunciant-contemplative follower of the Christ is not daunted by any of these charges, since both have already taken their leave of the everyday world and its values. Patience and loving-kindness may violate the standard rules by which the everyday world is governed, but what the renunciant-contemplative seeks has never been subject to the standards of this world: "The love of the Father is not in those who love the world; for all that is in the world . . . comes not from the Father but from the world. And the world and its desire are passing away, but those who do the will of God live forever" (1 John 2:15–17). The Dharma, too, runs counter to the churning stream of the everyday world of saṃsāra. As Bhikkhu Bodhi notes,

> though violence, either overt or subtle, may hold sway over the world in which we are afloat, the Buddha's path to freedom requires of us that we make a total break with prevailing norms. Thus one of the essential steps in our endeavor to

57 Many modern English-speaking Christians will recognize "Holy, holy, holy Lord, God of power and might" from the Sanctus in the eucharistic liturgy. This was the translation agreed on by a joint commission of English-speaking liturgists in 1973. But the classical English translation for *dominus deus sabbaoth* is "Lord God of hosts," with hosts, of course, meaning "armies." In 2011, the English translation of the Roman Missal went back to "Lord God of hosts."

> reach the abode of safety is to "lay down the rod," to put away violence, aggression and harmfulness towards all living beings.[58]

The Buddha identified "killing, imprisonment, confiscation, censure, or banishment" as so many ways of holding the rod with a view to maintaining some semblance of power and, in so doing, indicated that every form of asserting one's position over another—even civilly sanctioned ones—is to be set aside.[59]

Anger cannot be a prelude to good, as advocates of a righteous anger might claim, because it is not a prelude to *anything*, for, being blind, one sees *nothing*. As a way of distancing oneself from the world and the everyday people who comprise it, it cuts to the core the very possibility of any positive engagement with others at all. In both the Evagrian and the Dharmic understanding, there is simply no place for anger or ill will at all on the part of those who aspire to stillness. Always prone to agitation, always poised to pick up the gauntlet when thrown, as long as conditions of any kind and people of any stripe are able to provoke thoughts of anger or ill will in me, I can know no lasting peace. That such peace is bought in the coin of surrendering one's everyday response to such situations should not be news to the Christian: "Peace I leave with you; my peace I give to you. I do not give to you as the world gives. Do not let your hearts be troubled, and do not let them be afraid" (John 14:27). It will not be news to the pursuer of the Dharma, either: nirvāṇa, the cessation of tṛṣṇā, is frequently referred to in the *Nikāyas* as *the fearless*.[60] With no self to hold on to, both the fear of it becoming otherwise and the fear of it being harmed or annihilated simply do not arise.

Not getting what I want and having to endure what I do not want is, for most people—the aspiring renunciant-contemplative included—one of the most frustrating situations imaginable. If one is to continue on the path, it is important not only to overcome sensory desire and anger, but also to overcome the sense of loss that can easily arise in their absence. That sense of loss, too, reflects an all-too-tempting misunderstanding of myself and the world, one that, left unaddressed, will also obstruct the renunciant-contemplative on her way. It is not a coincidence that the next logismos Evagrius should address is sadness, to which we now turn.

58 Bodhi, *Dhamma Reflections*, 88.

59 Bodhi, *Numerical Discourses*, 291.

60 See Bodhi, *Numerical Discourses*, 550–52.

CHAPTER FIVE

The Querulous Spirit of Sadness

Evagrius's fifth logismos, sadness, might seem out of place in an inventory of obstructive mind states. Sadness, after all, seems to be an aftereffect, something that follows on the heels of something that *makes me* sad, much as pain follows from stepping on a protruding nail. The pain is not the problem, the nail is; so if sadness has arisen, that feeling should not be the problem, but rather whatever has prompted it. And just as I will want to see that nails are properly driven into wood to avoid such mishaps in the future, I will want to see conditions properly ordered so I do not become sad as a result of them. My sadness, I might be inclined to think, is *not my problem*, but a measure of the unsatisfactoriness of the conditions I happen to encounter. I may have abandoned sensual desire and I may have curbed my boiling irascibility, but—gosh darn it—this is all still a rather unsatisfactory state of affairs all the same. Fix the world, so the thought goes, and my sadness in the face of it will disappear.

But by ranking sadness among the logismoi, Evagrius signals that, however much sadness might be simply an emotional state that seems to arise naturally in conjunction with circumstances, there is still both a deceptive and a tempting aspect to it. Sadness is deceptive in that it takes such *feelings* of unsatisfactoriness as indicators of *actual* flaws or deficiencies. It then takes such thoughts about those flaws, feeds them, and keeps them alive by implicating far more than the particular situation in question. Now, rather far-flung thoughts enter the picture concerning how the whole world should be arranged, how everyone should act, or even how God ought to be disposed toward me and my place in the world. Of course, these thoughts do not actually do anything to change conditions, so I end up even sadder than before. Soon enough, it begins to seem that nothing—and no one, not even God—can ever measure up to my standards.

Sadness is tempting because these cultivated thoughts of unsatisfactoriness do nothing quite so much as reinforce my sense of self. Evagrius was quite clear on the point that "all the demons teach the soul to love pleasure; only the demon of sadness refrains from doing so. Instead, he corrupts the thoughts of those in the place by cutting off and drying up every pleasure of the soul by means of sadness."[1] So even though "pleasure follows every thought except for thoughts of sadness,"[2] we are nevertheless tempted by it; it is the very *absence* of pleasure that gives sadness its allure, as odd as that might sound at first blush. When "nobody knows the trouble I've seen; nobody knows my sorrow," as it is put in the widely known spiritual, my sadness certainly marks me out as special. Now I simply *have* to hold on to it, because if I were free of it, I would not be quite so special any longer. Seen in this light, sadness *is my problem*. It is not just an unfortunate psychophysical state that would call for therapeutic intervention and treatment as a coping mechanism (since it does not look like the world or the people around me are going to change any time soon). Instead, like all of the other logismoi, sadness is something to be seen through and abandoned along with the root thought of self that gives it rise—at least, of course, if one is to continue on the path toward communion with God in pure prayer.[3]

Still, sadness seems to be out of place among the logismoi for reasons internal to Evagrius's own teaching as well. One of the more puzzling aspects of his treatment of sadness has to do with his claim that, unlike the other logismoi, there is a form of sadness that is not entirely troublesome, but, in point of fact, has a beneficial quality to it: "Godly sadness calls the soul back with tears, refusing the joy and sadness of the opposing side, and it worries over approaching death and judgment; little by little it opens to accept this."[4] Evagrius here echoes Paul: "For godly grief produces a repentance that leads to salvation and brings no regret, but worldly grief produces death" (2 Cor 7:10).

---

1 Evagrius, *On Thoughts* 12; Sinkewicz, 161.

2 Evagrius, *Reflections* 51; Sinkewicz, 215.

3 Daniel G. Opperwall effectively distinguishes between Evagrius's understanding of sadness as a logismos and modern attempts to psychologize it. Opperwall, "Chained to Grievance, Rotten to the Roots: Evagrius and John Cassian on Sadness," *StPatr* 115 (2021): 374.

4 Evagrius, *Eulogios* 7.7; Sinkewicz, 34.

The question that faces anyone taking up Evagrius's treatment of sadness is this: Is this beneficial, "godly" sadness an aspect of the logismos of sadness, and, if so, what does that imply for an understanding of the logismoi generally? Or, if godly sadness is not an aspect of the logismos of sadness, what else must Evagrius have had in mind? Before exploring the full scope of this logismos, we need to settle the issue of Evagrius's seeming departure from the basic character of what it means to be a logismos at all in his identification of a beneficial, godly sadness.

John Gavin suggests that Evagrius's inclusion of sadness among the logismoi, while also seeing a certain positive aspect in it, stems from a perceived need to be accountable to the scriptural tradition. On his view, sadness posed

> a certain challenge for Evagrius Ponticus and two of his followers, Diadochus of Photice and St. Maximus the Confessor. While all three thinkers understood "grief" to be a vice that obstructed spiritual progress, they had to reconcile such a position with [the] passage in St. Paul's *Second Letter to the Corinthians*. . . . How can there be a "godly grief" or, better, a "grief willed by God"?[5]

While it is true that Evagrius uses Pauline language here, it would be a loss to read Evagrius on this point as if he were simply, or even primarily, satisfying the demands of scriptural fidelity. Evagrius was not at all hesitant to highlight certain scriptural passages while completely ignoring others; indeed, many of his confreres did just the same.[6] Rather, he takes up the distinction because these two kinds of sadness are those faced by every renunciant-contemplative, particularly in the early stages of his or her spiritual development. One is beset by them because one is still torn between the satisfactions of the life one has left behind and the realization that one has not quite yet begun to experience the fruits of the new one.

Here we can turn to the *Nikāyas* for some assistance in sorting this out. While there is no equivalent for sadness among the nīvaraṇas, the Pauline/

5 John Gavin, "'The Grief Willed by God': Three Patristic Interpretations of 2 Cor 7:10," *Greg* 91 (2010): 427.

6 Douglas Burton-Christie, *The Word in the Desert: Scripture and the Quest for Holiness in Early Christian Monasticism* (New York: Oxford University Press, 1993), 166; David Brakke, "Reading the New Testament and Transforming the Self in Evagrius of Pontus," in *Asceticism and Exegesis in Early Christianity: The Reception of New Testament Texts in Ancient Ascetic Discourses*, ed. Hans-Ulrich Weidemann (Göttingen: Vandenhoeck & Ruprecht, 2013), 284–85.

Evagrian distinction between worldly grief and godly grief does have a clear parallel in the Dharma's distinction between the "grief based on the householder life" and the "grief based on renunciation" that arises in the early stages of renunciant-contemplative practice:

> When one regards as a non-gain the non-gain of forms cognizable by the eye that are wished for, desired, agreeable, gratifying, and associated with worldliness—or when one recalls what was formerly not obtained that has passed, ceased, and changed—grief arises. Such grief as this is called grief based on the household life.[7]

By contrast, grief based on renunciation arises in conjunction with the awareness that one still has a long way to go before realizing the aim of one's aspiration:

> When, by knowing the impermanence, change, fading away, and cessation of forms, one sees it as it actually is with proper wisdom that forms both formerly and now are all impermanent, suffering, and subject to change, one generates a longing for the supreme liberations thus: "When shall I enter upon and abide in that base that the noble ones now enter upon and abide in?" In one who generates thus a longing for the supreme liberations, grief arises with that longing as condition. Such grief as this is called grief based on renunciation.[8]

In either case, grief (*domanassa*) is a disagreeable mental state (*vedanā*). While *feeling* might be one way to describe it, it is not a sensation related to the body, but rather one particular to the mind. In the *Nikāyas*, grief is frequently mentioned in conjunction with sorrow, lamentation, pain, and despair, and in the commentarial literature it is "always associated with antipathy and grudge, and [is] therefore karmically unwholesome (*akusala*)."[9] It is never good.

So what did the Buddha see that Evagrius also saw in making these distinctions? Both the Buddha and Evagrius would have been all too familiar with the disorientation that entering the renunciant life brings with it. Whereas the life of an everyday person is built around the exercise of one's own will in accordance with one's desires, all of that is stripped away upon entering into homelessness, and sadness is a not unexpected consequence.

We find this kind of sadness portrayed in the *Nikāyas* as the "four perils" that can beset a person who has recently entered into the holy life or, as it is

7 Ñāṇamoli and Bodhi, *Middle Length Discourses*, 1068.

8 Ñāṇamoli and Bodhi, *Middle Length Discourses*, 1069.

9 Nyanatiloka, *Buddhist Dictionary*, 57.

put here, "entered the water."[10] Upon entering the water, the metaphor goes, the aspirant becomes vulnerable to the peril of waves, the peril of crocodiles, the peril of whirlpools, and the peril of fierce fish. The peril of waves is encountered when a bhikkhu—reflecting on the fact that he is now instructed how to comport himself, when as a layman he had instructed others in their behavior—is displeased and considers returning to his previous life. When he further notes that he is now told by his fellow monks when and what to eat—and he recalls that he used to eat whatever and whenever he wanted, without needing anybody's permission—he falls prey to the peril of crocodiles. Should he find himself on the alms round looking around and seeing others enjoying themselves, he considers that the homeless life is much too exacting. He might understand that giving unbridled rein to sensual pleasures would be unbecoming, but he entertains the idea of splitting the difference between the two: "My family has wealth. I can both enjoy that wealth and do meritorious deeds. Let me now give up the training and revert to the lower life so that I can both enjoy that wealth and do meritorious deeds."[11] Now he is in the peril of whirlpools, swirling somewhere in a no-man's land between renunciant and everyday life. Or, finally, he is on the alms round and, seeing women loosely attired, is overcome with lust and considers leaving the ranks of the bhikkhus. Such is the peril of fierce fish. Succumbing in this way to the four perils, he gives up pursuing the renunciant path of the bhikkhu and takes his place among the lay disciples.

Recall that, in the course of the gradual training, once the bhikkhu had submitted to the training rules and had learned to live accordingly, he was then counseled to engage in mindfulness and full awareness of every movement and bodily state in order to abandon "memories and intentions based on the householder life."[12] This involved a conscious act of forgetting all that had, until now, come to pass: not as an induced amnesia, exactly, but as a refusal to continue rehearsing past events as if they had ongoing bearing on one's present self-understanding. The sutras speak of "nurturing delight" in past memories as a way of keeping the past *alive*:

> How, bhikkhus, does one revive the past? One nurtures delight there thinking, "I had such material form in the past." One nurtures delight there thinking, "I

---

10 Bodhi, *Numerical Discourses*, 502–5.

11 Bodhi, *Numerical Discourses*, 504. We will see this theme of splitting the difference again in conjunction with the discussion of restlessness-remorse.

12 Ñāṇamoli and Bodhi, *Middle Length Discourses*, 950–51.

> had such feeling in the past," . . . "I had such perception in the past," . . . "I had such formations in the past," . . . "I had such consciousness in the past." That is how one revives the past.[13]

"Nurtures delight" here is not simply the memory that this or that happened, but rather the "relishing of past experiences with thoughts of craving."[14] To the simple recollection of a past event, tṛṣṇā has been added, pulling one out of direct engagement in the present moment and, in so doing, reinforcing the conceit of a self that can somehow transcend it. The bhikkhu subject to the four perils finds himself beset by grief based on the householder life, not because that life is still in point of fact exercising a hold on him but because he simply will not let his delight in those cherished memories go.

The cultivation of memory is also central to Evagrius's understanding of worldly sadness:

> When it is through the frustration of one's desires, it occurs in this way. When certain thoughts gain the advantage, they bring the soul to remember home and parents and one's former life. And when they observe that the soul does not resist but rather follows right along and disperses itself among thoughts of pleasures, then with a hold on it they plunge it into sadness with the realization that the former things are no more and cannot be again because of the present way of life. And the miserable soul, the more it allowed itself to be dispersed among the former thoughts, the more it has now become hemmed in and humiliated by these latter ones.[15]

The longer one spends dwelling on the past, the more fully embellished the memories become until they obscure the present moment with things that are no more and can never be again. It is not simply enough to take leave of one's former life when taking up the renunciant-contemplative path; one has to dispel any recollection of that previous life as anything that ever held sway to begin with. There can be no looking back if one is to follow one's Lord:

> As they were going along the road, someone said to him, "I will follow you wherever you go." And Jesus said to him, "Foxes have holes, and birds of the air have nests; but the Son of Man has nowhere to lay his head." To another he said, "Follow me." But he said, "Lord, first let me go and bury my father." But Jesus said to him, "Let the dead bury their own dead; but as for you, go and proclaim the kingdom of God." Another said, "I will follow you, Lord, but let me first say

---

13 Ñāṇamoli and Bodhi, *Middle Length Discourses*, 1039–40.

14 Ñāṇamoli and Bodhi, *Middle Length Discourses*, 1344n1215.

15 Evagrius, *Praktikos* 10; Sinkewicz, 98.

> farewell to those at my home." Jesus said to him, "No one who puts a hand to the plow and looks back is fit for the kingdom of God." (Luke 9:57–62)

The only solution is to fully surrender to things as they stand. Just as the antidote to grief based on the household life is revulsion with respect to past memories, the antidote to worldly sadness is apatheia, the cultivation of dispassion with respect to the memory of those former attachments.

Ascesis comes to the aid of one still suffering from worldly sadness, since "hatred towards pleasures silences worldly sadness"[16]:

> An abstinent person does not experience sadness in the absence of food, nor does the chaste person experience sadness in the lack of a licentious pleasure; similarly the person free of anger in not attaining vengeance, or humble person when deprived of human esteem, or the person free of avarice when he suffers a loss—for such people have decisively turned away from the appetite for these things.[17]

The point is clear: if I want to steer clear of the debilitating nature of worldly sadness, I do well to steer clear of the appetitive drives and mind states that give rise to it. When I am no longer beset by gluttony in the present, I will not hold to memories of abundant food in the past. When I surrender the quick resort to anger in the present, I will not be inclined to rehearse instances of harm and insult long since passed.

Both Evagrius and the Buddha contrast this first kind of sadness with the second, godly sadness or grief based on the renunciant life. Unlike the first kind of sadness, which was based on the persistence of memory, the second kind of sadness arises in conjunction with hope. Because I am not where I want to be, I nurture hope that I will be different in the future:

> And how, bhikkhus, does one build up hope upon the future? One nurtures delight there thinking, "May I have such material form in the future." One nurtures delight there thinking, "May I have such feeling in the future," . . . "May I have such perception in the future," . . . "May I have such formations in the future," . . . "May I have such consciousness in the future." That is how one builds up hope upon the future.[18]

In the case of the noble disciple, sadness follows hope upon seeing clearly one's dukkha-laden samsaric state, imagining one's liberation from it in the

16 Evagrius, *Exhortations* 1.5; Sinkewicz, 218.

17 Evagrius, *Eight Thoughts* 5.12; Sinkewicz, 82.

18 Ñāṇamoli and Bodhi, *Middle Length Discourses*, 1040.

selflessness of nirvāṇa, and being dissatisfied that one is not there just yet. In the case of the Christian monk, sadness attending on hope arises in conjunction with longing for communion with God while one's mind is still obscured by one's self-love and its attendant obstructive thoughts, and becoming sad in light of that.

Such hope might seem to be a good thing, since it gives one an indication of the direction one should be taking. But one knows that already, and comparing one's present and future states does not provide any further insight, but only induces sadness. If I know full well that I have not come to the end of the path because I am still mired in attachments and delusions, what does *bemoaning* that fact contribute to overcoming them? Far from adding further insight into my condition or helping me along the path, hope actually clouds my awareness and gets in the way of what needs to be done. Hope, as it turns out, is just another form of aversion and, like its kin, anger, blinds one to the present moment. "To hope," Norman Fischer points out, "means to reject the experience of this moment, and therefore hope can be a kind of cowardice. Rather than face what's going on right now, we focus our attention on later, when things will hopefully be much more pleasant than they are at the present moment."[19] Not wanting one's present state, but not yet in conformity with some hoped-for future state, "sadness, along with fear and anger, arises because one is divided, caught between two worlds, unable to move forward or backward."[20]

The end to both worldly *and* godly sadness is to leave aside any thoughts of before or after and to face squarely the demands of the renunciant-contemplative life in the present with full concentration and resolve. "If you want to be free of sadness," Evagrius writes, "be zealous in pleasing God."[21] That zeal frees the monk *from* the world and *for* God by diverting attention from one's former and future self to the fulfillment of the commandments now. In the same way, for the noble disciple of the Buddha, the "full awareness" of one's bodily, affective, and mental states in ardently cultivated mindfulness clears away both the clouds of grief based on the householder life and that based on renunciation. As the backward-running ("I was this way") and

19 Norman Fischer, "Acupressure Point of the Heart," in *All the Rage: Buddhist Wisdom on Anger and Acceptance*, ed. Andrea Miller (Boston: Shambhala, 2014), 74.

20 Douglas Burton-Christie, "Evagrius on Sadness," *Cistercian Studies Quarterly* 44 (2009): 402.

21 Evagrius, *Maxims* 3.7; Sinkewicz, 231.

forward-running ("I shall be this way") currents of tṛṣṇā abate, the memories and intentions based on the householder life disappear, along with any hopes of how I imagine things will eventually turn out.[22]

This is where any close parallel ends between the sadness that Evagrius addresses and the sadness taken up in the *Nikāyas*. Because the nīvaraṇas become the focus of meditative awareness only after one has become solidly established in the ethical dimension of the holy life, and because the grief addressed in the *Nikāyas* concerns the bhikkhu still in the process of that establishment, no further mention of something like grief is made in conjunction with the nīvaraṇas.

So what did Evagrius see that the Buddha did not in counting sadness among the logismoi? In the most general terms, sadness is the name Evagrius gives to those demonic thoughts that reflect a misunderstanding of the nature of loss:

> Sadness is one who dwells over loss, who is familiar with frustrated acquisition, a forerunner of exile, remembrance of a family, a deputy of want, a kinsman of acedia, a complaint of exasperation, a reminder of insult, and a darkening of the soul, dejection in morals, drunkenness of prudence, a soporific remedy, a cloud of form, a worm in the flesh, sadness of thoughts, a people in captivity.[23]

Now, everyone is subject to the vicissitudes of gain and loss. "You win some, you lose some," we say, as if to remind ourselves of the obvious. Sadness arises in response to that obviousness as a kind of lament that more could not have been won or that so much had to be lost. It creates scenarios of how much better it would be if the gains were more substantial and lasting, and the losses fewer and further between. It wonders why things *have to be* the way they are.

Sadness pursued and intellectualized gives rise to theodicy, the attempt to answer the question of why a God who is all-powerful and all-good would create a world that is so deeply riddled with misfortune and evil, a world where evildoers fare well and the upright suffer. "This stinks!" the sad person says. "Could God not have made it otherwise?" Surely God *could* have, since God can do anything. So then why *didn't* God?

Philosophers and theologians may attempt to come up with satisfying answers to such questions. That is what philosophers and theologians do.

---

22 This point will be more fully developed in conjunction with restlessness-remorse in chap. 6.

23 Evagrius, *Vices* 4; Sinkewicz, 63.

But the renunciant-contemplative is not interested in tight arguments, and simply having come to some intellectually sound conclusion is a far cry from overcoming one's obstructive mind states. As Evagrius puts it, "For knowledge of God, one needs not a debater's soul, but a seer's soul."[24] It simply does not matter how sound or unsound the arguments that attempt to reconcile God's goodness with the miserable state of the world might be. The point of the contemplative life is to see into the very impulse to ask such questions in the first place.

Theodicy becomes an issue only for those who hold their own desires to be the standard for what is right, fitting, and just, and, in so doing, relegate God's standards to the back burner. "Through sadness," Seth Stadel notes, "the demons convince the monk that his own desires are more important than God's desires."[25] They are able to do this because the monk, even after confronting sense desire and anger, is still not entirely free of the passions:

> A prisoner of barbarians is bound in irons; a prisoner of the passions is bound with sadness. Sadness has no strength unless the other passions are present, as a fetter is without strength unless there is someone to attach to it . . . for sadness is constituted by the frustration of an appetite, and an appetite is joined to every passion.[26]

Or again, "Sadness sometimes occurs through the frustration of one's desires, or sometimes it follows closely upon anger."[27] Evagrius speaks of these passions as the monk's "possessions":

> But the monk with many possessions has bound himself with the fetters of his worries, as a dog is tied to a leash, even when he is forced to move off elsewhere. He carries around the memories of possessions as a heavy burden and a useless weight; he is stung with sadness and is mightily pained in thoughts. He has abandoned his possessions and is lashed with sadness.[28]

---

24 Evagrius, *Kephalaia Gnostica* 4.90, translated in Harmless and Fitzgerald, "Sapphire Light," 513. Ramelli's translation reads somewhat differently, although the point is the same: "The knowledge of God needs, not a dialectical soul, but (the faculty of spiritual) vision" (Ramelli, Kephalaia Gnostika, 244).

25 Seth M. Stadel, "Prayer without Anger and Sadness: The Syriac Adaptation of Evagrius' *Chapters on Prayer*," *ParOr* 45 (2019): 353.

26 Evagrius, *Eight Thoughts* 5.8–10; Sinkewicz, 82.

27 Evagrius, *Praktikos* 10; Sinkewicz, 98.

28 Evagrius, *Eight Thoughts* 7; Sinkewicz, 79.

Material possessions are, of course, included here, but anything—and anyone—I happen to hold dear counts as a possession, at least as far as being a ground for sadness goes. It is not the nature of the object or person in question so much as the *kind* of attachment I have come to develop for it. Put simply, I want to control those things and persons I am attached to. When circumstances, which are ultimately under God's control, prove to be different from what I would have happen, I am sad because they reveal that I am not in control after all.

We see how Evagrius illustrates this in what we might call "The Case of the Tardy Brother" in *To Eulogios*. The case begins straightforwardly enough: "When for the sake of his office the brother who lives with you goes on a trip, renew his memory according to the custom of your prayers." It is right and fitting to pray for travelers, and the Divine Liturgy includes among its opening petitions a prayer for all travelers, along with intercessions for all those who are sick, suffering, and imprisoned.[29] It is simply a mark of Christian charity to be mindful of all those who are in uncertain, dangerous, or unhealthy conditions and to express confidence in the providential hand of God with respect to them. "But," Evagrius continues, "do not hold him in your imagination beyond measure, lest perhaps the demons seize from you the beginning of disquiet and sharpen it to an even finer point. . . . They know in fact that out of excessive concern about one's brother they can shape feelings of sadness and so trouble the ruling faculty."[30]

It is one thing to commend *all* who travel or who are sick to the Lord's care. It is altogether another to single out *one particular person* among them—the one whom I am particularly solicitous of—and expect that God will have particular concern for *that* person. Asking God to keep in his care all who are sick is not the same as asking God to grant a speedy recovery to Uncle Charlie, who is suffering from shingles. In the first case, I am not keeping tabs on anyone's health situation, the speed of their recovery, or, indeed, whether they have in fact recovered. In the second, I am all too aware of Uncle Charlie's condition, can count the number of days he has been in pain, and can note any signs of improvement. If his condition does not improve, or, still more troubling, worsens yet, I might begin to despair of God's mercy, as it would seem that God has not answered my prayer.

29 David L. Frost, trans., *The Divine Liturgies of Saint John Chrysostom and Saint Basil the Great* (Cambridge: Aquila, 2015), 15, 63.

30 Evagrius, *Eulogios* 28; Sinkewicz, 55.

Such is the case with the traveling brother. He has gone off on an assignment. I know the distance there and back, how long the trip takes, and how long it should take him to settle his affairs and get back to the monastic compound. But when he does not arrive back when I think he should, I am not at all pleased. If my sadness at his delay is not kept in check, it can soon enough morph into anger: "Further, [the demons] quietly enkindle complaints of tardiness, as if the brother was neglectful regarding the urgency of his office, so that the much-disquieted yearning might perhaps even turn into hatred."[31] The hope that nothing bad happen to him on his journey now turns into a personal affront that he is late, and the move is made from an expression of concern upon his return—"How are you? Did you encounter difficulties?"—to an accusation—"Where the hell have you been?" It was not enough for him to arrive back safe and sound whenever that was to come to pass; he was to be back at *this* time and under *these* conditions. The "beginning of disquiet" has been now been sharpened to a very fine point indeed. The "excessive concern" Evagrius notes, then, is not a matter of being *overflowing* with concern but of being *overly exacting* in its application.

It is telling that Evagrius sets these reflections down under the heading "Pure Prayer," as if to underscore his general claim that pure prayer, as communion with God, is not obstructed by concerns about this or that. For Evagrius, prayer is "a state of mind destructive of every earthly mental representation,"[32] and must be distinguished from petition, "a converse of the mind with God accompanied by supplication [comprising] assistance or request for good things."[33] One who petitions for particular outcomes is still maintaining some distance from God by muddying the waters with extraneous representations foreign to that communion. Even though those representations have an air of loving concern about them, they, like all representations, have their root source in self-love. While I may be praying for my brother or my Uncle Charlie, it is *my* brother and *my* Uncle Charlie, and it is the satisfaction of *my wish* for them that is the subject of my petitions. When those petitions do not seem to receive the answers I was hoping for and I become sad (and possibly angry at God) as a result, it is not because

31 Evagrius, *Eulogios* 28; Sinkewicz, 55–56.

32 Evagrius, *Reflections* 26; Sinkewicz, 213.

33 Evagrius, *Reflections* 28; Sinkewicz, 214.

God is or is not responding to my requests but because I had no particular business asking for them in the first place:

> Do not pray for the fulfillment of your own wishes, for they do not necessarily accord with the will of God. But pray rather as you were taught, saying: "Your will be done" in me (Matt. 6:10). And in every matter entreat him in this way that his will be done, for he wills what is good and beneficial for your soul, but you are not necessarily looking for this.[34]

Evagrius himself seems to have run into this difficulty. Often enough, he admits, he had asked God for what he wanted, "forcing the will of God and not leaving it up to him to arrange for what he knows will benefit me." When he ended up getting exactly what he asked for, however, he found that he was "very annoyed" with himself, since, as he said, "it did not work out for me as I thought it would."[35]

An individual can only see things from their own limited vantage point, and whatever particulars they are concerned with will only ever be but the tiniest fraction of the whole sweep of the universe. I may not have that infinite perspective at my disposal, but I can at least set down any pretense to that perspective in fashioning my own plan for things. The surest way to do that is to become dispassionate with respect to all things—from my presuppositions of how the next hour should go to my presuppositions concerning the fate of the world. Everyday life is brimming over with such presumptions. The tardy brother or Uncle Charlie's health is only the tip of the iceberg, and the "excessive concern" that arises in conjunction with either of those is of a piece with such concern in conjunction with anything else. One need not hear but a fraction of the day's news before a sorrowful *o tempora! o mores!* rises in response. But circumstances, people, nations, religious bodies, and associations of all kinds come into being and pass away, and focusing my attention and worry on what is transitory and finite cuts to the quick the very mind that would participate in the infinite mind of God. For this reason, Evagrius also counsels the monk to beware of "the thoughts of sadness that come to us concerning transitory affairs, sinking the intellect into great affliction and killing it."[36]

Taking leave of the world in voluntary exile might spare the monk such concern and such sorrow, but coming face to face with the demons in solitude

34 Evagrius, *Prayer* 31; Sinkewicz, 196.
35 Evagrius, *Prayer* 32; Sinkewicz, 196.
36 Evagrius, *Antirrhetikos* 4.74; Brakke, 117.

brings forth its own occasion for sadness: that one has to confront the demons at all. This sadness, too, stems from the frustration of one's own attachments—not the everyday attachments of desire and anger but the attachment one has in the desire to grow closer to God. This is a sadness that arises in "the soul that wants, through its withdrawal from the world, to grow strong in the fear of God, but is hindered by the fear that comes from the demons."[37] Evagrius is quite graphic in his inventory of the demonic phantasmagoria: there are those that hiss, and those that have eyes that flash like fire; some appear like snakes, while others pop up out of thin air "like Ethiopians."[38] Whatever one makes of such descriptions, there can be no doubt that confrontation with the demons is terrifying, their grotesqueries matched only by the unpredictability of their arrival and strength of their number. "Why," the monk wonders, "has God let me be subject to this onslaught?"[39] Soon he is searching for specific reasons he has to undergo such trials,[40] and if it is not clear how all of this came about, he searches for some comfort in knowing "what is to happen to the demons on the day of judgment and what is the generation of torment to which they are to be handed over" in recompense for the torment they have caused him.[41] In the end, the monk may be so mired in such sadness that suicide might seem like the only way to escape it.[42]

Whatever resemblance the Evagrian logismos of sadness has to other forms of mental and spiritual affliction, it is perhaps best considered as a kind of deep *spiritual whininess* that, left unchecked and subsequently cultivated, leaves one incapable of any kind of satisfaction in the renunciant-contemplative life—or indeed in any life—at all. This whininess is the negative corollary of a sense of entitlement. In considering myself deprived of my wish list of how things ought to be, I cast about for alternatives that, in their turn, also prove elusive to my control. Now the very lack of control itself becomes the problem: "The monk is faced with the daunting task of coming to terms not only with all that is not as he would have it in his present life *but also* with the possibility that

37 Evagrius, *Antirrhetikos* 4.19b; Brakke, 103.

38 Evagrius, *Antirrhetikos* 4.13, 4.14, 4.18, 4.34; Brakke, 102–3, 107. As Brakke notes, *Ethiopians* was the general term used by the Egyptians to refer to anyone with black skin. In this case, it is the demons' blackness that is so distressing to the monk.

39 Evagrius, *Antirrhetikos* 4.7; Brakke, 101.

40 Evagrius, *Antirrhetikos* 4.17; Brakke, 103.

41 Evagrius, Antirrhetikos 4.56; Brakke, 112.

42 Evagrius, Antirrhetikos 4.72; Brakke, 116.

certain cherished dreams of the future will never be realized."[43] As Douglas Burton-Christie writes, sadness in the *Antirrhetikos* "seems to have less to do with the frustration of desire and more to do with discouragement or loss of hope that comes from being subjected to forces beyond one's control."[44] For one who, until now, has sought to control things out of self-love, finding that one's self is ultimately powerless—unable to control circumstances, control others, or control God—is certainly going to make one sulk.

Sadness in the early stages of renunciant-contemplative life is combatted by strengthening one's resolution and getting down to the business at hand. Overcoming sadness as a logismos involves cutting to the root the assumptions that one falls back on and seeing them as the misapprehensions that they are. It involves a fundamental reordering of the way in which one views the world, a revaluing of those things that, up to this point, have been occasions for one's sadness. That reordering begins by surrendering the presumption of setting one's agenda ahead of God's inscrutable ways, and the surest way to do that is surrender all agendas of every kind. But if this is done only as a grudging resignation to the brute facticity of the world, one will still not have overcome the obstacle, as least not *as a Christian*. Whereas both the Stoic and the Christian will, through apatheia, come to see that circumstances are (as Epictetus puts it) "not up to us,"[45] that realization will bring the Christian more than equanimity and peace—it will bring *joy* as well.

Joy is the very antithesis of sadness:

> Joy is the destruction of sorrow and thanksgiving for misfortunes, a vision that comes from prayers and gladness that comes from ascetic works, happiness from doing good, an ornament of renunciation, a receptacle of hospitality, a refuge of hopes, nourishment of ascetics, an encouragement for mourners, a consolation for tears, a help for affliction, a supporter of love, a partner in patience.[46]

Ceaseless joy goes hand in hand with ceaseless prayer: "Rejoice always, pray without ceasing," as Paul urges his readers (1 Thess 5:16–17). This is a Christian disposition in that it is drawn from the example of Christ, who endured the cross "for the sake of the joy that was set before him" (Heb 12:2). The cross

43 Burton-Christie, "Evagrius on Sadness," 405

44 Burton-Christie, "Evagrius on Sadness," 405–6.

45 Epictetus, *Handbook*, 11.

46 Evagrius, *Vices* 4; Sinkewicz, 63.

is not a means to an end; rather, it is the very expression of joy in the midst of suffering:

> Let the joy of peace be the law written in our heart, rooting out sadness, driving away hatred and destroying wrath, dissolving acedia; for hiding in peaceful forbearance and thanksgiving and overflowing in perseverance, the joy of peace is a sea of virtues, drowning by the cross the resistance of the devil.[47]

Just as sadness is not, as a logismos, principally an emotion, neither is the joy that counteracts it; as Hausherr puts it, this joy is "a disposition, a 'state' that will make you forget every lower joy."[48] It is a joy that only those who have surrendered their will to the will of God, even unto the prospect of death, can ever taste.[49]

This joy that counters sadness is also one filled with *gratitude*, and it is telling that each of the descriptions of joy just mentioned includes thanksgiving as one of its characteristics. Without an uncompromising gratitude for all things, pure prayer will not be forthcoming, for "prayer is the issue of joy and thanksgiving."[50] Indeed, it accompanies joy and prayer in Paul's exhortation to ceaseless prayer as well: "Rejoice always, pray without ceasing, give thanks in all circumstances; for this is the will of God in Christ Jesus for you" (1 Thess 5:16–18). No particular circumstances are singled out here, save perhaps those that, until now, have been most particularly odious:

> In afflictions be especially thankful, because through them you will perceive more clearly the grace of assistance; for by thus shaking off with thanksgiving the afflictions that come upon you, you will not darken the most radiant beauty of perseverance. When the demon has cracked the whip against your flesh, it will be found to provide you with the greatest reward if you accept the blow as a pretext for thanksgiving.[51]

---

47 Evagrius, *Eulogios* 6.6; Sinkewicz, 53–54.

48 Irénée Hausherr, SJ, *Les Leçons d'un contemplatif. Le Traité de l'Oraison d'Evagre le Pontique* (Paris: Beauchesne, 1960), 184.

49 Many centuries later, Francis of Assisi would make the same point quite descriptively in his account to Brother Leo of what "perfect joy" entails. See Regis J. Armstrong, OFM, J. A. Wayne Hellman, and William J. Short, eds., *The Prophet*, vol. 3 of *Francis of Assisi: Early Documents* (New York: New City, 2001), 449–50.

50 Evagrius, *Prayer* 15; Sinkewicz, 194.

51 Evagrius, *Eulogios* 8.8; Sinkewicz, 35. Here there is a parallel in the *Nikāyas* in the case of the Bhikkhu Puṇṇa, who exemplified the *kṣānti pāramitā*, the perfection of patient forbearance, in being ready to bear with gratitude the rough treatment he was bound to receive at the hands of the Sunāparantans. See Bodhi, *Connected Discourses*, 1168–69.

Or again, "He who is clothed in the purple of afflictions, that is, in perseverance . . . will with unceasing thanksgiving shake off the raindrops of these thoughts from his inner self."[52] Just as the joy that overcomes the logismos of sadness is not an emotion, neither is the thanksgiving that goes along with it. A disposition of gratitude that sees all circumstances—the painful *and* the pleasant, those sought *and* those unsought, the gains *and* the losses—as grounds for thanksgiving is not something that mere feelings can be counted on to bring to the fore; instead, it is the fruit of wisdom and insight. Of course, it is easy to feel grateful for the good things of life, and the exhortation to "count one's blessings" is a reminder to do just that. But I do not need to *count* my blessings when I look on *everything* with gratitude, including those things that bring me low. The ability to pick and choose among circumstances—being grateful for and rejoicing in some, while being saddened by others—still reflects the conceit of the self that has set its standard of how the world should run down to its least particulars.

Sadness cuts against my ability to look out on the world with any kind of perduring joy. Joy, along with peace, is vitally integral to the renunciant-contemplative life. Such joy and peace "enlighten the eye of the intellect for the contemplation of the superior goods."[53] So, too, does a thoroughgoing, abiding gratitude:

> When your mind out of a great longing for God gradually withdraws, as it were, from the flesh and turns aside all mental representations deriving from the senses or from memory or from temperament, being filled with both reverence and joy, then consider yourself to be near the frontiers of prayer.[54]

I will not be able to continue to practice as a contemplative as long as I am presenting God with a laundry list of everything that I find unsatisfactory. The prayer of the angry person may have been "an abominable incense offering" and "an irritating noise" when presented before the Lord, but the prayer of the whining petitioner is not going to land much differently. Jesus certainly did suggest that one should doggedly persist in presenting one's case before God, as in the Gospel parable of the widow before the unjust judge (Luke 18:1–8). But if one's case is built on the premise that one's own assessment of the situation is superior to anything God may have already had in mind, then

52 Evagrius, *Eulogios* 2.2; Sinkewicz, 30.
53 Evagrius, *Eulogios* 6.6; Sinkewicz, 33.
54 Evagrius, *Prayer* 61; Sinkewicz, 199.

it, too, is bound to be an irritation that has no place in an obstructionless communion with God. The judge may long abide the widow, but that does not at all mean they are of one mind and one heart.

Kevin Corrigan suggests that "the elimination of sadness in the later 7 sins' tradition is a bigger loss than we have ever recognized."[55] Given the richness and depth of Evagrius's treatment of sadness, that seems right. When spiritual whininess is not cast as an impediment to communion with God, the sense of entitlement that it reflects is certain to gain the upper hand. Spiritual practice then takes on the form of constant supplication for this or that, and God is imagined as something of an all-powerful Santa Claus. When things do not go my way, I assume God to be absent; when things happen that, despite my petitions, cause me harm or difficulty, I assume God to be indifferent or callous or even somewhat sadistic. So deep is the thought that unsatisfactory conditions demand nothing short of an overhaul that many religions have found a way to include it as a mainstay of their self-understanding. In Judaism it is *tikkun olam*, or *repairing the world*. In Christianity it takes the form of a rather robust agenda of social, economic, political, and environmental action framed within the language of responsibility, stewardship, and care for creation. All of them can be read as so many attempts to overcome sadness over the state of the world by taking over the job that God has presumably failed to execute properly.

That being said, it is easy to see why sadness would have fallen off the roster. Finding joy in what had previously prompted sadness and offering thanksgiving in the midst of tribulation are not everyday dispositions, nor are they easy to come by. They require the surrender of the self and its agenda—acts that most are either unwilling or unable to make. So much of social and political life is now dedicated to responding to and alleviating personal and communal forms of sadness, and perhaps that is the best that one can do for a body of everyday persons. For the renunciant-contemplative, however, treating that sadness as something that warrants changing conditions, rather than taking it as an obstacle to be overcome despite conditions as they are, is to cut oneself off from the peace and stillness that characterizes the fullness of life in God.

Satan's counsel to Antony, "Let them watch after themselves and stop censuring me for no reason!,"[56] is to be taken to heart. The monk has no one

55 Corrigan, *Evagrius and Gregory*, 88.

56 Athanasius, *Life of Antony*, 62.

to blame but himself for his sadness—not the demons, since they have no power beyond that which one hands over to them, and certainly not God, who merely allows the demons to do their work in order to test the aspirant's commitment. A monk who, falling ever more deeply into sadness, blames either speaks falsely. It is his own stubborn insistence that the world answer to his own demands of it that is to blame. If the Son of Man has nowhere to lay his head, neither will the mind of the monk who would follow him. The stillness one seeks is not one that can be measured by a standard of material, emotional, or intellectual satisfaction, and certainly not by any sense of mastery or control. Only when one has renounced all—even to the point of renouncing the thought that things could or should be other than they are—will one come to know that stillness in which the presence of God can be known. Just as sunlight cannot penetrate deep water, "the light of contemplation does not illuminate a heart overcome by sadness."[57]

57 Evagrius, *Eight Thoughts* 22; Sinkewicz, 83.

CHAPTER SIX

The Maelstrom of Perfection: Restlessness-Remorse

Bhikkhu Mahākoṭṭhita once approached Sāriputta, one of the Buddha's senior disciples, and put to him a series of questions regarding the relationship between living the holy life and its possible effect on one's future state. In particular, he wanted to know whether the practice had any effect on the positive or negative consequences of one's previous actions. In response to every version of the question that Mahākoṭṭhita could think of, Sāriputta answered, "Certainly not, friend." Frustrated, Mahākoṭṭhita fired back: "Then for what purpose does one live the spiritual life under the Blessed One?" Sāriputta replied, "One lives the spiritual life under the Blessed One, friend, for the purpose of knowing, seeing, attaining, realizing, and penetrating what one has not known, seen, attained, realized, and penetrated"[1]—the Noble Truths of dukkha, its cause, its end, the path to its end, *and nothing else.*

It is easy to understand both Mahākoṭṭhita's questions and his frustration at Sāriputta's answers. Frequently enough, meditative or contemplative practice is undertaken with the expectation of getting something out of it, whether that be tranquil mind states, mystical visions, or whatever one happens to associate with such concepts as enlightenment, realization, or salvation. If one is unsure about—or just not interested in—such ends, one might engage in some form of practice simply as a way to alter one's state, ranging anywhere from overcoming addictions to tinkering with personality traits, from becoming more relaxed generally to mitigating the effects of medical

1 Bodhi, *Numerical Discourses*, 1267–69.

or psychological conditions. Some have even gone so far as to suggest that the world as a whole would be a much better place, and its social ills greatly diminished, if only more people devoted themselves to prayer or meditation.[2] And if such this-worldly benefits were not enough, it is a common feature of many religions that a robust life of prayer and devotion can have some influence on mitigating the consequences of one's moral failings, even unto life after death.

As Sāriputta's responses to Mahākoṭṭhita make clear, however, the Dharma makes no room at all for such means-ends calculations in the pursuit of the holy life. In fact, the Buddha expressly denies that any kind accruable benefits are to be expected as a result of practice: "This holy life, bhikkhus, does not have gain, honour, and renown for its benefit, or the attainment of virtue for its benefit, or the attainment of concentration for its benefit, or knowledge and vision for its benefit. But it is this unshakeable deliverance of mind that is the goal of this holy life, its heartwood, and its end."[3] Anyone hoping the Dharma will make them some kind of better person—or at least better their lot—will have been amply forewarned that such expectations are bound to be disappointed and that holding on to them can only obstruct the attainment of what the Dharma does, in point of fact, have to offer.

The concerns underlying questions like Mahākoṭṭhita's arise from the nīvaraṇa of restlessness-remorse. Restlessness-remorse is, along with sloth-torpor, one of the two composite hindrances among the nīvaraṇas, hindrances that manifest in two distinct, yet interconnected, ways. Like the other hindrances, these two composite hindrances conceal reality and keep the aspirant from pressing onward out of fear of losing the self. Unlike the other three, which arise from mistaken thoughts about things and people, restlessness-remorse and sloth-torpor are distinctive in that they arise from mistaken thoughts about the nature and purpose of renunciant-contemplative practice itself. They are particularly pernicious because, if left unaddressed, they will drive the practitioner to leave the path, either by engaging in extraneous and unskillful activities or by failing to carry out those things that are particularly integral and skillful in coming to stillness and realization.

---

2 The International Society for Contemplative Research, for instance, looks at exploring "the role of contemplative practices in the advancement of social justice, racial equity, and conflict resolution." See "What Is Contemplative Research?," www.contemplativeresearch.org/what-is-contemplative-research. They are far from alone.

3 Ñāṇamoli and Bodhi, *Middle Length Discourses*, 290.

Restlessness-remorse concerns the former, and it functions as a unified hindrance in that its components are two sides of the same disposition, the drive for a kind of perfection or purity. Like the other nīvaraṇas, it is cunning because it gets certain things somewhat right: there *are* good and bad actions, certain things *are* conducive toward realization while other things are not, and there *is* a difference between the noble disciple and an everyday person. But, still under the sway of tṛṣṇā, one then takes that observation and comes up with a roster of determinate characterizations of what good action, realization, or being a noble disciple *must be like*.

From here, one might go in one of two directions. On the one hand, one might undertake actions that, so it is hoped, will causally produce such desired outcomes. When those activities fail to bring about their results in short order (as fail they will), one then continues to cast about for other form of practice that, this time, might succeed in accomplishing the task. Of course, this too will fail, and so the cycle continues. On the other hand, one might lose the impetus to practice by becoming worried that one will never be able to attain such an outcome because of one's past deeds. If one could go back in time, one would undo the deeds themselves, but since that is not possible, one now undertakes activities that, again so it is hoped, might at least undo their effects. Since effects follow inexorably from their causes, this, too, proves itself to be a fruitless enterprise, and until one is able to see that, one remains bound to an unproductive dwelling on the past that undercuts the resolve and the energy needed for pressing forward.

These perfectionist views are fundamentally mistaken because they rest on a misunderstanding of the nature of causality (*karma*):

> There is no such thing as saying: "By this discipline or practice or austerity or holy life I will bring my unripened kamma to fruition, or I will gradually make this ripened kamma go away." Neither of these things is possible, because pleasure and pain have been measured out with a measure limited by the round of birth-and-death, and there is neither increase nor decrease, neither excellence nor inferiority. Just as a ball of string when thrown runs till it is all unravelled, so fools and wise run on and circle round till they make an end of suffering.[4]

Because causality cannot be circumvented, practice cannot create an exemption from it. The unshakable deliverance of mind toward which it conduces is a thoroughgoing awareness of, openness to, and insight into that inexorable

4 Walshe, *Long Discourses*, 95.

chain of causes and conditions, not a tool for bending or breaking a link, so to speak, that might modify the course of that chain. In one ignorant of the nature of causality and the nature of practice, restlessness-remorse gives rise to a misapplied kind of zeal that can easily slide into a fanaticism of one kind or another, and away from stillness and any prospect of genuine insight.

In the *Nikāyas*, being subject to restlessness-remorse is likened to being blown about in the wind: "Suppose, brahmin, there is a bowl of water stirred by the wind, rippling, swirling, churned into wavelets. If a man with good sight were to examine his own facial reflection in it, he would neither know nor see it as it really is."[5] One is blown about because one is still taking one's cue from dharmas that fluctuate and change rather than simply letting them rise and fall as they will. (Sloth-torpor, as we will see in chapter 7, moves in the other direction, prompting one to slack off or quit altogether when one feels like one has been somehow shortchanged with regard to the promise of the life one has set out to lead.) As the winds of restlessness-remorse blow in two different directions, one toward the future and the other toward the past, we need to look at the components individually before taking up the conjoined pair as a single hindrance.

Setting out on the renunciant-contemplative path in accordance with the Dharma involves a basic understanding of the distinction between good and bad actions and an acknowledgment that these actions have consequences, beneficial or detrimental, that follow in their wake.[6] Without that, one would not even bother. The aspirant's initial inkling that "the household life is close and dusty, the homeless life is free as air"[7] is enough to take that first step, but the neophyte knows nothing about what the life of practice is actually like, nor can he or she possibly know what it will ultimately require.

This is true enough for any intended plan of action generally. I might sign on for a course of training based on the kind of career I hope to pursue, but until I am actually engaged in it, I can only project how it all might go. I might imagine a life as a physician, calling forth images of treating patients, performing surgery, or delivering babies, and I think I might like to do that myself. So I apply for medical school, get accepted, and begin my studies. Along the way there are several checkpoints by which I can assess my progress: course

5 Bodhi, *Connected Discourses*, 1612–13.

6 Ñāṇamoli and Bodhi, *Middle Length Discourses*, 935.

7 Walshe, *Long Discourses*, 99.

grades, graduation from medical school, licensing exams, residency, board certification, and so on. While my projected image of "being a physician" will certainly have been modified in the process, I will have no doubt that, once all of that is finished, I and others will be able to discern that I am indeed a physician, and that each of the steps will have done their work in producing that desired outcome.

The liberation of the mind is not like this, however. The steps of the gradual training from beginning to end do not *add up* to or *produce* realization as much as they *clear the ground* of any obstructions that stand in its way. Because the clear, radiant mind is nothing other than one's true nature—a nature that greed, anger, and delusion have only obscured—the Noble Path is a course of attrition, not accumulation, a process of surrender, not attainment. And as insight involves seeing directly into the emptiness of the self, this business I call *me* manifests no discernible attribute by which I might determine "I am enlightened" or "I am not enlightened." Even in attainment, I might never *know* that I have attained.[8]

Without any discernible signs to indicate whether one is making steady progress, one who feels the need to identify such signs is likely to be left feeling rather adrift. As a way of finding some bearings, one might take to noting changes in bodily or affective states: if what I am doing makes me feel better, I might think, I must be doing something right; if what I am doing is making me feel worse, then I must be doing something wrong. Those in the early days of practice will often be heard making comments to the effect that they "feel much more at ease" when they practice or that they "act more mindfully"—and perhaps they do. Nothing about that, however, indicates anything about the stillness of the mind or insight, and focusing on such states leaves one open to becoming concerned lest one begin to feel worse or act differently:

> The uninstructed worldling, who is not a seer of the noble ones and is unskilled and undisciplined in their Dhamma, who is not a seer of superior persons and is unskilled and undisciplined in their Dhamma, regards form as self or self as possessing form, or form as in self, or self as in form. That form of his changes and alters. With the change and alteration of form, his consciousness becomes preoccupied with the change of form. Agitation and a constellation of mental

---

8 Thirteenth-century Zen teacher Dōgen puts it like this: "Do not suppose that what you realize becomes your knowledge and is grasped by your consciousness. Although actualized immediately, the inconceivable may not be apparent. Its appearance is beyond your knowledge." Dōgen, *Moon in a Dewdrop: Writings of Zen Master Dōgen*, ed. Kazuaki Tanahashi (New York: North Point, 1977), 72.

> states born of preoccupation with the change of form remain obsessing his mind. Because his mind is obsessed, he is frightened, distressed, and anxious, and through clinging he becomes agitated.[9]

In taking up and abandoning the nīvaraṇa of sense desire, one is freed from attachment to discrete phenomena. In confronting and abandoning ill will, one is freed from aversion to such phenomena. In confronting and working through the nīvaraṇa of restlessness-remorse, one is freed from attachment or aversion to *changes* in phenomena. While change is a fact of conditioned existence, one still bound by tṛṣṇā is not content with the mere fact of change; one wants *positive* change, an indication of spiritual *progress* that fulfills some kind of expectation related to how one is faring, some measure of spiritual *profit*.

One practical manifestation of this mind state that is consistently identified in the textual sources is putting great store in things such as ceremonial rituals and observances. A staple of many religious systems is the performance of certain activities that, simply through their performance, are considered efficacious in bringing about some kind of spiritual outcome for the practitioner.[10] This was certainly true of Brahmanic practice at the time of the Buddha. One of those rituals involved ablution in the waters of certain rivers in order to wash away sins. Once, when a brahmin approached the Buddha wondering whether he, too, would take part in this ritual (in this case at the Bāhukā River), the Buddha responded: "'Why, brahmin, go to the Bāhukā River? What can the Bāhukā River do?' 'Master Gotama, the Bāhukā River is held by many to give liberation, it is held by many to give merit, and many wash away their evil actions in the Bāhukā River.'" The Buddha replied that he was not going to the river and added:

> Bāhukā and Adhikakkā,
> Gayā and Sundarikā, too,
> Payāga and Sarassati,
> And the stream Bahumati—
> A fool may there forever bathe
> Yet will not purify dark deeds.[11]

---

9 Bodhi, *Connected Discourses*, 865.

10 The classic Christian formulation of this is *ex opere operato*.

11 Ñāṇamoli and Bodhi, *Middle Length Discourses*, 120–21.

Bathing in water removes dirt from bodies, but it does not remove unskillfulness from previous actions or turn unskillful actions into skillful ones. Right conduct does:

> It is here, brahmin, that you should bathe,
> To make yourself a refuge for all beings.
> And if you speak no falsehood
> Nor work harm for living beings,
> Nor take what is offered not,
> With faith and free from avarice,
> What need for you to go to Gayā?
> For any well will be your Gayā.[12]

The point is that no ritual, specific pilgrimage site, or water from any source can do what right conduct can do. Only right conduct can bring about the fruits of the holy life—and nothing else.

While religiously prescribed rituals might be misguided and ineffectual distractions from the work that needs to be done, the Buddha points out that even more detrimental are those private rituals and observances one might set for oneself. I might resolve to meditate in the presence of some object or some sound, perhaps, or restrict myself to certain foods, or take to reciting a personal mantra or something of the kind. Further, I might mix in practices from other traditions and make up a kind of religious potpourri, a little from here and a little from there, creating what I fancy as my own uniquely personal spiritual practice. Taking note of how any of these make me feel when I do them (for how else could I measure their effectiveness?), I keep at them as long as I feel good doing them and discard them as they fail to make me feel better. But since all I am working with are my fluctuating conditioned states, I will find myself forever tinkering with minutiae:

> Having undertaken observances by himself,
> a person goes up and down, attached to perception.
> But having realized the Dhamma with knowledge,
> the wise one, broad in wisdom, does not go up and down.[13]

12 Ñāṇamoli and Bodhi, *Middle Length Discourses*, 121.

13 Bodhi, *Suttanipāta*, 295.

Up and down, down and up, now this, now that—all the while never settling into that stillness and equipoise of mind that was the aim of practice to begin with. It is in part in light of such considerations that the Buddha saw adherence to rites and rituals of any kind as a defilement of the mind (*saṃyojana*), a way of putting something in the place of what has been, or at least is in the process of being, discarded.

All the nīvaraṇas are likened to sieves,[14] and this is most assuredly the case with restlessness. Because one does not see immediate results, one fidgets. Rather than realizing that one needs to stop chasing after this or that state, one thinks one needs to keep doing something in order to get somewhere. But where there is, quite literally, *nothing* particular to accomplish, the drive to accomplish *anything at all* can only lead to a wasteful sapping of resources. Spiritual power (*bala*) remains undeveloped when subject to restlessness, since whatever strength it might have for conducing to liberation is squandered on actions that have no bearing on the aim of practice to begin with. One does not attain the still, unshakable deliverance of mind by being shaken all over the place.

In the *Nikāyas*, the account of the Bhikkhu Soṇa exemplifies what happens when one cannot seem to overcome this hindrance. Once when Venerable Soṇa was alone in seclusion, the following course of thought arose in his mind:

> I am one of the Blessed One's most energetic disciples, yet my mind has not been liberated from the taints by non-clinging. Now there is wealth in my family, and it is possible to enjoy my wealth and do meritorious deeds. Let me then give up the training and return to the lower life, so that I can enjoy my wealth and do meritorious deeds.[15]

Soṇa had followed the path of surrender without any discernible signs of progress, so he figured he should do something that seemed to guarantee results. Since there was nothing wrong with doing good works, that seemed like a reasonable course to take (of course it did not hurt that he would also be able to enjoy his wealth at the same time).

The Buddha, having discerned Soṇa's thinking on the matter, approached him and asked whether he was indeed considering disrobing and reentering the household life. When he answered affirmatively, the Buddha pressed him on the matter. It seems Soṇa had been rather accomplished at the lute back in

14 Ñāṇamoli and Bodhi, *Middle Length Discourses*, 239.

15 Bodhi, *Numerical Discourses*, 932.

the day, so the Buddha used the lute as a metaphor to make his point. When a lute's strings are too tight, it is not well tuned and easy to play; when its strings are too loose, it is also not well tuned and easy to play. Only when the strings are adjusted in a balanced way, neither too loose nor too tight, is it well tuned and easy to play. The same is true with spiritual practice: "If energy is aroused too forcefully this leads to restlessness, and if energy is too lax this leads to laziness. Therefore, Soṇa, resolve on a balance of energy, achieve evenness of the spiritual faculties, and take up the object there."[16] Soṇa had taken his own agitation over his lack of any signs of progress to be a sign that the training was faulty rather than an indication of his own unskillful approach to it. Just as one does not throw out an untuned lute but tunes it instead, Soṇa should not abandon the path but simply adjust his approach.

The second component of the conjoined nīvaraṇa of restlessness-remorse is a tenseness that gives rise to agitation pursued in the opposite temporal direction: namely, the past. Instead of focusing on what might be done to further future spiritual perfection, as one does with restlessness, with remorse one dwells on those things that one has done or left undone in the past. In the place of restlessness's "Let me try this to make myself feel better," remorse's expression is "If I hadn't done that, I wouldn't be in such a bad state now."

Here we need to tread very gingerly, for at various times the Buddha points out that reviewing one's own failings—as well as the failings of others, one might add—is a good and worthwhile undertaking. One particularly instructive instance in the *Nikāyas* concerns the bhikkhu Devadatta. Devadatta was the Buddha's cousin and had come to the view that the training rules should be even stricter than they were. When the Buddha did not agree with him, Devadatta tried to kill the Buddha on three different occasions in an effort to gain control of the saṅgha. When those plots failed, Devadatta left the saṅgha with five hundred bhikkhus. While his actions were still fresh in the memories of those assembled, the Buddha pointed out that Devadatta was "bound for the plane of misery, bound for hell," where he would remain "for an eon, unredeemable." His point, however, was not to pillory Devadatta, who by this time had since died, but to review for the assembly those kinds of

16 Bodhi, *Numerical Discourses*, 933. Bodhi notes that the Chinese parallel text has a somewhat different rendition of this counsel: "Therefore you should practice by taking up [the object] in a balanced way; do not cling, do not be heedless, and do not grasp marks" (*Numerical Discourses*, 1763n1368).

things that steer one off the path: gain, loss, fame, disrepute, honor, lack of honor, evil desires, and bad friendship.[17] It was Devadatta's resolute refusal to overcome these and correct his own behavior that had been his downfall, and the Buddha was rehearsing these as a way of counseling the bhikkhus to be on the alert should they arise in them, the better to avoid them from taking root or, if they had, the better to overcome them as quickly as possible.[18]

Contrast the tale of Devadatta with the account of Angulimāla. Angulimāla was "murderous, bloody-handed, given to blows and violence, merciless to living beings. Villages, towns, and districts were laid waste by him. He was constantly murdering people and he wore their fingers as a garland."[19] On one occasion the Buddha took to the road in Angulimāla's direction despite repeated warnings from the locals. When Angulimāla saw him coming his way, he knew he had an easy mark: "Men have come along this road in groups of ten, twenty, thirty, and even forty, but still they have fallen into my hands. But now this recluse comes alone, unaccompanied, as if forcing his way. Why shouldn't I take this recluse's life?" Running after the Buddha with all due speed, he found that he could not overtake the Buddha, who simply kept walking at a normal pace. Finally, Angulimāla shouted, "Stop, recluse! Stop, recluse!" to which the Buddha replied, "I have stopped, Angulimāla, you stop too." The Buddha continued,

> Angulimāla, I have stopped forever,
> I abstain from violence towards living beings;
> But you have no restraint toward things that live:
> That is why I have stopped and you have not.

Then Angulimāla took his swords and weapons, cast them into a pit, and asked to go forth as a bhikkhu, and the Buddha accepted him.

Not long after, the locals heard that Angulimāla was staying with the Buddha and the rest of the assembly in Anāthapiṇḍika's Park, and they appealed to their king, Pasenadi, to apprehend him. So Pasenadi set out with five hundred

---

17 These are often referred to as the "eight worldly dharmas" that circle around and around without end. One caught up in them finds oneself in a kind of maelstrom, forever buffeted now in this direction, now in that. For this reason they are also referred to at times as the "eight winds."

18 Bodhi, *Numerical Discourses*, 1118–19.

19 Ñāṇamoli and Bodhi, *Middle Length Discourses*, 710.

cavalry. Arriving before the Buddha, Pasenadi asked him to hand Angulimāla over. But the Buddha asked him what he would do if he were to discover that Angulimāla had gone forth, and Pasenadi replied that he would treat him as any other bhikkhu, offering him respect, robes, food, shelter, and medicinals, and arranging for his protection. "But," Pasenadi continued, "how could such an immoral man, one of evil character, ever have such virtue and restraint?" When the Buddha pointed to a bhikkhu standing nearby and indicated that he was, indeed, Angulimāla, the king was alarmed at first, but then, composing himself, he offered him many fine things and lauded the Buddha for taming him where force and weapons could not. Still, some time later, it happened that when Angulimāla was out on the alms round, someone threw a clod at him, someone else threw a stick, and yet another threw a shard at him, cutting his head. The Buddha, seeing the bleeding Angulimāla approaching, said, "Bear it, brahmin! Bear it, brahmin! You are experiencing here and now the result of deeds because of which you might have been tortured in hell for many years, for many hundreds of years, for many thousands of years."[20] Coming to realization did not exempt Angulimāla from the inevitable consequences of his past actions.

We had occasion to look briefly at hiri-ottappa in chapter 1. There, we saw that the twofold conscience of moral shame and moral dread supported the diligent observance of the precepts and training rules, and it was the proximate cause for overcoming sense desire. It is preemptive in orientation: "He should not do anything, however slight, because of which other wise people might criticize him," as it is put in the *Mettā Sutra*.[21] As the "bright guardians of the world," hiri and ottappa set up the checkpoint to determine which actions shall pass and which not, not because of any negative consequences that might follow from them ("I might be censured"), but because the actions are themselves unworthy of the company of the noble ones ("I am doing something censurable"). There is power in hiri-ottappa, just as there is in faith, energy and wisdom.[22]

Remorse, by contrast, is an impotent dwelling on deeds already done or left undone. Buddhaghoṣa glosses on it as follows:

> A contemptible act is *kukata*; the state of [a displeased mind, produced by making] such an act [its object] is "worry" (*kukkucca*). It has repentance as

20 Ñāṇamoli and Bodhi, *Middle Length Discourses*, 710–15.

21 Bodhi, *Suttanipāta*, 179.

22 Bodhi, *Numerical Discourses*, 819.

> characteristic, sorrow at deeds of commission and omission as function, regret as manifestation, deeds of commission and omission as proximate cause, and it should be regarded as a state of bondage.[23]

As the commentary continues, "The mode of worrying is 'fidgeting.' The state of one beset by worry is 'over-scrupulousness.'"[24] Where the fidgeting associated with restlessness manifests in an attachment to rituals and observances in order to make good things happen, the fidgeting associated with remorse manifests as a rigid moralism in order to keep bad things from happening.

In the Buddha's time, some among the Jains championed this kind of rigid moralism.[25] We see this in the course of a conversation between the Buddha and a certain local chief, Asibandhakaputta, who was a lay disciple of the nigaṇṭhas (another name for the Jains). Asibandhakaputta took the lead:

> Venerable sir, Nigaṇṭha Nātaputta teaches the Dhamma to his disciples thus: "Anyone at all who destroys life is bound for a state of misery, bound for hell. Anyone at all who engages in sexual misconduct is bound for a state of misery, bound for hell. Anyone at all who speaks falsehood is bound for a state of misery, bound for hell. One is led on [to rebirth] by the manner in which one usually dwells." It is in such a way, venerable sir, that Nigaṇṭha Nātaputta teaches the Dhamma to his disciples.[26]

One can well imagine the kind of fear such a view can instill in someone who is taken with it. When one single offense is enough to seal my fate, I am going to be quite fretful indeed. To avoid such dire consequences, there is no limit to the measures I will take to ensure that the least transgression has no chance of arising. Unrelenting scrupulousness, then, would seem to be a sure course of action; it is better to be safe than sorry.[27]

---

23 Buddhaghoṣa, *The Expositor* (Atthasālinī)*: Buddhaghoṣa's Commentary on the Dhammasaṅgaṇī, The First Book of the Abhidhamma-Piṭaka*, trans. Pe Maung Tin (Delhi: Motilal Banarsidass, 2016), 343. Nyanatiloka translates *kukkucca* as "scruples" (*Buddhist Dictionary*, 90).

24 Buddhaghoṣa, *Expositor*, 491.

25 Mahavira, considered the founder of the Jains, was a contemporary of the Buddha.

26 Bodhi, *Connected Discourses*, 1341.

27 One can see the impetus for the rise of the Digambara, or "sky-clad," sect of Jainism in this view. The Digambaras were so called because, in an effort to avoid killing or harming the least thing, they (but only the males) went about without clothing. In addition, they carried a *picchi*, a broom made of fallen peacock feathers, with which to sweep the ground in front of them as they walked and to clear any spot where they might sit. Mahavira himself is iconographically portrayed naked.

But the Buddha's response here is telling: "What do you think, headman? In the case of a person who destroys life, if one compares one occasion with another, whether by day or by night, which is more frequent: the occasions when he is destroying life or those when he is not doing so?" Asibandhakaputta concedes that the occasions when one is destroying life are, by comparison, quite few indeed, and the same holds for any other breaches of moral conduct. To say that one action is enough to seal one's fate is to set that action apart from everything else one is doing. All of those actions together, those that are morally good as well as those that are morally evil, set in motion causal chains that have to play themselves out. Asserting that one can determine exactly how that ensemble will fall out at some future point in time (projecting the outcome of those causal chains) is to make a knowledge claim that is unwarranted. Assessing a person's moral quality by the state the person happens to be in (reading a particular causal chain arising from a past action into the present) is also a baseless exercise.[28] No matter what one has done in the past, and no matter how one has responded to it, the point is simply not to violate the precept going forward.

There is no question here of atonement, discharging a debt, or setting the scales to balance—some of the common metaphors that are used in conjunction with remorse. It is frequently pointed out that there is no concept of sin in the Dharma, if by *sin* one understands some kind of stain that needs to be washed away. Lapses of body, speech, and mind occur, but no sort of penalty or punishment is incurred through them:

> He reflects thus: "In many ways the Blessed One criticizes and censures the destruction of life, and he says: 'Abstain from the destruction of life.' Now I have destroyed life to such and such an extent. That wasn't proper; that wasn't good. But though I feel regret over this, that evil deed of mine cannot be undone." Having reflected thus, he abandons the destruction of life and he abstains from the destruction of life in the future. Thus there comes about the abandoning of that evil deed; thus there comes about the transcending of that evil deed.[29]

When I turn left instead of right, I simply turn around and head in the right direction; I do not have a debt to pay to anyone for having done so. That my trip now takes longer is not an imposition come from elsewhere and meted

28 See the *Mahākammavibhanga Sutra* (The Greater Exposition of Action) for an extensive discussion of these points. Ñāṇamoli and Bodhi, *Middle Length Discourses*, 1058–65.

29 Bodhi, *Connected Discourses*, 1343.

out by another but a natural consequence of having wasted time going in the wrong direction. I cannot retrieve that lost time, so trying to do something in order to get it back is not an option. And, of course, berating myself for having taken a wrong turn does nothing to get me to my destination.

Remorse for one's actions—as opposed to the simple recognition of the unskillfulness of one's actions—is a taint in that it indicates ongoing ego attachment. In considering myself a worse person for having committed some evil act, someone who needs to be made righteous, I actually reinforce the conceit of a self:

> The conceit of inferiority, like other forms of pride that arrogate oneself above others, is a subtle form of self-affirmation. Conceit, as it is generally understood, is waving one's flag or banner highest over others and drawing attention to oneself. Even if one is asserting one's inferiority, one is still engaged in a display of self-advertisement. At a more subtle level, both pride and self-contempt are wrong views of the self, an idea rendered explicit in the idea of the "I am" conceit.[30]

I may still, like Devadatta, end up in a hell state or, like Angulimāla, find myself on the receiving end of mudballs, sticks, and sharp projectiles, but these are simply the unhappy consequences of unskillful *actions* now taking their course. None of that adds up to any kind of assessment of a *self* who now has to somehow earn his way back to parity with others.

Like all the other nīvaraṇas, restlessness-remorse does not arise out of nowhere but has a particular nutritive ground. In this case, that nutritive ground is "unsettledness of mind":

> And what, bhikkhus, is the nutriment for the arising of unarisen restlessness and remorse and for the increase and expansion of arisen restlessness and remorse? There is, bhikkhus, unsettledness of mind: frequently giving careless attention to it is the nutriment for the arising of unarisen restlessness and remorse and for the increase and expansion of arisen restlessness and remorse.[31]

As Bhikkhu Bodhi notes, unsettledness of mind (*cetaso avūpasama*) is, denotatively, "restlessness and remorse themselves."[32] If this seems to border on a tautology—ending the arising of restlessness and remorse is accomplished

30 Maria Heim, "The Conceit of Self-Loathing," *Journal of Indian Philosophy* 37 (2009): 62.

31 Bodhi, *Connected Discourses*, 1568.

32 Bodhi, *Connected Discourses*, 1900n57.

by ending the arising of restlessness and remorse—it is only seemingly so: for it is careless, rather than careful, attention to restlessness and remorse that keeps them in play.

In the *Uddesavibhanga Sutra*, the Buddha, unsolicited, offers advice on how to maintain that kind of attention:

> Bhikkhus, a bhikkhu should examine things in such a way that while he is examining them, his consciousness is not distracted and scattered externally nor stuck internally, and by not clinging he does not become agitated. If his consciousness is not distracted and scattered externally nor stuck internally, and if by clinging he does not become agitated, then for him there is no origination of suffering.[33]

"Stuck externally" relates to gratification based on the sign of some sense form (*viññāṇa*); "stuck internally" relates to gratification based on the sign of some internal form (*citta*).[34] In conjunction with sense desire, attachment to the sign of the beautiful was investigated and abandoned. In conjunction with ill will, it was the sign of the repulsive. Overcoming restlessness-remorse involves abandoning attachment to any signs of *purity*:

> They do not construct, they have no preferences,
> they do not assert: "[This is] ultimate purity."
> Having loosened the knot of grasping that has been tied,
> they do not form desires for anything in the world.
>
> For a brahmin who has transcended the boundary,
> who has known and seen, nothing is tightly grasped.
> Not excited by lust or attached to dispassion,
> he does not grasp anything here as supreme.[35]

Just as beauty and repulsiveness refer to nothing inherent in things themselves, ascriptions of purity or impurity likewise have nowhere to land—not in actions, not in states of affairs, and not in anything I might look at and call *myself*. *I* cannot be better, worse, or even equal to others, since such evaluation belies an ongoing attachment to self.

---

33 Ñāṇamoli and Bodhi, *Middle Length Discourses*, 1074.

34 Ñāṇamoli and Bodhi, *Middle Length Discourses*, 1350n1252.

35 Bodhi, *Suttanipāta*, 295.

We find this expressed through an interchange between two disciples, Khema and Sumana, and the Buddha. Khema went first:

> Bhante, when a bhikkhu is an arahant, one whose taints are destroyed, who has lived the spiritual life, done what had to be done, laid down the burden, reached his own goal, utterly destroyed the fetters of existence, one completely liberated through final knowledge, it does not occur to him: "There is someone better than me," or "There is someone equal to me," or "There is someone inferior to me."

The Buddha agreed, and Khema took his leave. Then Sumana approached the Buddha: "Bhante, when a bhikkhu is an arahant, one whose taints are destroyed, . . . one completely liberated through final knowledge, it does not occur to him: 'There is no one better than me,' or 'There is no one equal to me,' or 'There is no one inferior to me.'" The Buddha agreed with Sumana as well. Whether there is someone or no one equal to me does not matter, since attainment is not measured by comparison of *persons*. It is enough that there is attainment; it is not necessary to add commentary about *who* has attained or not, because, at bottom, there is no discernible *who* involved at all. Since claims of superiority, inferiority, and equality only ever refer back to the aggregates, to *whom* would they even apply? After Khema and Sumana had both left, the Buddha said to the other bhikkhus, "Bhikkhus, it is in such a way that clansmen declare final knowledge. They state the meaning but don't bring themselves into the picture."[36]

Restlessness-remorse is born of a similar evaluative system now applied to oneself. In the case of restlessness, "me now" is set in comparison with an anticipated "me in the future," and the thought arises, "I will be superior in the future if I do this now." In the case of remorse, "me now" is placed alongside "me in the past"; having done something that led to an unfortunate situation in the present, the thought "I am worse than I was before I committed that act" arises.

As the sutra indicates, one should not be overly hasty in thinking this adds up to something like "me now" is *the same as* or *equal to* "me at some other time" and then going on to think that it does not matter one way or another whether I practice diligently or commit unskillful and immoral actions. It simply means removing the self as the point of reference:

> Because of this one should not think oneself better,
> Nor should one consider oneself inferior or equal.

36 Bodhi, *Numerical Discourses*, 922.

> Being affected in various ways,
> One should not persist in positioning oneself.[37]

The essential emptiness of the self precludes its being placed in any kind of relation to anything or anyone at all. That being the case,

> a brahmin does not speak of purity by another,
> by the seen and the heard,
> by good behavior and observances, by the sensed.
> Untainted by merit and by evil he has discarded
> what was taken up without creating anything here.[38]

Discarding everything without putting anything in its place is nothing other than the practice of renunciation with which the aspirant began:

> Standing to one side, the young deva Subrahmā addressed the Blessed One in verse:
>
> "Always frightened is this mind.
> The mind is always agitated
> About unarisen problems
> And about risen ones.
> If there exists release from fear,
> Being asked, please declare it to me."
>
> [The Buddha responded:]
>
> "Not apart from enlightenment and austerity,
> Not apart from restraint of the sense faculties,
> Not apart from relinquishing all,
> Do I see any safety for living beings."[39]

"Relinquishing all," of course, is nothing other than relinquishing the conceit of the self. When the conceit of the self is relinquished, there is simply nothing

37 Bodhi, *Suttanipāta*, 312.
38 Bodhi, *Suttanipāta*, 294.
39 Bodhi, *Connected Discourses*, 149.

by which to compare, contrast, or even equate oneself with others or with projections of a future or past self.

If unsettledness of mind is the ground of restlessness-remorse, settledness of mind is its counteragent:

> Bhikkhus, I do not see even one other thing on account of which unarisen restlessness and remorse does not arise and arisen restlessness and remorse is abandoned so much as pacification of the mind. For one with a pacified mind, unarisen restlessness and remorse do not arise and arisen restlessness and remorse are abandoned.[40]

Six things are said to lead to such pacification: much learning, investigation, familiarity with the Vinaya, association with mature people, good friendship, and suitable talk.[41] We will have occasion to look at learning, investigation, good friendship, and suitable talk below, in conjunction with the nīvaraṇa of indecision. Here our focus is on familiarity with the Vinaya and association with mature practitioners.

Recall that the precepts and training rules of the Vinaya are *given* to the aspirant; one does not come up with them on one's own but *receives* them, just as they are, and simply follows them. Straightforward adherence to the precepts and training rules is a skillful way of avoiding the "going up and going down" that marks the attempt to find some kind of sweet spot of practice on my own. One should do no less than follow them, but there is no need to do more than what they prescribe, either. Even if it is not clear how following these training rules does the job, it is not one's place to gainsay them, add to them, or detract from them. The only exception to this is the concession that a homeleaver may engage in certain additional ascetic trainings known as the *dhutaṅga* practices.[42] Those finding themselves with some extra degree of

---

40 Bodhi, *Numerical Discourses*, 92.

41 *Sāratthappakāsinī*, referenced in Bodhi, *Connected Discourses*, 1909n96. See, too, Soma Thera, *The Way of Mindfulness: Being a Translation of the Satipaṭṭhāna Sutta of the Majjhima Nikāya; Its Commentary, the Satipaṭṭhāna Sutta Vaṇṇanā of the Papañcasūdanī of Buddhaghosa Thera; and Excerpts from the Līnatthapakāsanā Ṭikā, Marginal Notes of Dhammapāla Thera on the Commentary* (Whitefish, MT: Kessinger, 2010), 127–28. The Vinaya is the collection of sutras dealing with the Pāṭimokkha, the monastic training rules, and other matters of virtuous conduct.

42 There are thirteen *dhutaṅga* practices: (1) to wear patched-up robes, (2) to wear only three robes, (3) to go for alms, (4) not to omit any house while going for alms, (5) to eat at one sitting, (6) to eat from the alms bowl, (7) to refuse all further food, (8) to live in the forest, (9) to live under a tree, (10) to live in the open air, (11) to live in a cemetery,

zeal may discharge that by restraining themselves further than the training rules themselves would demand, but here, too, there are limits on the eagerness an aspirant might entertain. No one is to engage in them for renown, for the purpose of satisfying any kind of greed for gain of any kind, or even for looking for something else to do.[43]

Restlessness-remorse can afflict anyone, but one new to the practice or still young in years is particularly susceptible to it, much as in any other area of life. Age has a way of tempering youthful zeal, and associating with those who are mature in the practice can serve to temper one's as yet overeager enthusiasm. Most everyone past a certain number of years of life or practice can look back and see how much time, energy, and investment went into trying to make something of oneself. For one just setting out on the renunciant-contemplative path, hearing from those more advanced in years can provide a helpful perspective for sorting out what is more important from what is less important over the long haul. The zeal of the novice, like the zeal of new converts generally, runs the risk of burning up its fuel all at once. It might make an impressive display, but it has little chance of perduring. Practice that can stand the test of time is not a matter of pyrotechnics but of a slow, steady flame.

Restlessness-remorse is a kind of bondage. Tethered to fears arising from past actions and hopes with respect to future states, one is forever yanked in one direction or the other. The Buddha likens freedom from restlessness-remorse to liberation from enslavement: "Just as a man might be a slave, not his own master, dependent on another, unable to go where he liked, and after some time he might be freed from slavery, able to go where he liked, might think: 'Before this I was a slave . . .' And he would rejoice and be glad about that."[44] That freedom is nothing but the aim of the holy life itself:

> Let not a person revive the past
> Or on the future build his hopes;
> For the past has been left behind
> And the future has not been reached.

(12) to be satisfied with whatever dwelling, and (13) to sleep in the sitting position (and never lying down). See Nyanatiloka, *Buddhist Dictionary*, 53.

43 See Buddhaghoṣa, *Path of Purification*, 55–77, for a fuller discussion of these practices and the restrictions placed on them.

44 Walshe, *Long Discourses*, 102.

Instead with insight let him see
Each presently arisen state;
Let him know that and be sure of it,
Invincibly, unshakeably.[45]

Mahākoṭṭhita's fret and worry about the outcomes that accrue from practice are quelled once Sāriputta's answer is finally realized.

45 Ñāṇamoli and Bodhi, *Middle Length Discourses*, 1039.

CHAPTER SEVEN

Facing the Prospect of Emptiness: Acedia and Sloth-Torpor

By any common metric, the life of a renunciant-contemplative is tedious and boring. Bearing with the same living conditions, the same food, the same routine, and many of the same faces week after week, and month after long month, can wear down even the most dedicated. If one adds to this that, again by any common metric, such a life is rather unproductive, unremarkable, and unrewarding, it can seem as though one is thoroughly wasting one's time. And when one further realizes that there really is no end to this life, that one never *graduates*, so to speak, from the practice, perseverance can wane and vigor diminish. The counsel to remain resolutely grounded in each present moment, the sure antidote to restless-remorse and sadness, can feel like a not-so-subtle form of torture when the present has nothing very interesting—and quite a lot that seems rather inane—to offer again and again and yet again. Even if one pursues the path as a householder, any effort made with respect to the practice is sooner or later going to run out of steam as the novelty wears off, tedium sets in, and the lack of any appreciable markers of success continually stares one in the face. Soon enough, an attitude of "Who cares?" can set in, leading the aspirant to go listlessly through the motions of the practice day after seemingly interminable day.

The truth, of course, is that no one does care. Because such a life is, to the common understanding, only virtuous in the most supererogatory of ways (and then only when it is not seen as downright idiotic), one incurs no wider social criticism for abandoning it. In fact, one might sooner be praised than censured by one's family and former acquaintances—even if they are coreligionists—were one to give up the practice and return to one's everyday life and way of doing things. Both the Christian and Buddhist traditions are filled with lore describing attempts by friends and family to keep a son or daughter, friend, or other relative from abandoning the life of the everyday person or, if it was already too late for that, to try to lure the aspirant back. Even if the aspirant had succeeded in freeing oneself from social and family obligations—or one's family and friends had finally given up trying to convince one otherwise—the aspirant might soon enough find that this "Who cares?" hides a much deeper, more insidious thought. It is not just that practice is monotonous and boring; all kinds of things are, but we stick with them because there is some point to doing so, some kind of payoff, in the end. Soon enough, however, the aspirant slowly begins to realize that renunciant-contemplative practice is not like those other enterprises. Offering nothing but more of the same, without any kind of noticeable gain whatsoever, not only does the practice seem rather tedious and inane, but it comes to be experienced as *soul-crushingly* so, such that leaving it all behind seems like the most reasonable thing to do.

Evagrius calls this phenomenon the demon of *acedia*, a term that, while not a neologism of his own, nevertheless received at his hand a new, distinctive sense. As Christopher Joest writes:

> In secular Greek it meant *carelessness*, *indifference*, or quite simply *lack of interest in something*. In Origen the term turns up once in a commentary on the story of the temptation of Jesus in the desert, wherein acedia is listed between sleep and cowardice. . . . In monastic literature before Evagrius, the word is found only in chapter 36 of Athanasius' *Vita Antonii*, where it is placed between *hatred for asceticism* and *grief*. Coptic writings translate the word with *sluggishness* or the *weakening of the heart*; Syriac writings have *remorse* or *weakness of the spirit* or even *annoyance*. All these characterizations are echoed by Evagrius.[1]

It is perhaps because of this rather wide range of meaning that, if recent publications are any indication, acedia has gripped the contemporary imagination more than any of the other logismoi.[2] Many are swift to equate it with boredom,

1 Christoph Joest, "The Significance of *Acedia* and *Apatheia* in Evagrius Ponticus Part I," *American Benedictine Review* 55 (2004): 137.

2 Some of the titles in this area include Kathleen Norris, *Acedia and Me: A Marriage, Monks, and a Writer's Life* (New York: Riverhead, 2008); Jean-Charles Nault, *The Noonday Devil: Acedia, the Unnamed Evil of Our Times*, trans. Michael J. Miller (San Francisco: Ignatius, 2015); and R. J. Snell, *Acedia and Its Discontents: Metaphysical Boredom in an Empire of Desire* (Kettering, OH: Angelico, 2015).

depression, and ennui generally, while still others see it as a particularly keen affliction of modern life with all of its conveniences, comforts, and ready distractions. While all of these may well be distressing phenomena, "one is hard pressed to find an intelligible definition of acedia that corresponds to a recognizable psychological or existential condition" when viewed in the context of renunciant-contemplative practice, as Andrew Crislip points out.[3] Indeed, the phenomenal manifestations of acedia Evagrius enumerates are hard to understand as deep vexations if they are viewed other than as the mark of a demon whose only aim is to sap contemplative practice of its lifeblood.

In the Dharma, this mind state is called sloth-torpor. While it has not captured the contemporary imagination as much as acedia has, it is just as much of an obstacle in the path of the Dharmic renunciant-contemplative as acedia is for the Christian counterpart. Much like acedia, sloth-torpor covers a range of mind-body states. Sloth (thīna) refers to its more mental manifestations;[4] it is described in the commentarial literature as "indisposition, unwieldiness of mind; adhering and cohering; clinging, cleaving to, stickiness; stolidity, that is, a stiffening, a rigidity of the mind." Torpor (*middha*) covers much of the same kind of experience, but in conjunction with its more bodily manifestations; it is characterized as "indisposition and unwieldiness of sense, a shrouding, enveloping, barricading within; torpor that is sleep, drowsiness, slumbering, somnolence."[5] The water-related analogy used to describe it the *Nikāyas* only begins to capture the oppressive nature of this nīvaraṇa: "Suppose, brahmin, there is a bowl of water covered over with water plants and algae. If a man with good sight were to examine his own facial reflection in it, he would neither know nor see it as it really is. So too, brahmin, when one dwells with a mind obsessed by sloth and torpor."[6]

A similar, though perhaps more compelling, analogy might be that of a bog. Covered over with plant life, the water below is cut off from light and oxygen, those very things that give it the ability to sustain life. Such wet plant

3 Andrew Crislip, "The Sin of Sloth or the Illness of the Demons? The Demon of Acedia in Early Christian Monasticism," *HTR* 98 (2005): 145.

4 In the Dharma, body and mind are understood not as two radically distinct entities, but as aspects of one continuous functioning. An experience is therefore more or less mental, more or less bodily, in nature.

5 [Caroline] Rhys Davids, trans., *A Buddhist Manual of Psychological Ethics: Translation of the First Book of the* Abidhammapiṭaka entitled Dhammasaṅgaṇī *(Compendium of States or Phenomena)* (Delhi: Motilal Banarsidass, 2016), 288.

6 Bodhi, *Connected Discourses*, 1612.

cover is also heavy, and once it has grown in can it only be removed with a great deal of effort. As one is deprived of energy-sustaining resources and burdened with such a heavy load, even the very thought of doing something about this hindrance just seems like one more burden that, in the end, does not seem to be worth the time and effort.

As these analogies make clear, "Who cares?" would be the very mildest verbal expression of this obstacle. More to the point would be something along the lines of "This is all *bullshit*," with all the spleen such an expression is meant to convey. All too often the life of prayer or meditation is portrayed as something of an extraordinarily idyllic state, carried out in beautiful natural surroundings or serene buildings, the pleasing sounds of chanting and the fragrant smell of flowers and incense filling the air. In truth there is no glamor in it, anything initially pleasing about it soon enough loses its patina, and there is nothing particularly interesting or novel that awaits the practitioner just around the corner. Acedia and sloth-torpor prove themselves to be particularly pernicious obstacles to renunciant-contemplative life because they have to do with the seeming *pointlessness* of such a life.[7] Until one has seen into that pointlessness and roused the determination to push past it, one will not be in a position to pursue the path through to the end.

Evagrius's description of acedia covers a wide range of manifestations, from simple laziness to thoughts of being thoroughly oppressed:

> Acedia is an ethereal friendship, one who leads our steps astray, hatred of industriousness, a battle against stillness, stormy weather for psalmody, laziness in prayer, a slackening of ascesis, untimely drowsiness, revolving sleep, the

7 One might go so far as to claim that they are banes specific to renunciant-contemplative practice. This is certainly true in the case of thīna-middha, since it is only ever identified as an obstacle in conjunction with the cultivation of samādhi. Just how exclusive acedia is to renunciant-contemplative practice is a matter of some dispute. Gabriel Bunge makes the point that "acedia is by no means an exclusive disease of anchorites," suggesting it is an obstacle for everyday Christians generally. Bunge, *Despondency: The Spiritual Teaching of Evagrius Ponticus on Acedia*, trans. Anthony P. Gythiel (Yonkers, NY: St. Vladimir's Seminary Press, 2011), 23. I would counter that while it is certainly not a bane unique to anchorites as opposed to, say, cenobites, mendicants, or committed lay practitioners, it is nevertheless particular to renunciant-contemplatives rather than to everyday people at large. Moreover, acedia as described by Evagrius and many of the other Desert Elders is not the same as *sloth*, even though sloth would later come to be listed among the seven sins. Acedia is lassitude toward the demands of the contemplative life, not just general laziness with respect to everyday life.

> oppressiveness of solitude, hatred of one's cell, an adversary of ascetic works, an opponent of perseverance, a muzzling of meditation, ignorance of the scriptures, a partaker in sorrow, a clock for hunger.[8]

One of the distinguishing characteristics of acedia—and certainly its most vexing—is the range and fluidity of its domain. Unlike gluttony and fornication, which have the belly and the libido as instigators, or avarice, anger, and sadness, which rise in response to the actions of others or states of affairs generally, acedia has no clearly defined source, except the many particularities of renunciant-contemplative life itself. One would be at pains to identify one mental image that any given moment of acedia can be traced to, and this can be nothing short of disconcerting for one who, up to this point, has been navigating the spiritual life in opposition to the business of the world and the push and pull of one's own embodied states though ascetic practices. We see this illustrated in the many examples of the functioning of acedia Evagrius provides.

The daily routine of the desert monk was nothing if not materially boring.[9] The day-to-day business that carries the householder from waking to sleeping was gone; in its place were hours upon hours of solitude, punctuated only briefly twice a day by reciting a few psalms, giving some attention to one's handiwork, and securing whatever meager provisions were necessary. One day would blend into the next, and, if not for the weekly synaxis, every day was pretty much the same, even down to the recitation of the same psalms over and over again. Only the movement of the sun brought any observable sense of the day's passing, and even that was not much to go on:

> First of all, [the demon of acedia] makes it appear that the sun moves slowly or not at all, and that the day seems to be fifty hours long. Then he compels the monk to look constantly towards the window, to jump out of the cell, to watch the sun and see how far it is from the ninth hour, to look this way and that.[10]

The ninth hour was the time for the daily meal. Not that the monk needed to be particularly hungry; it was just that eating was at least *something* to look forward to in order to fill in the time and punctuate the day.

---

8 Evagrius, *Vices* 6.4; Sinkewicz, 64.

9 For a sense of what such a life entailed, see Lucien Regnault, *The Day-to-Day Life of the Desert Fathers in Fourth-Century Egypt* (Petersham, MA: St. Bede's, 1999).

10 Evagrius, *Praktikos* 12; Sinkewicz, 99. The monk has a particular interest in the time of day since it indicates when he will get his next meal.

Every once in a while, a stranger or fellow monk might happen by, spicing up the otherwise rather solitary life of the monk with a bit of novelty. But unless the monk was an abba who might receive the occasional disciple, no one was likely to call and provide the kind of distraction he was looking for. Still, this did not stop the monk from keeping watch all the same: "The eye of the person afflicted with acedia stares at the doors continuously, and his intellect imagines people coming to visit. The door creaks and he jumps up; he hears a sound, and he leans out the window and does not leave it until he gets stiff from sitting there."[11] Even the arrival of a thief, one can imagine, would have been a welcome sight to the acedia-stricken monk.[12]

If no one was coming to visit, perhaps some reading might prove stimulating enough and offer some new insight or at least a memorable turn of phrase.[13] So the monk would turn away from the window, pick up a book, and begin to peruse it, only to find that this, too, was just as mind-numbing as everything else:

> When he reads, the one afflicted with acedia yawns a lot and readily drifts off to sleep; . . . turning his eyes away from the book, he stares at the wall and again goes back to reading for awhile; leafing through the pages, he looks curiously for the end of texts, he counts the folios and calculates the number of gatherings. Later, he closes the book and puts it under his head and falls asleep.[14]

One solution would be to give up reading altogether: "Look," acedia whispers, "such-and-such holy old man knew only twelve Psalms, and he pleased God."[15] Words were such a bother that perhaps, instead of reading, the monk would imagine that God could just as easily infuse his mind with wisdom directly, giving rise to "the thought of listlessness that shuns the reading of and meditation on spiritual words and which advises us to ask the Lord that we might learn the Scriptures through his Spirit."[16]

---

11 Evagrius, *Eight Thoughts* 14; Sinkewicz, 84.

12 The sayings of the Desert Elders are filled with accounts of thieves. See, for instance, Wortley, *Anonymous Sayings*, 487.

13 What we know of today as *lectio divina* is the medieval development of this early practice of using the Scriptures as the basis for prayer.

14 Evagrius, *Eight Thoughts* 15; Sinkewicz, 84.

15 Evagrius, *Antirrhetikos* 6.5; Brakke, 134.

16 Evagrius, *Antirrhetikos* 6.8; Brakke, 135.

As the tedium and solitude continued unabated, the monk would begin to nitpick every last aspect of his life in the desert:

> And further, he instills in him a dislike for the place and for his state of life itself, for manual labor, and also the idea that love has disappeared among the brothers and there is no one to console him. And should there be someone during those days who has offended the monk, this too the demon uses to add further to his dislike (of the place). He leads him on to a desire for other places where he can easily find the wherewithal to meet his needs and pursue a trade that is easier and more productive; he adds that pleasing the Lord is not a question of being in a particular place: for scripture says that the divinity can be worshiped everywhere.[17]

Like a child who blames the ball when she fails to kick it ("stupid ball") the monk would find fault in everything and everyone around him ("dumb cell," "bad brothers," "lousy work"), and come to blame the life of practice itself as the culprit down to every one of its least aspects.

Or perhaps the monk was tossed in the other direction, and rather than berating his conditions or his brothers, he began to berate himself. Why was he here in this isolated place focused on his own practice when he could be doing something for the well-being of others, he might ask. When the life of Mary looked increasingly uninteresting and one was not finding much that is satisfying in this "better part," the temptation arose to lead the life of Martha, since at least being busy and having all of the fret and worry that goes with it gives one *something* to hang on to (Luke 10:38–42). Having nothing to show for one's ascesis and prayer life, feeding a few people, alleviating someone's hardship, or even securing some converts could seem like perfectly fine substitutes and at least provide some immediate satisfaction.[18]

One of the most cunning aspects of acedia is that many of the things it conjures in the mind of the monk are, in themselves, perfectly reasonable by everyday standards and are indeed often even commendable as a way of living a Christian life. There is nothing wrong with visiting the sick or engaging in other acts of charity—in fact, they are commanded in the Gospels (Matt

17 Evagrius, *Praktikos* 12; Sinkewicz, 99. The reference is to John 4:21–24.

18 It is hard to resist the observation that the present-day emphases on social services, activism for social change, and the like are just so many structural bulwarks against the slightest manifestation of acedia in churches and other religious communities. The concern that liturgies and prayer services be engaging (better: *entertaining*) would need to be included here as well; heaven forbid one should find prayer or meditation boring or repetitive.

25:31–46). There is no general requirement that a Christian confine oneself to a cell or even a particular settlement, city, or region—the apostles spread throughout the known world proclaiming the faith, again consistent with Gospel command (Matt 28:16–20). The careful monk would know better: "A person afflicted with acedia proposes visiting the sick," Evagrius notes, "but is fulfilling his own purpose."[19] A monk given to acedia is "quick to undertake a service, but considers his own satisfaction to be a precept."[20] As we saw already in conjunction with the first stages of the training, and again in conjunction with the logismoi of gluttony and avarice, the thought of laying aside the life of ascesis and prayer in order to better serve the needs of others is nothing other than the work of the tempter dressed up as "Christian charity." Finally, while every Christian is invited to be moderate in matters of food and sex and to curb avarice and anger, what these early monks set out to do went far and beyond the counsels given to everyday members—or even the hierarchy—of the church.

Acedia is so cunning that it will even take that last observation and turn it into yet another way of undoing the monk. He might begin to despair that he is not really doing enough, so he begins to entertain the thought that even greater ascetic feats are called for:

> The demon of acedia [suggests] to the persevering (ascetic) an extreme withdrawal, inviting him to rival John the Baptist and Antony, the very first of the anchorites, so that, unable to bear the prolonged and inhumane withdrawal, he flees with shame, abandoning the place, and the demon then makes his boast, "I prevailed over him" (Ps 12:5).[21]

If acedia were simply sloth, the monk would not even think of increasing his austerities. But in trying to combat acedia through taking on more than he can do, the monk opens himself to almost certain failure. Now the renunciant-contemplative life seems even more oppressive, prompting him to question its value at all. When addressed in this way, acedia "takes away [the monk's] hope by showing [him] how very difficult the monastic life is and that a human being can scarcely endure its way of life."[22] Not that the monastic

---

19 Evagrius, *Eight Thoughts* 7; Sinkewicz, 84.
20 Evagrius, *Eight Thoughts* 8; Sinkewicz, 84.
21 Evagrius, *On Thoughts* 35; Sinkewicz, 178.
22 Evagrius, *Antirrhetikos* 8.14; Brakke, 136.

life is really *that* difficult; it is just that in making it seem so the monk has a ready excuse to abandon it.

Once the novelty experienced at the start of the renunciant-contemplative life wears off and acedia sets in, the prospect of doing this for the rest of one's life only adds insult to injury. When hours seem like days, days seem like months, and months seem like years, as soon as acedia "reckons for me a long time and years of [this] wretched life" and "a prolonged old age,"[23] one might feel quite trapped indeed. When the prospect of decades of the life is overwhelming, it is time to focus resolutely on the present moment, and nothing commends itself to that kind of focus as much as manual labor. Already in *Foundations*, Evagrius anticipated the demon of acedia in his initial counsel to the neophyte concerning work: "Give thought to working with your hands, if possible both night and day. . . . In this way you can also overcome the demon of acedia and eliminate all the other desires inspired by the enemy. The demon of acedia lies in wait for laziness and 'is full of desires,' as scripture says (Prov. 13:4)."[24] Manual labor shifts one's attention from an abstract consideration of the passage of time to the demands of the job to be done. Each step of the labor process is a task complete in itself, and there is a clear, discernible end to that step. Time can seem to fly when one is engrossed in a task: "Set a measure for yourself in every work and do not let up until you have completed it. Pray with understanding and intensity, and the spirit of acedia will flee you."[25] Of course, acedia is so cunning that it can take even one's daily work and turn it into yet another pretext for abandoning the ascetic life. It might provoke the thought "that hates the manual labor of the skill that it knows, and wants to learn another skill by which it will be better supported and which will not be so arduous."[26]

The monk risks being defeated by acedia to the degree to which he finds these thoughts compelling enough actually to use them as reasons to abandon the contemplative life altogether. At first, this might simply manifest as the thought that he should "take a little break and make an extended visit to our home and kinfolk."[27] What is a little time off from such a lifelong enterprise? Surely a few weeks' vacation could do some good, he might think. Or maybe

23 Evagrius, *Antirrhetikos* 8.25, 8.32; Brakke, 139–40.
24 Evagrius, *Foundations* 8; Sinkewicz, 9.
25 Evagrius, *Eight Thoughts* 18; Sinkewicz, 85.
26 Evagrius, *Antirrhetikos* 6.1; Brakke, 133.
27 Evagrius, *Antirrhetikos* 8.39; Brakke, 142.

Christ was wrong when he said, "Whoever comes to me and does not hate father and mother, wife and children, brothers and sisters, yes, and even life itself, cannot be my disciple."[28] Once home, however, and finding oneself back in the midst of all of the everyday concerns of those around him, it would be doubly hard to now leave them a second time.

The key to overcoming acedia is to remain steadfast and persevere through and despite these thoughts, not giving them the least quarter. Evagrius could not praise perseverance enough as an antidote for acedia:

> Perseverance is the severing of acedia, the cutting down of thoughts, concern for death, meditation on the cross, fear firmly affixed, beaten gold, legislation for afflictions, a book of thanksgiving, a breastplate of stillness, an armour of ascetic works, a fervent work of excellence, an example of the virtues.[29]

Or again, "perseverance is the cure for acedia, along with the execution of all tasks with great attention [and the fear of God]."[30] The perseverance Evagrius has in mind is not simple willpower, an idea in one's head about how much one would *like* to persevere. Above all, it is a matter of actually keeping one's body confined to the cell:

> You must not abandon the cell in the time of temptations, fashioning excuses seemingly reasonable. Rather you must remain seated inside, exercise perseverance, and valiantly welcome all attackers, especially the demon of acedia, who is the most oppressive of all but leaves the soul proven to the highest degree. Fleeing and circumventing such struggles teaches the mind to be unskilled, cowardly, and evasive.[31]

In time, the demon will leave the monk's mind alone, once it sees how resolutely and consistently the monk refuses to budge from his physical position.

Acedia stands in a particular relation to the other logismoi in that it is, in Evagrius's estimation, the hardest of all to work through. Because of this, acedia is the logismos that, once overcome, decisively clears the path of the aspirant: "The demon of acedia, also called the noonday demon (cf. Ps. 90:6), is the most oppressive of all the demons. . . . No other demon follows immediately after this one: a state of peace and ineffable

---

28 Evagrius, *Antirrhetikos* 8.45; Brakke 143. The reference is to Luke 14:26.

29 Evagrius, *Vices* 6.4; Sinkewicz, 64.

30 Evagrius, *Eight Thoughts* 17; Sinkewicz, 85.

31 Evagrius, *Praktikos* 28; Sinkewicz, 102.

joy ensues in the soul after this struggle."[32] It is the last of the demons to be wrestled with, just before attaining (perfect) apatheia: "Perfect impassibility emerges in the soul after the victory over all the demons that oppose the practical life."[33]

Given the vagaries of acedia, it is easy to see why its overcoming is so decisive for attaining stillness. Acedia emerges as the misguided thought of *looking for something when in fact there is nothing to be found*—an attempt to latch onto imagined projections of what renunciant-contemplative life (and the communion with God it makes possible) supposedly *should be*, rather than settling wholeheartedly into what it *actually is*. When Evagrius describes acedia as "a relaxation of the soul,"[34] it must be understood that this is a particular kind of relaxation, namely, the relaxation of the soul *on the arduous path to formless, imageless prayer*. In effect, the monk gets lazy with acedia, clinging even now to mental projections despite their vexing nature, rather than pursuing the admittedly uncanny and hitherto unknown, unimagined, and immaterial life of God. This helps make sense of Evagrius's claim that "of the (various types of) thoughts, some travel along with us as monks; others (travel with us as) men of the world."[35] Because the everyday Christian would not have undertaken such a task—or even have been expected to—he or she could not be faulted for being lax in its pursuit.

Whatever similarities acedia bears to other states of mind and the thoughts that accompany them, it is a logismos only in light of one's aspiration, "an attack on [one's] very identity as a solitary."[36] Acedia is, as Guillaumont notes, "essentially the adversary of *hesychia*"[37] because it undercuts the very work required to attain it. If I am not interested in stillness, then acedia will not be an obstacle for me, whatever other things such listlessness renders difficult or impossible to accomplish as an everyday person. Although at times acedia might feel something like these, it is not some kind of punishment, nor is it a sign of failure.[38] The suffering it brings is "a gift given by the Spirit" out of

32 Evagrius, *Praktikos* 12; Sinkewicz, 99.
33 Evagrius, *Praktikos* 60; Sinkewicz, 108.
34 Evagrius, *Eight Thoughts* 6.1; Sinkewicz, 83.
35 Harmless and Fitzgerald, "Sapphire Light," 528.
36 Harmless and Fitzgerald, "Sapphire Light," 511.
37 Guillaumont, *Un philosophe au désert*, 183.
38 Evagrius, *Antirrhetikos* 8.54, 8.57; Brakke, 145–46.

solidarity with the suffering Christ.[39] If there are "peace and ineffable joy"[40] that follow upon overcoming acedia, they are nothing other than the joy of the cross (Heb 12:2), a joy that cannot be tasted any other way than by enduring it. Just as death and resurrection are not two but are bound together and interpenetrate in one paschal mystery, the joy of renunciant-contemplative life is inseparable from suffering through each and every one of the logismoi—and much more besides.

Sloth-torpor is the second of the conjoined nīvaraṇas. As with restlessness-remorse, each of its constituent elements is obstructive in its own right, but paired together they highlight two sides of a single form of ego attachment. Unlike restlessness-remorse, which involved an excess of zeal in anticipation of determinate outcomes, sloth-torpor emerges in the wake of the exasperation when one does not see much sign of progress in the practice, along with the despair that whatever lies at the end of the path just might not be worth all of the effort. Nyanatiloka indicates that sloth-torpor may on occasion be associated with "greedy consciousness."[41] This is a consciousness that remains on the lookout for some glimpse of the liberation promised by the Dharma, when in fact all one sees instead are the ongoing projections of one's own mind—and absolutely nothing beyond that. Soon enough, one finds it increasingly hard to put in any effort at all, and one will grab at the least excuse to just take it easy.

We find this point presented narratively in the *Khandhavagga Sutra* with respect to the case of the bhikkhu Tissa:

> Now on that occasion the Venerable Tissa, the Blessed One's paternal cousin, informed a number of bhikkhus: "Friends, my body seems as if it has been drugged, I have become disoriented, the teachings are no longer clear to me. Sloth and torpor persist obsessing my mind. I am leading the holy life dissatisfied, and I have doubt about the teachings."[42]

Tissa's fellow bhikkhus, solicitous for his state, reported the matter to the Buddha, who then had them tell Tissa to come and see him. In their conversation, the Buddha refreshes Tissa on the conditioned nature of the five skandhas (form, feeling, perception, volitional formations, and consciousness). If one

39 Evagrius, *Antirrhetikos* 8.51; Brakke, 145.

40 Evagrius, *Praktikos* 12; Sinkewicz, 99.

41 Nyanatiloka, *Buddhist Dictionary*, 183.

42 Bodhi, *Connected Discourses*, 929.

is not devoid of attachment to them, the Buddha reminds him, then "sorrow, lamentation, pain, displeasure, and despair" will arise; if one is devoid of attachment, then these do not arise. In effect, Tissa is mistaking his experience of sluggishness as an indication that he is not really getting anywhere at all, when, in fact, the sluggishness simply indicates where he needs to apply greater effort.

The Buddha goes on to show Tissa that the difficult circumstances prompting his distress are wholly to be expected; indeed, they are exactly the ones the Buddha himself passed through. Thus, there is no reason for Tissa to get disoriented when encountering difficulties, since he can take refuge in the fact that the Buddha has seen all this before and know that, despite everything thīna-middha throws in front of the aspirant, there *is* an end to it in due time.

> Suppose, Tissa, there were two men: one unskilled in the path, the other skilled in the path. The man unskilled in the path would ask the skilled man a question about the path, and the latter would say: "Come, good man, this is the path. Go along it a little way and you will see a fork in the road. Avoid the left-hand branch and take the right-hand branch. Go a little further and you will see a dense thicket. Go a little further and you will see a vast marshy swamp. Go a little further and you will see a steep precipice. Go a little further and you will see a delightful expanse of level ground."[43]

Pursuing the renunciant-contemplative path does not mean getting to take a detour around the thickets, swamps, and precipices that lie in wait; instead, it leads *right into* them. Without passing through these hazards, there is no expanse of level ground, no release to be found. For one, like Tissa, who left the close and dusty confines of householder life for the free and open life of the bhikkhu, this might not have been anticipated. Still, it is one thing to hear there is an end to all the fret and trouble, and quite another to dive wholeheartedly into it.

Because the Buddha was no stranger to the seemingly intimidating nature of the path that leads to that level ground, he was able to give Tissa some coaching on how to begin to muster the requisite resolve. The first step is to recognize the drugged and disoriented feeling as normal for anyone who is still only half-heartedly approaching the practice:

> When one is unguarded in the doors of the sense faculties, immoderate in eating, and not intent on wakefulness; when one lacks insight into wholesome qualities

43 Bodhi, *Connected Discourses*, 930.

> and does not dwell intent on the endeavor to develop the aids to enlightenment in the earlier and later phases of the night, one's body seems as if it had been drugged, one becomes disoriented, and the teachings are no longer clear to one. Dullness and drowsiness obsess one's mind. One lives the spiritual life dissatisfied and has doubt about the teachings.[44]

Mediocre efforts yield mediocre results in any area of life, and the same is true for the practice of the holy life.

One of the indicators of sloth-torpor's hold is therefore an inadequate or incomplete grasp of the teachings. One might pick up on a word or phrase here or there, think there is something to it, and assume that one has attained some level of wisdom. In a tradition where meditation is a key component of practice, words such as *tranquility*, *peace*, and *ease* are bound to be taken at face value by those unwilling to put much effort in. Soon enough, one might imagine that relaxation is the point of the exercise:

> Having eaten as much as he wants until his belly is full, a bhikkhu yields to the pleasure of rest, the pleasure of sloth, the pleasure of sleep. When a bhikkhu . . . yields to the pleasure of rest, the pleasure of sloth, the pleasure of sleep, his mind does not incline to ardor, effort perseverance, and striving. Since his mind does not incline to ardor . . . and striving, this [is a] bondage of mind.[45]

If one thinks that the path is meant to be easy, then any relaxing state will be taken to be a sign that one has gotten somewhere when, in fact, one is only relishing one's somnolence. Thiradhammo Bhikkhu calls sloth-torpor the "tranquility trap": "While the mind may be tranquil, it is often lacking in clarity or energy. This kind of calm is closer to lethargy than to vibrant tranquility."[46] Both sleep states and samādhi states may be called *tranquil*, but the tranquility of the one is not the tranquility of the other.

Here we see why thīna-middha is a conjoined nīvaraṇa, intimately linking a stilled, inactive body with a stilled, unprobing mind. It may manifest as sloth or laziness, but it is a laziness that obtains when one's mind is caught

44 Bodhi, *Numerical Discourses*, 684–85. Here we see the importance of successfully mastering the early stages of the gradual training. Each one of them was already an occasion to combat sloth-torpor.

45 Bodhi, *Numerical Discourses*, 821.

46 Thiradhammo, *Working with the Five Hindrances*, 120.

up in the delight of a kind of tranquility that is more akin to sleep than to unshakable deliverance of mind:

> Bhikkhus, there are these eight grounds for laziness. What eight?
>
> Here, a bhikkhu has to do some work. It occurs to him: "I have some work to do. While I'm working, my body will become tired. Let me lie down." He lies down. He does not arouse energy for the attainment of the as-yet-unattained, for the achievement of the as-yet-unachieved, for the realization of the as-yet-unrealized. This is the first ground for laziness.[47]

The remaining grounds for laziness—having done some work, having to make a trip, having made a trip, having gone for alms and not gotten enough food, having gone for alms and gotten enough food, being ill, and recovering from illness—follow similarly.[48] In all these cases, the bhikkhu is faced with something taxing: but rather than just getting on with it and moving on to the next thing, he preemptively lies down and takes a nap, without making good use of the present moment to cultivate his practice. Though his body may be lying down rather than working, it is his mind that has already given up. In the *Nikāyas*, this is described as "a mind that is constricted internally": "And what, bhikkhus, is mind that is constricted internally? It is a mind that is accompanied by sloth and torpor, associated with sloth and torpor."[49] The slothful body is an outward expression of the constricted mind.

The bhikkhu's laziness here does not consist in simply taking naps when tired or resting up in conjunction with an illness or after a hard day's work. Sleep itself is not the problem. Everyone sleeps—even the Buddha. Once when he was retiring after spending most of the night in walking meditation, Māra approached him as he was lying down and chided him:

> "What, you sleep? Why do you sleep?
> What's this, you sleep like a wretch?
> Thinking 'The hut's empty' you sleep:
> What's this, you sleep when the sun has risen?"

47 Bodhi, *Numerical Discourses*, 1226.

48 Bodhi, *Numerical Discourses*, 1226–27.

49 Bodhi, *Connected Discourses*, 1739.

But the Buddha could not be baited:

> "Within him craving no longer lurks,
> Entangling and binding, to lead him anywhere;
> With the destruction of the acquisitions
> The Awakened One sleeps:
> Why should this concern you, Māra?"[50]

Resting one's all-too-frail human body, as Rhys Davids notes, is as free of moral taint "as the folding up of leaves and blossoms at night."[51] Taking a satisfied *delight* in that sleep and using that as an excuse not to press on, however, is an obstacle to one's liberation. Since things such as needing to do some work, taking a trip, or getting sick are bound to happen, the reflective bhikkhu takes advantages of those moments of not traveling, not working, and not being ill to rouse energy.

Still, sometimes the body seems to have a mind of its own and inclines toward sleep all the same. Before succumbing completely, perhaps one can take measures to rekindle some energy and snap out of it. Such was the advice the Buddha gave to the bhikkhu Moggallāna. Once the Buddha saw the Venerable Mahāmoggallāna starting to doze. Approaching him, the Buddha asked:

> "Are you dozing, Moggallāna? Are you dozing, Moggallāna?"
>
> "Yes, Bhante."
>
> "Therefore, Moggallāna, you should not attend to or cultivate the object you were attending to when you became drowsy. By such means, it is possible that your drowsiness will be abandoned.
>
> "But if you cannot abandon your drowsiness in such a way, you should ponder, examine, and mentally inspect the Dhamma as you have heard it and learned it. . . .
>
> "But if you cannot abandon your drowsiness in such a way, you should recite in detail the Dhamma as you have heard it and learned it. . . .
>
> "But if you cannot abandon your drowsiness in such a way, you should pull both ears and rub your limbs with your hands. . . .
>
> "But if you cannot abandon your drowsiness in such a way, you should get up from your seat, rub your eyes with water, survey all the quarters, and look up at the constellations and stars. . . .

---

50 Bodhi, *Connected Discourses*, 200.

51 Rhys Davids, *Buddhist Manual of Psychological Ethics*, 289n1.

> "But if you cannot abandon your drowsiness in such a way, you should attend to the perception of light. . . .
>
> "But if you cannot abandon your drowsiness in such a way, you should undertake [the exercise of] walking back and forth, perceiving what is behind you and what is in front, with your sense faculties drawn in and your mind collected."

The Buddha concluded by telling Moggallāna that if none of that should work, he should just lie down and sleep, get right up after he had awakened, and not relish the fact that he had just had a nap.[52] Sleep may have been exactly what Moggallāna needed, but that conclusion was unwarranted on the basis of the first signs of drowsiness. Active measures to test that initial drowsiness, like rubbing the eyes and looking at some light, are always available tools at the bhikkhu's disposal; he just needs to make the effort to use them.

Sloth-torpor, like the other hindrances, is overcome by cutting off its food supply, and the Buddha's advice to Moggallāna already indicates the how to begin to make that happen:

> And what, bhikkhus, is the nutriment for the arising of unarisen sloth and torpor and for increase and expansion of unarisen sloth and torpor? There are, bhikkhus, discontent, lethargy, lazy stretching, drowsiness after meals, sluggishness of mind: frequently giving careless attention to them is the nutriment for the arising of unarisen sloth and torpor and for the increase and expansion of arisen sloth and torpor.[53]

It is not the tiredness itself, but rather the unwillingness to do something about it, that shows the nīvaraṇa to be operative. Discontent happens. Drowsiness after meals happens. It sometimes happens that the mind is sluggish. Careful attention means recognizing these moments as such without attachment or rejection; careless attention means reading them as indicative of something about oneself ("I am because of this"). It is the mind being weighed down through ego attachment leading to torpor with respect to further pursuit of the path—and not the yawning and stretching—that is itself the hindrance.

---

52 Bodhi, *Numerical Discourses*, 1059–60.

53 Bodhi, *Connected Discourses*, 1568.

The only way to counter the hindrance is to rouse energy and determination, even in the face of such states, by surrendering any attachment to them:

> Bhikkhus, I do not see even one other thing on account of which unarisen dullness and drowsiness do not arise and arisen dullness and drowsiness are abandoned so much as the element of instigation, the element of persistence, the element of exertion. For one who has aroused energy, unarisen dullness and drowsiness do not arise and arisen dullness and drowsiness are abandoned.[54]

There is a difference between recognizing that the teaching-and-practice is good and wholeheartedly embracing it. The Buddha himself had noticed this in his own development: "Before my enlightenment, while I was just a bodhisatta, not yet fully enlightened, it occurred to me too: 'Good is renunciation, good is solitude.' Yet my mind did not launch out upon renunciation and become placid, settled, and liberated in it, though I saw it as peaceful."[55] It was only with the increasing recognition of the dangers of sensual pleasures that he actively pursued it. If one has difficulty mustering that energy and determination, it is perhaps because one is still not convinced that the tṛṣṇā-laden and dukkha-filled life is all that bad—or that it is worth the effort to be liberated from it.

Sloth-torpor is the adversary of samatha no less than acedia is the adversary of hesychia. Samatha serves as a sure point of departure for the further pursuit of the path because it is a *dynamic* stillness infused with determination, or what the tradition identifies as spiritual energy (*vīrya*). Etymologically, *vīrya* refers to manliness or virility or courage (its Latin cognate is *virtus*, from *vir*, or "man");[56] it is one of the perfections (*pāramitās*), and it is one of the seven factors of enlightenment (*vīrya-sambojjhaṅga*). It is sometimes translated as *heroic willpower.*[57] This is not the heroic willpower of some Nietzschean *Übermensch*, setting his ego as the measure of all things, but the heroic willpower of one who

---

54 Bodhi, *Numerical Discourses*, 92.

55 Bodhi, *Numerical Discourses*, 1310.

56 Sexist overtones notwithstanding, one subject to thīna-middha might be encouraged to "man up." A more universally applicable exhortation might be "to grow a spine."

57 Johnathan C. Gold, "Freedom through Cumulative Moral Cultivation: Heroic Willpower (*Vīrya*)," *Journal of Buddhist Ethics* 25 (2018): 741.

presses on in divesting his ego from all such pretenses. It is a willpower that, while fearless, is not brazen.

The Buddha's own analogy for thīna-middha demonstrates how this is so:

> A person who is imprisoned during a festival day is unable to see the beginning or the middle or the end of the festivities. When released on the following day, he hears people saying, "Oh, how delightful yesterday's festival was! Oh, those dances and songs!" he will not reply. And why not? Because he did not enjoy the festival himself.
>
> In the same way, even if a very eloquent Dharma discourse is being given, one overcome by sloth and torpor would not know its beginning, middle, or end. If after the discourse, he hears it being praised: "How pleasant it was to listen to the Dharma! How interesting the subject was and how good the similes!" he will not reply. And why not? Because of his sloth and torpor, he did not enjoy the discourse. In this way, sloth and torpor are like imprisonment.[58]

Two people may be sitting next to one another in the meditation hall. Both are physically still, and the minds of both have settled down from their everyday chattering. But the one, seeing this as the be-all and end-all of practice, savors the moment and tries to hold on to it; the other, knowing that this state frees her for probing the teaching and pressing on toward insight, now applies herself energetically to realizing what the Dharma teaches. Later, when the talk is being given, the one still remains content with his balmy state, does not attend to what is being said, and finds it confusing or irrelevant. The other, however, is now primed to listen, learn from, and apply what is being taught, finds it encouraging, and is eager to test it out for herself. That the one should languish in the practice while the other thrives follows as a matter of course. Here we find perhaps one of the best examples of the metaphor the Buddha used to describe the nīvaraṇas generally. Recall that the hindrances were likened to a shawl:

> "It is just as if this River Aciravatī were brimful of water so that a crow could drink out of it, and a man should come along wishing to cross over . . . and were to lie down on this bank, covering his head with a shawl. What do you think, Vāseṭṭha? Would that man be able to get to the other side?" "No, Reverend Gotama."
>
> In the same way, Vāseṭṭha, in the Ariyan discipline these five hindrances are called obstacles, hindrances, coverings-up, envelopings.[59]

---

58 *Majjhima Aṭṭhakathā* 2:318; cited in in Tan, "Nīvaraṇa: Mental Hindrances," 7.

59 Walshe, *Long Discourses*, 191.

The shawl of sloth-torpor is the warm, fuzzy blanket that keeps me cozy and snug in the cold confines of my own ego attachment. The fearlessness that overcomes the nīvaraṇa is simply the fearlessness of tossing that aside and intrepidly plunging into the as yet unplumbed waters.

Sloth-torpor is the most tenacious of the five hindrances and the last to be overcome. It is eliminated only with the attainment of the fourth jhāna, the highest level of samādhi: "In the case of the hindrances, the hindrance of uncertainty is eliminated by the first knowledge. The three, namely lust, ill will and worry, are eliminated by the third knowledge. Stiffness and torpor and agitation are eliminated by the fourth knowledge."[60] The state of mind that marks the fourth jhāna—equanimity—is precisely the quality that allows one to overcome sloth-torpor:

> Sāriputta entered upon and abided in the fourth jhāna, which has neither pain-nor-pleasure and purity of mindfulness due to equanimity. And the states in the fourth jhāna—the equanimity, the neither painful-nor-pleasant feeling, the mental unconcern due to its tranquility, the purity of mindfulness, and the unification of mind; the contact, feeling, perception, volition, and mind; the zeal, decision, energy, mindfulness, equanimity, and attention—these states were defined by him one by one as they occurred; known to him those states arose, known they were present, known they disappeared.[61]

Now, having come to that level expanse of ground—which the Buddha had described, but which one had not yet experienced for oneself—one *knows* that the struggle and effort is worthwhile, and the very idea of holding back and not dedicating one's all to the practice will not even arise.

Acedia and sloth-torpor are endemic to the renunciant-contemplative life. It is a testament to both the Buddha and Evagrius that they identified this obstacle as an altogether expected—even *necessary*—one to work through on the path to stillness. Confronting acedia or sloth-torpor and cutting through its oppressive weight definitively uproot any lingering romanticism about the renunciant-contemplative life, along with any misplaced or shallow expectations one might have put on it. Even if one practices not as a celibate but as a householder, one will have encountered these obstacles any time one has set aside dedicated periods for concerted practice—perhaps not the first time or the third, since it is all so new, but certainly after the twentieth, fiftieth, or

60 Buddhaghoṣa and Ñāṇamoli, *Path of Purification*, 715–16.

61 Ñāṇamoli and Bodhi, *Middle Length Discourses*, 900.

five-hundredth time, or beyond. If one has not yet confronted them—if one is still finding the practice pleasingly tranquil or relaxing—then perhaps one has not yet begun to dig into the practice with any degree of sincerity or effort.

Both the Buddha and Evagrius knew that renunciant-contemplative life was not for the weak of resolve or the faint of heart. It requires *grit*, and grit is not something one is born with, but must be cultivated and developed in conjunction with slogging through the rough terrain of practice. Much like gentleness and loving-kindness, perseverance and *virya* must be *demonstrated* in the process of overcoming the hindrance that stands in their way with a resolve that can only come from within. No one can make me gentle, no one can make me patient, and no one can muster for me the determination to see the path through to the end.

The good news is that I do not have to pull these out of the ether, for they have been there all along. They are aspects of my true nature that I have enclosed within the confines of a self that would try to deny that nature, settling for "chilling out" and "zoning out," as we might say today. Freedom from sloth-torpor is thus like being freed from prison: "Just as a man might be bound in prison, and after a time he might be freed from his bonds without any loss, with no deduction from his possessions. He might think: 'Before this I was in prison . . . ,' and he would rejoice and be glad about that."[62] Seeing through this obstacle, I come to see that I was the one who had put myself in the prison in the first place through my own insistence on a petty and superficial form of ease and tranquility.

62 Walshe, *Long Discourses*, 101–2.

CHAPTER EIGHT

Indecision, the Wasteland

In the *Nikāyas*, we hear of the plight of the Kālāma people, who lived in the town of Kesaputta in northern India. It seems they had been visited by a succession of religious adepts, all of whom claimed their doctrine to be the true teaching. Each outdid the others in trumpeting the correctness of their tenets and pointing out the inadequacies of the rest, leaving the Kālāmas bewildered as to what was true. But now the Buddha had come to town, so they sought his advice on how to sort it all out: "We are perplexed and in doubt, Bhante, as to which of these good ascetics speak truth and which speak falsehood." The Buddha was not at all surprised at their confusion: "It is fitting for you to be perplexed, Kālāmas, fitting for you to be in doubt. Doubt has arisen in you about a perplexing matter." But if they had been expecting the Buddha to simply declare a winner in the contest of doctrines, they were soon to be disappointed. Instead, they were told to sort things out for themselves.

Buddhism is often trumpeted in contemporary circles as a skeptic's dream religion, and the first part of the Buddha's instruction to the Kālāmas would seem to underwrite just such a view:

> Come Kālāmas, do not go by oral tradition, by lineage of teaching, by hearsay, by a collection of scriptures, by logical reasoning, by inferential reasoning, by reasoned cogitation, by the acceptance of a view after pondering it, by the seeming competence [of a speaker], or because you think: "The ascetic is our guru."[1]

The criticism of assent based on appeals to authority, tradition, or oral or written testimony is a staple of rational humanism generally, and the Buddha's

1 Bodhi, *Numerical Discourses*, 280.

advice would not call any of that into question. But it is important to note that even cool, rational thinking—so often put forth as the antidote to the perplexity that arises from reliance on received tradition and the testimony of others—is here quietly lumped in with the rest. Even the most penetrating philosopher has no tools in her box that can definitively free one from the kind of doubt in question here, for there is always the prospect of a better argument, a new data set, or another, yet unexplored tack that might be taken. As long as these remain in play, one will never settle into the kind of work that needs to be done.

Of course, the Buddha did not just tell them to figure it all out on their own, as if that were enough; rather, he offered instruction in a sure way to do that: "But when, Kālāmas, you know for yourselves: 'These things are unwholesome; these things are blameworthy; these things are censured by the wise; these things, if accepted and undertaken, lead to harm and suffering,' then you should abandon them."[2] One needs to discover the truth of the matter at hand, not through discursive analysis, but through one's own direct awareness, unclouded by the fear of what that awareness might portend for one's self-conception. It is confidence in *that* counsel that the nīvaraṇa *vicikicchā* seeks to undermine.

Frequently rendered *doubt* or *perplexity*, *vicikicchā* covers both skepsis and indecision, but the *Nikāyas* and commentaries treat it more often as indecision. Both forms of doubt are, of course, inimical to the renunciant-contemplative life, though in rather different ways. Skepsis keeps one from even starting down the path. It is the kind of skepticism shown by the Kālāmas when confronted with so many diverse doctrinal claims; in the face of such a smorgasbord of views, one does not know even where to begin. It is the same kind of skepticism shown, however implicitly, in the summary judgment that any and all spiritual paths are equally good (we would not even be hearing about the Kālāmas if they had just nodded along with each presentation they heard, said it was just as fine as the others, and then went home). Such a perspective can only be had by looking at all of them from a position of some remove, and as long as one

---

2 Bodhi, *Numerical Discourses*, 280. This is, of course, not the whole of the solution to the Kālāmas' doubts; the Buddha was addressing them as everyday persons of goodwill, not as lay disciples, so there is no discussion of the holy life or even of the Noble Truths. See Bodhi, "A Look at the Kālāma Sutta," in *Dhamma Reflections*, 61–65, for a clear, nuanced reading of the *Kālāma Sutra*.

is doing that, one is not actually walking *any* path, let alone the path of the Dharma.

Indecision, by contrast, is a matter of trying to keep one foot each on two different paths, hedging one's bets, so to speak, by not quite fully committing in one direction or another. It renders one immobile at a crossroads. Unlike skepsis, which, to borrow a modern metaphor, would lead one to doubt the very existence of the cake, indecision is a case of wanting to both eat it *and* not eat it, so one chews away without knowing whether to swallow or spit it out. One is in large part certain as to which things are wholesome and which are blameworthy but, despite that, still holds out the possibility that there might be *something* praiseworthy in the unpraiseworthy or *something* skillful in the unskillful. This is not because one is otherwise impartially interested in these matters abstractly, but because one is still on the lookout for a way of circumventing the plain truth that all things—and one's self in particular—are conditioned, impermanent, and not worth investing in. Indecision, like all of the other nīvaraṇas, is yet another way of keeping up the conceit of the self. It is of indecision that Chögyam Trungpa writes, "You do not trust any possible alternatives and do not want advice or any way out. You doubt the teachings, the teacher, and the Buddhadharma. You even doubt the simple, sensible norms of everyday existence."[3] No matter *what* one doubts, the *doubting self* is still there, standing stock-still at the intersection. Put simply, "doubt arises in one who has not abandoned craving."[4]

As with all of the other nīvaraṇas, ego-sustaining tṛṣṇā is the root cause of indecision, and this accounts for why rational thinking was included in the Buddha's advice to the Kālāmas. Nothing quite reinforces the sense of self more than thinking does.[5] Descartes only confirmed, in his own time, what the Dharma had long taught. Pursue thinking long enough, and you will lose a sure grasp of your body, your senses, the objects of sense perception, and even other humans and God—but the self remains more firmly ensconced than ever. *Cogito ergo sum* might prove to be the bedrock of certain knowledge, but the only thing one ends up knowing for certain is one's thinking self, and all the rest is added back in only insofar as it supports that thinking self

3 Chögyam Trungpa, *The Truth of Suffering and the Path of Liberation* (Boston: Shambhala, 2009), 48.

4 Bodhi, *Connected Discourses*, 1076n136.

5 Keren Arbel notes, "Thinking is a manifestation of the sense of self; it is that which sustains, at least, the grossest sense of 'me' and 'I.'" Arbel, *Early Buddhist Meditation: The Four* Jhānas *as the Actualization of Insight* (New York: Routledge, 2016), 87.

in its ongoing exercise. Since indecision is nothing but that thinking process run rampant, overcoming indecision brings the practitioner one step further to the deliverance of mind that is unshakable, because one is free of all *thought* about it.

In the *Nikāyas*, indecision is described as a kind of unsettledness resulting from keeping all kinds of mental flotsam and jetsam afloat: "Suppose, brahmin, there is a bowl of water that is turbid, unsettled, muddy, placed in the dark. If a man with good sight were to examine his own facial reflection in it, he would neither know nor see it as it really is. So too, brahmin, when one dwells with a mind obsessed by doubt."[6] In effect, doubt keeps one ruminating on matters that thinking is utterly unequipped to resolve. Because one never finds any resolution for these thoughts, because one continues chewing and chewing on them without ever managing to swallow, one cuts off any prospect of receiving the nutrition they contain. This aligns with yet another characterization of indecision in the *Nikāyas*, where it is described as a "mental barrenness,"[7] like a poor tract of land on which nothing worthwhile can grow. The commentaries only amplify its debilitating qualities: "It is this kind of doubt, this working of doubt, this dubiety, puzzlement, perplexity, distraction, standing at cross-roads; collapse, uncertainty of grasp; evasion, hesitation, in capacity [*sic*] of grasping thoroughly, stiffness of mind, mental scarifying, that is called [doubt]."[8]

Like all the other nīvaraṇas, indecision has a particular nutritive ground from which it draws its impetus: "And what, bhikkhus, is the nutriment for the arising of unarisen doubt and for the increase and expansion of arisen doubt? There are, bhikkhus, things that are the basis for doubt: frequently giving careless attention to them is the nutriment for the arising of unarisen doubt and for the increase and expansion of arisen doubt."[9] In the *Nikāyas*, five specific bases are mentioned in conjunction with indecision: doubt about the Buddha, doubt about the Dharma, doubt about the Saṅgha, doubt about the training, and resentment against one's companions in the holy life.[10]

---

6 Bodhi, *Connected Discourses*, 1613.

7 Bodhi, *Numerical Discourses*, 819–20. The Pali is *cetokhila*. Bhikkhu Bodhi points out that the *Majjhima Nikāya Aṭṭhakathā* describes *cetokhila* as "rigidity, rubbish, or a stump in the mind" (Ñāṇamoli and Bodhi, *Middle Length Discourses*, 1202n217).

8 Rhys Davids, *Buddhist Manual of Psychological Ethics*, 239.

9 Bodhi, *Connected Discourses*, 1568.

10 Bodhi, *Numerical Discourses*, 819–20.

Reviewing each of these allows us to see the full extent of this hindrance's reach.

Doubt about the Buddha does not arise in conjunction with the question whether there was a human being, someone named Siddhartha Gotama, who was born in Lumbini, died in Kushinagar, and along the way taught and attracted any number of disciples. As sketchy as the historical record is, at least that much seems to be a settled enough matter. Instead, it arises in conjunction with the question of whether such a person could even be *a Buddha* to begin with. A Buddha is one to whom the epithets of a Buddha—"accomplished, fully enlightened, perfect in true knowledge and conduct, sublime, knower of worlds, incomparable leader of persons to be tamed, teacher of gods and humans, enlightened, blessed"—properly apply.[11] Indecision questions whether any of that can ever be ascribed to *anyone*, because a life free of all defilements, unbounded by saṃsāra, fully aware of the rising and falling of worlds, unobstructed, and traceless seems incompatible with being a living human being at all.[12]

The Buddha was well aware of the propensity to such doubt, and he anticipated the strong likelihood that bhikkhus who had not yet come to realization would fall into it. Just as in the case of the Kālāmas, he had some advice on how to settle it: "Bhikkhus, a bhikkhu who is an inquirer, not knowing how to gauge another's mind, should make an investigation of the Tathāgata in order to find out whether or not he is fully enlightened."[13] Now, such a bhikkhu has not yet developed the wherewithal to know and understand enlightenment for himself, and he is in no position to ascertain it directly in another. The Buddha thus invites the bhikkhu to work with what he can know—dharmas, or observable phenomena. In a series of investigative questions relating to particular dharmas, a bhikkhu is led little by little to muster confidence in the Buddha *as a Buddha*. Are there any defiled states cognizable in the Tathāgata through the eye or the ear? No. Are there any mixed states in him, part defiled and part not, cognizable through the eye or the ear? No.

11 Ñāṇamoli and Bodhi, *Middle Length Discourses*, 118–19.

12 The Christian parallel would, of course, concern not whether there was a person from Nazareth named Jesus who taught and was crucified under Pontius Pilate, died, and even rose from the dead, but whether said person can be *the Christ*—the second person of the eternal Godhead, one in being with the Father, the Logos without whom nothing came into being, fully human *and* fully God.

13 Ñāṇamoli and Bodhi, *Middle Length Discourses*, 415.

Are there cleansed states to be found in him? Yes. Did the Tathāgata come to them only recently or over a long time? Over a long time. If he has come to some renown and fame, are the dangers connected with renown and fame present in him?[14] No. Is the Tathāgata without fear and not restrained by fear? Yes. Does he avoid sensual pleasure because he, having destroyed lust, is now without lust? Yes.

The investigation goes on to probe not only the states of the Buddha's person, but also his relations with those around him. In a group made up of well-behaved and poorly behaved people, does he despise the poorly behaved? No. If there is a bhikkhu who has been taught, does that bhikkhu trace his confidence in the Dharma to the Buddha himself as one who is fully enlightened? Yes. For those without firsthand access to the person of the Buddha and his qualities (as is the case for all of us today), it is perhaps this last question that is most decisive. Have we perchance met someone who exhibits in some good measure the qualities of a Buddha and acknowledges that it is through the Buddha's teaching that he or she has attained this much? Yes. If that is the case, then one can have reasonable assurance that confidence in the Buddha is not misplaced: "Bhikkhus, when anyone's faith has been planted, rooted, and established in the Tathāgata through these reasons, terms, and phrases, his faith is said to be supported by reasons, rooted in vision, firm; it is invincible by any recluse or brahmin or god or Māra or Brahmā or by anyone in the world."[15] Although the inquirer has not come to know the mind of Buddha directly for him- or herself, he or she can now proceed with resolve toward that fuller insight in the ease of stillness.

Doubt about the Dharma is the failure to maintain an unwavering confidence in it as being "well proclaimed by the Blessed One, visible here and now, immediately effective, inviting inspection, onward leading, to be experienced by the wise for themselves."[16] To be sure, there are many appealing things in what the Buddha taught, and one need not have taken the threefold refuge, or even think the Buddha was all that special, to appreciate them. But such appreciation does not add up to confidence in anything, let alone the Dharma, since it is the enjoyment of a pithy comment, perhaps, and not the liberating potential of the teaching that the aficionado is most interested

14 We will have occasion to review such dangers in conjunction with the discussion of vainglory in chap. 9.

15 Ñāṇamoli and Bodhi, *Middle Length Discourses*, 418.

16 Ñāṇamoli and Bodhi, *Middle Length Discourses*, 119.

in. Confidence in the Dharma is manifest in the willingness to abandon any particular thoughts or feelings about the teaching and to let it permeate one's view of things as they are.

The Buddha and his disciples frequently said of the Dharma that it is "good in the beginning, good in the middle, and good in the end, with the right meaning and phrasing," and that it "reveal[s] the holy life that is perfectly complete and pure."[17] Still, anything taught is only as effective as one's receptivity to it, and *how* one receives it has much to do with *what one thinks* one is receiving. This is why the Buddha had fully anticipated the likelihood of a poor reception of the teaching when he noted that those who are as yet "fired by lust, obscured by darkness, will never see this abstruse Dhamma, deep, hard to see, subtle, going against the stream."[18] One who harbors doubts about the Dharma should therefore first of all check whether one is actually perceiving the Dharma to begin with, or whether one's defilements are already skewing the teaching.

The *Nikāyas* describe five qualities in a hearer that keep one from grasping the subtleties of the Dharma:

> Bhikkhus, possessing five qualities, even while listening to the good Dhamma one is incapable of entering upon the fixed course [consisting in] rightness in wholesome qualities. What five? One disparages the talk; one disparages the speaker; one disparages oneself; one is unwise, stupid, obtuse; one imagines that one has understood what one has not understood.[19]

The first two qualities reflect a surly, resistant attitude from the outset; one will never have confidence in anything, let alone the Dharma, while persisting in such a frame of mind. Here, one cannot even be said to be doubting the Dharma, strictly speaking, since one is not even focused on the teaching, but on the rhetorical skill of the speaker as manifest in the delivery.

The other qualities, however, concern unskillful views that the hearer holds about himself. When I disparage myself, I feign an incapacity for understanding the Dharma by thinking that I am not smart enough or sufficiently educated enough to grasp it. Even if I do not enjoy the most probing of intellects, there is nothing in the Dharma that requires a high IQ as much as concerted effort in the practice of rendering the mind wieldy

17 Bodhi, *Connected Discourses*, 1339.
18 Bodhi, *Connected Discourses*, 232.
19 Bodhi, *Numerical Discourses*, 765.

through renunciation—something most anyone can do, if they are willing, as submission to the gradual training shows. Any traces of obtuseness on the part of the disciple are owed more to willful resistance than to lack of information or conceptual sophistication, and perduring doubt about my own ability to comprehend the Dharma is nothing more than that resistance ossified.[20]

Certainly the most pernicious quality among the five is the last—imagining oneself to have understood what one has not understood. In any number of domains of everyday life, it may be sufficient to say, "This is the truth as I see it," and the perspectival and situated nature of most of our views about the world is now widely accepted as a given. From a Dharmic perspective, however, attachment to one's own views is precisely what defines saṃsāra as the realm of ignorance and vexation. One who would aspire to liberation cannot be content with the idea that one's idiosyncratic takes are the end of the matter on *anything*, let alone the Dharma. That this or the other aspect of the Dharma might happen to "make sense" to a person might well indicate that that person has failed to discern the point that is being made or, at least, that one has not yet plumbed the subtleties of it. The Dharma is never what one *thinks* it is.

Even if one might not doubt the reality of Buddhahood or the comprehensiveness and truth of the Dharma, one might still doubt that it is at all attainable by everyday people. One might be willing to concede that in one singular instance there was a human being who did, but that was the Buddha, and that was a one-off situation—and a long time ago at that. For the rest of us poor saps, so it might seem, the most we can do is acknowledge the uniqueness of the Buddha, hold him up as an exemplar, and offer such devotional exercises as we might be inclined to undertake.

But in taking refuge in the Three Jewels, one is also taking refuge in the company of those men and women who, in greater or lesser measure, came to the realization of the truth the Buddha knew and taught. These people, collectively, constitute the *āryasaṅgha*, the saṅgha of the noble ones:

> The Saṅgha of the Blessed One's disciples is practising the good way, practising the straight way, practising the true way, practising the proper way; that is, the

20 It goes without saying that the Dharma is not able to be grasped by children or the cognitively impaired, and only an unthinking practitioner of the Dharma will even try to get them to grasp it.

> four pairs of persons, the eight types of individuals.[21] This Saṅgha of the Blessed One's disciples is worthy of gifts, worthy of hospitality, worthy of offerings, worthy of reverential salutation, the unsurpassed field of merit for the world.[22]

All of these have demonstrated that the liberation offered by the Buddha is indeed attainable for human beings, for all of them have come to some degree of realization.

One might think that this is all well and good, but still be of two minds about the training that leads to such liberation. Already in the description of the gradual training, we see some of the initial resistance one might throw up against the constraints of the holy life, such as the objection that some of the training rules were unduly trivial. Beyond the triviality of a particular rule or precept, one may question the ability of the discipline as a whole to do its job, so to speak. One who is given to such indecision might fall again into restlessness-remorse and cast about for different or additional practices. As with restlessness-remorse, one is invited to abandon any thought of outcome and instead to attend closely to the skillfulness or unskillfulness of one's actions. Noting that ease ensues when the training is followed and dis-ease ensues when it is not, one can gain confidence enough in the training: "Cleansed by exertion . . . a noble disciple recollects his own virtuous behavior as unbroken, flawless, unblemished, unblotched, freeing, praised by the wise, ungrasped, leading to concentration."[23] Although one knows nothing of final attainment, one at least knows that much, and that is enough to press on.

Finally, resentment against one's companions manifests when a bhikkhu is "angry and displeased with his companions in the holy life, resentful and callous towards them."[24] This is clearly a kind of variation on ill will, and we will see it again in the discussion of vainglory and pride, but it also attests to a certain kind of indecision. Instead of looking at the work one must do and keeping one's nose to the grindstone, one looks around and takes note of all those unsatisfactory things that are always found among men and

---

21 The four pairs and eight types are those on the path to stream-entry and those who have realized the fruit of stream-entry, those who are on the path to once-returning and those who have realized the fruit of once-returning, those who are on the path to nonreturning and those who have realized the fruit of nonreturning, and, finally, those on the path to becoming arhats and those who have realized the fruit of arhatship. To the four pairs and eight types, the Mahāyāna adds the bodhisattvas.

22 Ñāṇamoli and Bodhi, *Middle Length Discourses*, 119.

23 Bodhi, *Numerical Discourses*, 297.

24 Ñāṇamoli and Bodhi, *Middle Length Discourses*, 194.

women, monastic or not. One might be inclined to overlook the shenanigans of everyday people as just more instances of samsaric wandering, but here we have fellow renunciants, and they are supposed to be *better* than those others, are they not? If not, does that not make them just as deluded as the rest or, worse, nothing but nefarious charlatans? In either case, they certainly do not measure up.

Are there bad monks? Of course there are. The Buddha himself was under no illusion that there would be schismatics among the bhikkhus, and even if it did not come to an all-out rift in the saṅgha, he pointed out that "there will be bhikkhus who are undeveloped in body, virtuous behavior, mind, and wisdom." Some of them will ordain others but not be able to guide them; others will fall into a "dark Dhamma" but not be able to discern that they have; still others will not incline toward hearing or understanding the Tathāgata's teaching but instead be taken in by poetry and pleasing words, bond with women, become fond of luxury, or be disinclined to solitude.[25] What was true for the Buddha's time is no less true today, and one can draw up a list as long as one's arm (and longer yet) of the countless sexual, financial, and abuse-related scandals that never seem to go away, not just in Buddhist communities but in religious communities of all kinds. One obstructed by indecision will have more than enough to chew on here. Clearly, one might think, the path is ineffective if there are those who, while claiming to follow it, still fall quite wide of the mark. If that is the case, one will be tempted to conclude, it cannot be worth following. So the doubter leaves, never to return.

Everyday people will think and act this way, and, as an account of an everyday way of thinking, it is perfectly understandable. The question here, however, is whether it is *skillful* for one who has set out on the renunciant-contemplative path. When presented with schismatic and inept bhikkhus, the Buddha offered that "it is enough for a bhikkhu to dwell heedful, ardent, and resolute" to attain what has not yet been attained, alone—*as an island*—if need be. A bhikkhu's task is simply to "recognize" and "make an effort to abandon" these practice-defeating circumstances should he encounter them.[26] Simply put, associate with the good bhikkhus, avoid the rest, and, in any case, do not dwell on it. One's own practice is not at all contingent on the practice

25 Bodhi, *Numerical Discourses*, 713–15.

26 Bodhi, *Numerical Discourses*, 712–13.

of others, and one's ability to keep the precepts does not rise and fall as a consequence of whether others do or not.

Doubts about the Buddha, the Dharma, the Saṅgha, and the training and resentment about one's companions are all, in a sense, practical doubts. It is easy to see how they might arise on the part of one considering whether to join the ranks of the noble disciples; or, if one had and was not yet established in it, one might find oneself pondering whether one might have made a mistake and ended up falling in with the wrong crowd altogether. Still, without being free from these doubts—without an unwavering confidence in the Buddha, the Dharma, the Saṅgha, and without holding one's companions dear—one cannot be counted among those renunciant-contemplatives of the Buddha's company—or indeed be considered much of a renunciant-contemplative of any kind at all, Buddhist or not.[27]

As troubling as these kinds of doubt are, still more troubling is the indecision that arises in conjunction with purely speculative concerns. Under the banner of teaching one thing, and one thing only—dukkha and its end—the Buddha made some rather bold claims about the nature of the self, the nature of the world, and the nature of true liberation from them. When he was once asked by one of his senior disciples, Moggallāna, whether he recalled ever having given a short summary of the Dharma, he responded with perhaps the boldest claim of them all:

> I do recall doing so, Moggallāna. Here Sakka, ruler of gods, came to me, and after paying homage to me, he stood at one side and asked: "Venerable sir, how in brief is a bhikkhu liberated in the destruction of craving, one who has reached the ultimate end, the ultimate security from bondage, the ultimate holy life, the ultimate goal, one who is foremost among gods and humans?" When this was said, I told him: "Here, ruler of gods, a bhikkhu has heard that nothing is worth adhering to.[28]

For one with a disputatious mind, the bait will be all too quickly taken. *Nothing*? Nothing *at all*?

Where the everyday mind might make out a kind of nihilism in such a statement and react accordingly by simply turning away, the claim that there is nothing worth adhering to will send the speculatively minded into

27 Ñāṇamoli and Bodhi, *Middle Length Discourses*, 159.
28 Ñāṇamoli and Bodhi, *Middle Length Discourses*, 347.

overdrive. So, in addition to the five grounds of doubt already identified, the *Dhammasaṅgaṇī* includes two more: thoughts about the past and future, considered separately or together, and doubts concerning the accuracy of the teaching on dependent origination.[29] These two issues emerged already in the Buddha's time as the key speculative obstacles to practice. They are interconnected, in that they both reflect a misunderstanding of the nature of things—and one's individual person in particular—as empty of abiding selfhood and hence not worth adhering to.

We see this exemplified in the *Cūḷamālunkya Sutra*. One day in his meditation, it occurred to the Bhikkhu Māluṅkyaputta that the Buddha had not pronounced anything definitive about a roster of classic metaphysical questions: whether the world is eternal, whether the world is finite or infinite, whether the soul and the body are the same or different, whether after death a Buddha exists, whether after death a Buddha both exists and does not exist, or whether after death a Buddha neither exists nor does not exist. Māluṅkyaputta wanted answers one way or the other, and he thought to himself: "If [the Buddha] declares to me either 'the world is eternal' or 'the world is not eternal' . . . then I will lead the holy life under him; if he does not declare these to me, then I will abandon the training and return to the low life."[30] So off he went to the Buddha and laid down his conditions for continuing in the practice.

The Buddha then reminded Māluṅkyaputta that he never said anything to the effect that, if someone followed him, he would provide the answers to these questions. In a deft move, he threw that ball back into Māluṅkyaputta's court: "That being so, misguided man, who are you and what are you abandoning?"[31] If Māluṅkyaputta was intent on surrendering the self and breaking free of saṃsāra, he would find that either answer—yea or nay—to any of those speculative questions would make his own practice impossible:

> Māluṅkyaputta, if there is the view "the world is eternal," the holy life cannot be lived; and if there is the view "the world is not eternal," the holy life cannot be lived. Whether there is the view "the world is eternal" or the view "the world is not eternal," there is birth, there is ageing, there is death, there is sorrow, lamentation, pain, grief, and despair, the destruction of which I prescribe here and now.[32]

---

29 Rhys Davids, *Buddhist Manual of Psychological Ethics*, 239. The *Dhammasaṅgaṇī* is the first book of the Abhidhamma Piṭaka, the collection of scholastic writings that attempt to systematize the teaching of the Buddha.

30 Ñāṇamoli and Bodhi, *Middle Length Discourses*, 533.

31 Ñāṇamoli and Bodhi, *Middle Length Discourses*, 534.

32 Ñāṇamoli and Bodhi, *Middle Length Discourses*, 535.

The same holds for the other pairs as well: if any dharma is eternal, no progress is possible, since a dharma's eternality implies the absence of change; if all dharmas are annihilated, no progress is possible, since nothing remains that can be identified as something that has changed.[33] Therefore the Buddha left all of this undeclared because "it is unbeneficial, it does not belong to the fundamentals of the holy life, it does not lead to disenchantment, to dispassion, to cessation, to peace, to direct knowledge, to enlightenment, to Nibbāna."[34] The Noble Truths, which do lead to all of those, are the only things he ever taught, because they are the only things that are needed.

Like extraneous particulate matter suspended in water, material for doubt may be present in the mind, but it is not of the mind itself, nor need the mind rely on it or take its cue from it in any way. The water is still there, but rather than maintaining a clear and transparent view that looks past the bits and pieces of gunk suspended in it, one rivets one's attention on that foreign material, hoping to discern something in it all the same. Such "careless attention" is the nutritive ground of doubt: "For one who attends carelessly, unarisen doubt arises and arisen doubt increases and expands."[35] One does not need a global theory of the universe; one simply needs to recognize the basic difference between better and worse states:

> And what, bhikkhus, is the denourishment that prevents unarisen doubt from arising and arisen doubt from increasing and expanding? There are, bhikkhus, wholesome and unwholesome states, blamable and blameless states, inferior and superior states, dark and bright states with their counterparts: frequently giving careful attention to them is the denourishment that prevents unarisen doubt from arising and arisen doubt from increasing and expanding.[36]

Unless and until one is certain that there even *is* a distinction in these states at all, one will be stuck at the fork in the road between them. The Buddha's advice to the Kālāmas and to anyone else beset by doubt is the advice he gave himself when he had set out on the path:

> Bhikkhus, before my enlightenment, while I was still only an unenlightened Bodhisatta, it occurred to me: "Suppose that I divide my thoughts into two

33 The Buddha here anticipates precisely the dispute held later among the Greek philosophers, with Parmenides holding to the eternality of being and Heraclitus holding to its infinite flux.

34 Ñāṇamoli and Bodhi, *Middle Length Discourses*, 536.

35 Bodhi, *Numerical Discourses*, 91.

36 Bodhi, *Connected Discourses*, 1600.

> classes." Then I set on one side thoughts of sensual desire, thoughts of ill will and thoughts of cruelty, and I set on the other side thoughts of renunciation, thoughts of non-ill will, and thoughts of non-cruelty.[37]

Then, whenever a thought of sensual desire, ill will, or cruelty would arise, he would reflect that such a thought leads to the affliction of himself and others, obstructs wisdom, and leads away from the path toward release. In the same way, whenever the thought of renunciation, non–ill will, or noncruelty would arise, he would reflect that it does not lead to the affliction of self and other, but instead aids wisdom and does lead on the path toward release.

This sorting exercise is also a skillful response to the various occasions of doubt first noted. There are bad monks and good monks; follow the good and ignore the bad. Being a Buddha seems like too high an aspiration? Aspire anyway. Unclear on this or that aspect of the Dharma? Probe it and learn what it has to teach, even if it does not make much sense on the first pass—or even the hundredth. Not sure about those who constitute the *āryasaṅgha*? Strive to be worthy of their company all the same.

The nīvaraṇa of doubt arises as a consequence of losing sight of the purpose and the strategy of the Dharma.[38] The Dharma, to say it yet again, is meant for one purpose and one purpose only: the ending of dukkha.[39] Dukkha, as Thiradhammo Bhikkhu points out, "is not merely a six-letter word, but a painfully poignant, personal and multifarious experience (if one dares to look at it)."[40] The Dharma is not a theory of the universe, a blueprint for social analysis or structuring, or a nascent form of what we today would call psychology. The teaching on dependent origination was intended as an aid in the liberation from suffering and not as a stand-alone set of propositions to be assessed simply on their merits. It is perhaps one of the persistent manifestations of indecision that so many attempts are made to render that teaching *understandable* by treating it as yet another variation on or contribution to the physical, social, or therapeutic sciences. All of that is just so much further gunk in the water, to pursue the metaphor, since none of it is relevant for freeing oneself of dukkha, and any of it may actually get in the way of liberation by introducing concerns that are wholly extraneous to the path. It is not

37 Ñāṇamoli and Bodhi, *Middle Length Discourses*, 207.

38 Here I am following Bhikkhu Bodhi's take on doubt in "Two Faces of the Dhamma," in *Dhamma Reflections*, 41–42.

39 Bodhi, *Connected Discourses*, 938.

40 Thiradhammo, *Beyond I-Making*, 146.

surprising that the Buddha was hesitant to teach the Dharma *at all*, since its reception was likely to be skewed in accordance with the attachments and predilections of most every hearer.

In the commentarial literature, six things are identified as being conducive to the abandonment of indecision: much learning, investigation, familiarity with the Vinaya, resoluteness, good friendship, and suitable talk. Since investigation, familiarity with the Vinaya, and resoluteness have already been taken up in conjunction with other nīvaraṇas, here we can focus on much learning, good friendship, and suitable talk.

The corpus of the teachings of the Buddha and the Dharma ancestors can be viewed as a treasury of so many attempts to cut through the naive realism through which everyday persons understand themselves and conduct their affairs. Like the scriptures of many religions, it teaches things that are not immediately apparent to the everyday mind, but to think that this means that the Dharma is some kind of esoteric revelation would be to miss the point. It is not that the Dharma comes from elsewhere; it is that one has simply been blind to what has been before one's eyes all along. In taking the time to probe the sutras, one learns to expand one's vision, to consider things in a new way. Learning the teaching, committing it to memory, and acting in light of it steel the resolve and strengthen the aspiration of the practitioner:

> He has learned much, remembers what he has learned, and accumulates what he has learned. Those teachings that are good in the beginning, good in the middle, and good in the end, with the right meaning and phrasing, which proclaim the perfectly complete and pure spiritual life—such teachings as these he has learned much of, retained in mind, recited verbally, mentally investigated, and penetrated well by view.[41]

Returning over and over again to the sutras and the teachings of the Dharma ancestors is a sure way to keep extraneous thoughts from taking flight, since most anything one might raise an issue about has already been addressed in one way or another in that body of wisdom.

Good friendship assists one in that learning process. When Ānanda asks Sāriputta how one comes to hear of the Dharma not yet heard, to not forget those that have been heard, and to recall them with ease, Sāriputta reminds

41 Bodhi, *Numerical Discourses*, 724.

Ānanda that he knows the answer to this already and invites him to spell out what he knows:

> Here, friend Sāriputta, a bhikkhu learns the Dhamma: the discourses, mixed prose and verse, expositions, verses, inspired utterances, quotations, birth stories, amazing accounts, and questions-and-answers. He teaches the Dhamma to others in detail as he had heard it and learned it. He makes others repeat the Dhamma in detail as they have heard it and learned it. He recites the Dhamma in detail as he has heard it and learned it. He ponders, examines, and mentally inspects the Dhamma as he has heard it and learned it. He enters upon the rains in a residence where there live elder bhikkhus who are learned, heirs to the heritage, experts on the outlines. From time to time he approaches them and inquires: "How is this, Bhante? What is the meaning of this?" Those venerable ones then disclose to him what has not been disclosed, clear up what is obscure, and dispel his perplexity about numerous perplexing points.[42]

To understand the Dharma, I need others. If left to figure all of this out on my own, I will run up against the limits of my abilities to think through anything, imagine that my limits are actually the limits of the Dharma, and pursue the path ineffectively or stray from it entirely. Admitting that I do not understand and placing myself under the guidance of those more advanced in the practice are not indications of personal failing, but a skillful way of developing myself. Much as the fortnightly confession of training rule infractions served to perfect me in the practice of the precepts, confessing one's ongoing ignorance and confusion to a Dharma elder serves to perfect my grasp of the teaching:

> When a bhikkhu's mind is obsessed and oppressed by doubt, and he does not understand as it really is the escape from arisen doubt, on that occasion he should approach an esteemed bhikkhu and say to him: "Friend, my mind is obsessed and oppressed by doubt, and I do not understand as it really is the escape from arisen doubt. Please teach me the Dhamma for abandoning doubt."[43]

It is worth noting that the counsel to approach an esteemed bhikkhu is given not only to one afflicted by indecision, but to one troubled by any of the other nīvaraṇas as well.

Though the life of the dharmic renunciant-contemplative afforded the aspirant much solitude, there were still plenty of occasions to talk with one's fellow bhikkhus. Often these conversations concerned matters related to the

42 Bodhi, *Numerical Discourses*, 923–24.

43 Bodhi, *Numerical Discourses*, 887.

practice itself, as we just saw. At other times, however, the conversations went all over the place:

> Now on [one] occasion, after their meal, on returning from their alms round, a number of bhikkhus had assembled in the assembly hall and were sitting together engaging in various kinds of pointless talk, that is: talk about kings, thieves, and ministers of state; talk about armies, perils, and wars; talk about food, drink, garments, and beds; talk about garlands and scents, talk about relatives, vehicles, villages, towns, cities, and countries; talk about women and talk about heroes, street talk and talk by the well; talk about the departed; miscellaneous talk, speculation about the world and the sea; talk about becoming this or that.

The Buddha was quick to point out the inappropriateness of such banter: "Bhikkhus, it is not suitable for you, clansmen who have gone forth from the household life into homelessness out of faith, to engage in various kinds of pointless talk, that is: talk about kings, thieves, and ministers of state . . . talk about becoming this or that."[44] What was true for those bhikkhus is true for anyone who would pursue the Dharma, homeleaver and householder alike. Most any conversation one might enter into will likely have to do with something on that list, since such talk is the warp and woof of everyday communication with others: the price of groceries, the town council's decision to close a neighborhood park, the latest advance in technology, fashion trends, and sports statistics.

Such talk is pointless in at least three respects. First, the content of such talk concerns nothing but the detritus of human life while coursing on in saṃsāra. It comes and goes like everything connected with wiles of everyday people and the vicissitudes of the worlds they construct. It may be *news* in that there are new particulars in play, but it is still for all that the *same old story*, since it is just another manifestation of the tṛṣṇā-driven formations of persons bound to their samsaric worlds. The names may change, but most every day there is some politician involved in scandal, some establishment robbed, some act of wanton violence perpetrated, some abandoned litter of kittens found and given a new home, or some centenarian being feted. Good news or bad news does not matter; all of it is nothing other than more bits and pieces in the water that draw attention away from the clear rays of sunlight.

Pointless talk also sows seeds of dissention, and Buddhaghoṣa includes "taking sides" among the various manifestations of indecision.[45] Taking sides

44 Bodhi, *Numerical Discourses*, 1424.

45 Buddhaghoṣa and Ñāṇamoli, *Path of Purification*, 479.

would seem to be the very opposite of indecision, since taking a side involves staking one's ground with respect to the matter at hand, and, in an everyday sense, this is certainly true enough. But taking sides about conditioned states of affairs reveals a latent doubt about impermanence and nonself. It assumes that there is, indeed, *a side to take*, presumably the one that is more stable, secure, and, to the mind of the side taker, much truer than its opposite, and that there is where one should put one's confidence and trust.

Finally, pointless talk shores up the conceit of the self, because it reinforces the idea that one is *defined* by one's opinion on some matter by on the side one takes:

> Whereas some ascetics and Brahmins remain addicted to disputations such as: "You don't understand this doctrine and discipline?—I do!" "How could *you* understand this doctrine and discipline?" "Your way is all wrong—mine is right!" "I am consistent—you aren't!" "You said last what you should have said first, and you said first what you should have said last!"[46]

Everyday persons put stock in cultivating and advancing their identities; that is the nature of being an everyday person. The noble disciple surrenders the conceit that any given phenomenon speaks to the creation of any identity at all and so is able to take a pass on weighing in on matters of any kind:

> Having abandoned what is taken up, not clinging,
> one does not create a dependency even on knowledge.
> Not taking sides among those who are divided,
> one does not fall back on any view at all. . . .
>
> How could anyone here in the world categorize him,
> that brahmin who does not cling to any view?[47]

The noble disciples who successfully go against the stream in pursuing renunciation and solitude have taken their leave of all that stuff and nonsense because they know all too well how easy it is to get sucked into and become embroiled in it, and they will have no doubt seen just how poorly that always seems to play out as far as one's relationship to the world and to others goes.

---

46 Walshe, *Long Discourses*, 71.

47 Bodhi, *Suttanipāta*, 295–96.

None of this reduces the noble aspirant to utter silence, however, since there are topics of conversation that are wholly suitable and not at all pointless:

> There are, bhikkhus, ten topics of discussion. What ten? Talk on fewness of desires, on contentment, on solitude, on not being bound up with others, on arousing energy, on virtuous behavior, on concentration, on wisdom, on liberation, on knowledge and vision of liberation. These are the ten topics of discussion.[48]

They are appropriate discussion topics because they concern those things that the holy life has only ever been about to begin with. Even here, however, such talk is not for just anyone, and both the speaker and the hearer need to have *standing* with respect to these topics. From the side of the speaker, one is not wise to speak of things of which one is oneself ignorant. Only "when a bhikkhu possesses five qualities, [is it] fitting for his fellow monks to hold a discussion with him. What five? Here a bhikkhu is himself accomplished in virtuous behavior . . . in concentration . . . in wisdom . . . in liberation . . . [and] in the knowledge and vision of liberation."[49] As it is put in the *Suttanipāta*:

> Without having discerned the Dhamma,
> without attending to the meaning under the learned ones,
> not understanding it oneself, immersed in doubt,
> how can one get others to perceive it?[50]

From the side of the hearer, one is not wise who, as we saw above, was not in a fit state to listen receptively and with understanding to what was being taught. If patient endurance is the test for assessing the degree of one's loving-kindness, one's ability to keep one's mouth or ears shut appropriately and to keep the mind still in the face of such matters are good tests of whether one has overcome doubt.[51]

There is no rest from doubt until one's "uncertainty about the Master who teaches the way, about the way, and about the fruit of the way, is abandoned

48 Bodhi, *Numerical Discourses*, 1424.

49 Bodhi, *Numerical Discourses*, 694.

50 Bodhi, *Suttanipāta*, 208.

51 As we will see in chap. 9, taking a side and trying to get others to see it—even if it is related to practice—is also a manifestation of pride. As here with respect to indecision, taking a side reveals a lack of confidence in the emptiness of the self. None of this is ever a matter of *being in the right*.

through the actual experience of the distinction attained."[52] Even the faith that helped one start on the path can only go so far. In an interchange between the Buddha and Sāriputta, we hear that when the Buddha asked, "Sāriputta, do you have faith that the faculty of faith, when developed and cultivated, has the Deathless [i.e., nirvāṇa] . . . as its final goal?" Sāriputta replied: "Venerable sir, I do not go by faith in the Blessed One about this. . . . I am one, venerable sir, by whom this has been known, seen, understood, realized and contacted with wisdom. I am without perplexity or doubt about this."[53] The Buddha approved his answer. The Buddha also expressed approval of another bhikkhu, Revata the Doubter, when he, too, had overcome his doubt:

> At one time the Lord was staying near Sāvatthī in the Jeta Wood at Anāthapiṇḍika's monastery. On that occasion the Venerable Revata the Doubter was sitting cross-legged not far from the Lord, holding his body erect and reviewing his own purification by overcoming doubt.
>
> The Lord saw the Venerable Revata the Doubter sitting cross-legged not far away, holding his body erect and reviewing his own purification by overcoming doubt.
>
> Then, on realizing its significance, the Lord uttered on that occasion this inspired utterance:
>
> Whatever doubt as to here or beyond
> In one's own or another's experience,
> The meditators abandon all these,
> The ardent ones living the holy life.[54]

Purifying oneself of doubt is a necessary step on the way to the realization of the Noble Truths, but simply overcoming this nīvaraṇa is not, of itself, their realization.[55] For that, one will need to press on further.

The invincibility of a mind not assailed by indecision is one that—like Sāriputta's or Revata's—is no longer reliant on the teaching of others, nor casting about in the public sphere for some kind of information. Such a mind is also no longer looking for intellectual satisfaction, as if living the holy life

52 Buddhaghoṣa and Ñāṇamoli, *Path of Purification*, 178.
53 Bodhi, *Connected Discourses*, 1689–90.
54 Ireland, *Udāna and the Itivuttaka*, 70.
55 Ñāṇamoli and Bodhi, *Middle Length Discourses*, 242–43.

were contingent on answers to unanswerable questions, and which, in any case, do nothing to further one's progress along the path. Instead, such a mind is wholly committed to the task at hand, the unshakable deliverance of mind:

> Offered to us as the irreplaceable means of deliverance, the Dhamma does not seek mere intellectual assent, but commands a response that is bound to be fully religious. It addresses us at the bedrock of our being, and there it awakens the faith, devotion and commitment appropriate when the final goal of our existence is at stake.[56]

As Bhikkhu Bodhi continues, "Once we have decided that the Dhamma is to be our vehicle to spiritual freedom, we have to step on board: we must leave our hesitancy behind and enter the course of training which will lead us from faith to liberating vision."[57] That hesitancy has only ever proven to be troublesome and binding, and one will never be free of indecision as long as one reserves something akin to the *right to doubt*. Such is the arrogance of the self that it sees itself as the sole judge of all things, as if reality had to pass its standards for it to accede to the truth of the matter. Far from being a kind of healthy skepticism or a useful intellectual tool, it is its own form of dogmatism, since it tenaciously holds to what, for it, is an absolutely unassailable position: its own rightful place as judge, jury, and executioner in the contest of competing thoughts and views.

The Buddha likened freedom from doubt to the freedom a traveler might enjoy having come through a treacherous journey and now being within eyeshot of a safe haven:

> Just as a man, laden with goods and wealth, might go on a long journey through the desert where food was scarce and danger abounded, and after a time he would get through the desert and arrive safe and sound at the edge of a village, might think: "Before this I was in danger, now I am safe at the edge of a village," and he would rejoice and be glad about that.[58]

Wholehearted and unwavering confidence in the Buddha, Dharma, and Saṅgha is the edge of that safe village where liberation and release are ultimately to be found. One may not have found one's way to the village square just yet, but at least one is no longer wandering confused in the wasteland, not knowing which way to turn.

---

56 Bodhi, "Two Faces of the Dhamma," 42.
57 Bodhi, "Two Faces of the Dhamma," 42.
58 Walshe, *Long Discourses*, 102.

Evagrius, for his part, does not categorize doubt among the logismoi. He does, however, refer to it briefly in *On Thoughts* in conjunction with discernment:

> If an anchorite should wish to receive knowledge of discernment from the Lord, let him first work diligently at the commandments that are in his power, omitting nothing and thus at the time of prayer "let him ask" for knowledge "from God who gives to all generously and without reproaching, but let him ask without doubting," and without being cast about by the waves of disbelief, "and it will be given him" (James 1:5–6).[59]

As James continues, "for the doubter, being double-minded and unstable in every way, must not expect to receive anything from the Lord" (Jas 1:7–8). Discernment is a virtue; doubt is not. Discernment is a gift from God; being double-minded is the disease of the still recalcitrant, fearful self.

As with so much that Evagrius wrote in conjunction with the obstacles to pure prayer, there appears to be an autobiographical aspect to his description of the irreconcilability of doubt and discernment. In the Coptic *Life of Evagrius*, the biographer Palladius of Galatia relates that when Evagrius had made his way to Jerusalem from Constantinople,

> blessed Melania the Roman joyfully welcomed him. But once again the Devil hardened his heart as in the time of Pharaoh, and his heart doubted and became divided; and on account of his boiling youthfulness and his very learned speech, and because of his large and splendid wardrobe (he would change clothes *twice a day*), he fell into vain habits *and bodily pleasure.*[60]

Melania, sensing what it would take to cure Evagrius of his double-mindedness (not to mention his love of his well-curated wardrobe), ended up sending him to Egypt to throw himself unreservedly into the renunciant-contemplative life. As Evagrius would come to know, living a life of ascesis and prayer puts an end to double-mindedness, because through the various aspects of the practical-gnostic life one's proclivities to *think* about everything and anything are undercut by the direct confrontation with those things the mind can only *be directly aware of*, unmediated by concepts or representations of any kind.[61]

---

59 Evagrius, *On Thoughts* 26; Sinkewicz, 171.

60 Tim Vivian, trans., *Four Desert Fathers: Pambo, Evagrius, Macarius of Egypt, and Macarius of Alexandria. Coptic Texts Relating to the* Lausiac History *of Palladius* (Crestwood, NY: St. Vladimir's Seminary Press, 2004), 78.

61 See Martin Laird, "The 'Open Country Whose Name Is Prayer': Apophasis, Deconstruction, and Contemplative Practice," *Modern Theology* 21 (2005): 141–55.

CHAPTER NINE

Delusions of Spiritual Success: Vainglory and Pride

In his discussion of acedia, Evagrius makes the claim that "no other demon follows immediately after" it.[1] It might come as a surprise, then, that there are still two more logismoi to consider. But Evagrius's claim is a technical one. From gluttony to acedia, all the logismoi have some kind of connection to one's constitution, to one's circumstances, or to renunciant-contemplative practice itself. The cultivation of apatheia is instrumental in overcoming them, because apatheia helps still the appetitive and irascible soul, and all of them connect in one way or another to the soul that is not wholly centered on God. But the "peace and ineffable joy [that] ensues in the soul"[2] after the struggle with acedia can, if one is not attentive, provide the occasion for still more obstructive thoughts to arise, thoughts tied neither to circumstantial nor to psychophysical conditions—the demons of vainglory and pride. Here there is no *causal* connection between the preceding logismoi and the onset of these two, since these arise "after the defeat of the remaining thoughts."[3] And while there may be nothing left of those other thoughts or their object domains for these two to feed on, that does not hinder vainglory and pride in the least. In fact, it only strengthens their hold.

Although they have no particular phenomenal material to work with, vainglory and pride still have a ground like all the other logismoi: the one

1 Evagrius, *Praktikos* 12; Sinkewicz, 99.
2 Evagrius, *Praktikos* 12; Sinkewicz, 99.
3 Evagrius, *Reflections* 57; Sinkewicz, 216.

thought that remains when the conditions for all other thoughts have been taken away—the root thought, the thought of the self. To be sure, the others had the conceit of the self attending them, too, but, unlike those others, vainglory and pride have *only* to do with the self—the estimation of myself as I see it reflected in the eyes of others around me, and the estimation I hold of myself even in my deepest solitude. Acedia may have been the most difficult of the logismoi to overcome, but vainglory and pride are the most sweeping, since there is nothing at all in the phenomenal world that can constrain them:

> Pride has no matter in that it is focused upon *nothing*, an empty ego that takes itself falsely to be *everything*. Vainglory, into which pride is reflected by contrast, is object-dependent in that it feeds upon "empty opinion" and swells in its attempt to devour *everything*, viz., a world of material adulation.[4]

In their free-ranging omnivorousness, vainglory and pride threaten to swallow up everything the renunciant-contemplative will have endured so much to attain and more besides.[5]

While vainglory and pride are not singled out for inclusion among the nīvaraṇas, we find them both following closely on the heels of the five in the commentarial literature. After reviewing the hindrances one by one, from sense desire through doubt, the *Suttanipāta* commentator adds by way of conclusion:

> Having dispelled that doubt, when they achieve some trifling distinction, conceit, denigration, and pride arise. Having dispelled these too, on account of some superior achievement of distinction, gain, honor, and praise arise. Infatuated with gain and so forth, teaching a counterfeit of the Dhamma, they achieve wrongly obtained fame. Established upon that, on account of their social class and so forth, they extol themselves and look down at others.[6]

For the practitioner of the Dharma, then, no less than for his or her Christian counterpart, the potential for vainglory and pride to stymie the attainment of stillness cannot be ignored but must be anticipated at every turn.

Evagrius addresses vainglory in two distinct contexts. The first pertains to the monk in the initial stages of his renunciant life. At issue here are the reasons

4 Corrigan, *Evagrius and Gregory*, 86–87.
5 See Evagrius, *On Thoughts* 14; Sinkewicz, 162.
6 Bodhi, *Suttanipāta*, 872–73.

why one is engaging in the practice in the first place: "Seek to scrutinize the suggested reasons for which you labour at ascesis," Evagrius counsels, "lest the goals of your attainments become corrupted through interior thoughts."[7] Like the soldier and the athlete, the renunciant who goes off into voluntary exile seeking God is often enough treated as some kind of hero, particularly if there is some measure of valued attainment connected with it. The soldier is awarded a medal for his courage, and the athlete receives a trophy for leading the pack in terms of her speed, agility, or talent. The religious adept likewise stands to receive fulsome praise, sycophantic worship, or other forms of adulation for attaining mystical visions, coming to some deep esoteric knowledge or insight, or maybe even just "acting like a good monk." The neophyte, seeing such praise from others as something worth striving for, runs the risk of taking those purported indicators of spiritual progress as guides for his own practice rather than the path to communion with God, which, as we have seen, does not admit of such potentially crowd-pleasing displays.

The second context deals with the monk who is in the subsequent stages of practice and has, in smaller or greater measure, overcome the preceding logismoi. In the case of the soldier or the athlete, both of whom are public persons, there is at least some clear, intersubjective measure of actual accomplishment—the number of enemies killed, perhaps, or being first across the finish line. The solitary renunciant-contemplative, by contrast, has long been hidden from the public eye, and his or her accomplishments (if one can even speak in such terms) are not the kind of thing one can simply point one's finger at. So if the monk has made any progress on this front, he might just be inclined to tell anyone who will listen about it in order to reap those anticipated rewards: "Whenever the anchorite's mind attains some small degree of impassibility, it then acquires the horse of vainglory and immediately rushes to the cities, getting its fill of the lavish praise accorded to its repute."[8] Even if one has not actually emerged from one's solitude, simply "fantasizing about social encounters"[9] is enough to give vainglory legs and thwart one's prayer.

Vainglory needs an audience, but it can only hold that audience as long as it has something to keep the crowd entertained. Because renunciant-contemplative practice leaves one with nothing much to show, vainglory

7 Evagrius, *Eulogios* 14; Sinkewicz, 40.

8 Evagrius, *On Thoughts* 15; Sinkewicz, 163.

9 Evagrius, *Vices* 7; Sinkewicz, 64.

prods the monk into a "pretense of industriousness"[10] in order to come up with something to put on display. This could take any number of forms, but the most ready-to-hand are those that involve speech:

> The thought of vainglory [compels] us to talk a lot about superfluous things—this excess becomes quickly apparent in monks who live in seclusion but who, due to vainglory, throw themselves into the affairs of the world and gladly welcome people who come to them to settle disputes they have with one another.[11]

The anchorite may restrict himself to the cell or the compound, but that does not stop him from effectively setting up shop there, welcoming all who come to call, and making a display of his purported wisdom and insight by weighing in on their affairs. Even if no one shows up, he, again in thought, can at least form some opinion or another about this or that on the basis of what he takes to be his superior wisdom, for vainglory "compel[s] the soul to speak in empty words, and that endeavor to entangle the intellect in transitory affairs, by which they set in motion in us either desire or anger."[12]

Just as pointless talk was a condition for indecision in the Dharma, speaking about such ephemeral matters gives the impression that one is somehow *credentialed* for having confronted and overcome (to some degree) the logismoi and attaining some impassability and stillness. Those supposed marks of success are then appealed to as the source of one's purported insight into just about anything else under the sun. Whatever else the renunciant-contemplative is, he or she is not at all what today we call a public theologian, one who, from a position of some attainment or understanding (whether actual or presumed matters little here), feels at liberty to comment on current events, matters of policy, social trends, or forms of cultural expression. If prayer is, as Evagrius maintains, a silent, unmediated, unobstructed communion with God, then the appellation *public theologian* can only be a contradiction in terms, since there is nothing at all public about communion with God or the still practice of prayer in which that communion takes place. If we add to this the fact that concern over the state of current affairs is but another form of "excessive concern" that only leads to sadness and from sadness easily enough to anger, we find yet another reason why it behooves the monk to steer clear of the temptation to weigh in on everyday goings-on.

10 Evagrius, *Vices* 7; Sinkewicz, 64.

11 Evagrius, *Antirrhetikos* 7.12; Brakke, 150.

12 Evagrius, *Antirrhetikos* 7.33; Brakke, 154.

One of the distinguishing characteristics of the first Christian monastics was not only that they were celibate and relatively isolated; they were also by and large not priests.[13] Exercising the office of the priesthood inevitably places one in the center of attention—presiding over the eucharistic liturgy, officiating at the dispensation of the other sacraments, taking over administration of a local church, becoming involved in the politics of the church at large, perhaps, and, of course, holding forth from the pulpit. If there were ever an opportunity for vainglory to get the audience it so desperately seeks, the ordained ministry would be a sure way to get it. The benefits of voluntary exile from the world of family and social life that had been so integral to setting out on and keeping at renunciant-contemplative practice could be undone unless one were to maintain a guarded distance from the ecclesiastical world as well. (None of this goes so far as to call the priesthood itself into question, and Evagrius recommended that "one should love priests next after the Lord, since they purify us through the holy mysteries and pray for us."[14] It simply calls the priesthood into question as a fitting occupation for one who would attain stillness.)

If its frequent mention during Evagrius's treatment of vainglory is any indication, the temptation to ordained ministry had to be fiercely combated by a renunciant-contemplative. It is a particularly wily aspect of this temptation that it often comes in the form of dreams.[15] In *Antirrhetikos*, Evagrius mentions this fact almost in passing: "While I was asleep at night, [the demon] made me the shepherd of a flock and, during the day, interpreted the dream for me saying, 'You will be a priest, and look, those who want you will soon come after you.'"[16] In *On Thoughts* he elaborates on this point, describing how the demon works:

> Generally speaking these are the sorts of dreams [vainglory] invent[s]. Frequently one sees oneself rebuking demons, healing certain bodily conditions, or wearing the clothing of a shepherd and pasturing a little flock. And immediately upon waking one gets a fantasy of the priesthood and then spends the entire day thinking through the things that involves.[17]

---

13 Regnault, *Day-to-Day Life of the Desert Fathers*, 162–71.

14 Evagrius, *Letter* 49.1; cited in Gabriel Bunge, *Spiritual Fatherhood: Evagrius Ponticus on the Role of the Spiritual Father*, trans. Luis Joshua Salés (Yonkers, NY: St. Vladimir's Seminary Press, 2016), 61.

15 For a detailed analysis of Evagrius's treatment of dreams, see Rubén Peretó Rivas, "Dreams in Evagrius Ponticus' Life and Teaching," *Vox Patrum* 37 (2017): 523–42.

16 Evagrius, *Antirrhetikos* 7.26; Brakke, 152–53.

17 Evagrius, *On Thoughts*; Sinkewicz, 173.

The undiscerning monk is wont to take such dreams as signs from God and imagine that, because his thoughts throughout the day have become so wrapped up in the idea of ministry, nothing short of a bona fide vocational "call" has taken place. That preoccupation, however, is a sure sign of the dream's demonic origin. "Angelic dreams are not like this," Evagrius points out, "but possess a great peace of soul, an ineffable joy, suppression of impassioned thoughts by day, [and] pure prayer . . . which slowly emerge under the Lord's influence and reveal the wisdom of the Lord."[18]

Following the promptings of vainglory with a view toward the priesthood could lead to falling back into the grips of the other logismoi as well. Vainglory has a ready ally in avarice, since in order to get the recognition I want, I might soon find myself using my available resources in order to get it. Simony, "the demon that advised us to acquire the priesthood through money,"[19] is an obvious case in point. But even if it does not come down to purchasing ordination outright, doing whatever one could to curry favor with the bishop with a view to ordination is to be avoided, too, and "the thought of vainglory that advises me to do something so that I might be honored with the priesthood"[20] is no less insidious simply because no money is involved. One who has attained to pure prayer has to keep guard, lest one think that one's attainments can function as credentials for addressing any matter, secular or religious. Renunciant-contemplative practice does not turn one into an expert on human affairs.

It is one of the common assumptions associated with religious practice that what has proven helpful for me should of course be helpful for others. However well-intended they may appear on the surface, attempts to make one's own practice known to others so that they, too, might enjoy its fruits often hide the subtle (or not-so-subtle) thought of one's own privileged position for being already in the know. An easy target for vainglory, then, is found in any thought the monk might have about touting the merits of renunciant-contemplative life to any and all who will listen. Vainglory, Evagrius writes, "advises us to go forth into the world at an improper time on the pretext that we might instruct the brothers and sisters and persuade them to [take up] the monastic life," and it stirs up "thoughts that compel us because of vainglory

---

18 Evagrius, *On Thoughts*; Sinkewicz, 173.

19 Evagrius, *Antirrhetikos* 7.36; Brakke, 155.

20 Evagrius, *Antirrhetikos* 7.40; Brakke, 156.

to make known our illustrious way of life."[21] Even if no words are spoken, thoughts that simply "entice us to go out into the world in order to benefit those who see us"[22]—as if just making sure they get a good look at a monk were doing them some kind of service—are also demonic ploys that play on the monk's vanity.

It is one thing to happen to be an example for others; it is another to *fancy oneself* an example for others. In practical terms, it is a sure recipe for disaster. Many are those who would presume to speak of the things of God and offer themselves as shining examples of the spiritual life, only to be brought low once the details of their lives become public knowledge. Whereas one might have compassion for the one who, in an open admission of weakness, still falls down, the other who, in the midst of trumpeting a presumed superior way of life, also falls down invites nothing but contempt.[23] It is hard enough to bear with someone still subject to sense desire, anger, and the rest; still more insufferable is the one who now parades her presumed spiritual *specialness* for all to see, even as her public display reveals in its very exercise the clearest mark of her lack of attainment.

Above all else, vainglory is an obstacle to an abiding communion with God. In addition to chasing after substitutes for God in human honor and praise, it also looks for any slight indicators of some kind of spiritual progress and presumes them to be signs from God, as if God were somehow rewarding my undertaking. I must be praying right, one given to vainglory might think, if God seems to afford me some glimpse of himself:

> When the mind finally achieves the practice of pure prayer free from the passions, then the demons no longer attack it on the left, but on the right. They suggest to it a notion of God along with some form associated with the senses so that it thinks that it has perfectly attained the goal of prayer. A man experienced in the gnostic life said that this happens under the influence of the passion of vainglory.[24]

---

21 Evagrius, *Antirrhetikos* 7.1, 7.20; Brakke, 147, 151.

22 Evagrius, *Antirrhetikos* 7.18; Brakke, 151.

23 Evagrius, *On Thoughts* 14; Sinkewicz, 162. Evagrius references Matt 12:45 ("Then it goes and brings along seven other spirits more evil than itself, and they enter and live there, and the last state of that person is worse than the first") and 2 Pet 2:20 ("For if, after they have escaped the defilements of the world through knowledge of the Lord and Savior Jesus Christ, they are again entangled in them and overpowered, the last state has become worse for them than the first").

24 Evagrius, *Prayer* 72; Sinkewicz, 200.

The problem with mystical visions is that they are still *states* and therefore are still a source of representations in the mind. And because God does not admit of representation, any purported vision of God is by its very nature *not* God.

Because "vainglory . . . attempts at circumscribing the divine in forms and figures,"[25] it is easy to see why Evagrius would label it the "author of heresies."[26] Thinking myself in possession of some special dispensation, I imagine myself to have a much deeper insight into the divine than those around me. As I must have attained something they clearly did not (otherwise they would have spoken about it in the same way I do), I make sure to spread the word. If there is a gathering of theologians, I will insinuate myself among them. If I have access to writing materials, I will send out descriptions of my newfound wisdom. So special am I that, should I find any who agree with me, I will take that as a sign of my deeper insight, but should I find others disagreeing with me, I will take that as further confirmation of my specialness, too, since they must assuredly be deluded. If there is one thing the heretic does *not* suffer from, it is self-doubt, and here we find the close connection between vainglory and pride. Pride is vainglory with an audience of one.

Pride can afflict anyone, no matter one's station in life or the nature of one's accomplishments. For one aspiring to communion with God, however, pride is particularly cunning precisely because it gets dressed up in religious language. At its root is "the thought of pride that said to me, 'I am the Lord's holy one.'"[27] Once I have entertained that thought, all constraints on the ego are cast aside, since I will think that *anything* I happen to think or do is blessed with God's favor. Such hubris, however, is the surest mark of the hold of this logismos:

> Pride is opposition to God, demonic fantasy, wicked jealousy, obscuring blindness, insolence in one's attitude, conceit of the flesh, false love of esteem, servitude to wicked thoughts, friendship with the demons, an eminent soul, an obvious siege by the adversary, an admonition to destruction.[28]

No other demon exercises quite the same stranglehold on the self. It was self-love that gave rise to the first of the logismoi, and it is self-love that continues to show itself here even after the other demons have been defeated.

---

25 Evagrius, *Prayer* 116; Sinkewicz, 206.

26 Evagrius, *Vices* 7; Sinkewicz, 64.

27 Evagrius, *Antirrhetikos* 8.1; Brakke, 159.

28 Evagrius, *Vices* 9; Sinkewicz, 65.

The chapters in *Antirrhetikos* each have a title indicating the particular logismos under consideration, but only the eighth, "Against the Cursed Thoughts of Pride," adds the adjective *cursed.* As a first counter to this thought, Evagrius reminds the reader of Genesis 3:14: "Cursed are you among all animals and among all wild creatures; upon your belly you shall go, and dust you shall eat all the days of your life." David Brakke suggests this rebuttal serves as a reminder to the monk that he is earth and ashes, as in *Eight Thoughts* 8.12 and *Exhortations* 1.6.[29] But perhaps it is not the monk that is being humbled here, but pride itself—accursed pride, the root logismos, the tempter *primus inter pares.* It is, after all, the serpent that God is addressing at that point in Genesis, and it is the serpent alone that is, in point of fact, cursed; Adam and Eve for their part are simply informed of the consequences they will have to face now that they have followed pride's bait. For them to be accursed would be to place them beyond salvation's pale.

The reminder of one's finitude, however, is well-taken. While the ascetic practices of the first renunciation appeared to lie within the monk's power to take up, much like the soldier and athlete for their part, Evagrius points out that even that first renunciation, no less than the renunciation of thoughts, was only ever the working of the Holy Spirit in conjunction with the monk's cooperation: "As for those who have received from grace the strength for ascetic labours, let them not think that they possess this from their own power, for the word of the commandments is for us the cause of all good things."[30] Evagrius proposed his own version of the "Kāli test" to determine just how far one has gone to eliminating the logismoi by one's own power:

> Whenever certain impure thoughts are chased away quickly, let us search out the cause. When has this occurred? Is it for want of the object, the matter being hard to acquire, or because of the impassibility present in us did the enemy have no strength against us? . . . It is necessary to know these things for the sake of our zeal and our strength, so that we may know if we have crossed the Jordan and are near the city of the palm trees or are still continuing in the desert and are being beaten upon by foreigners.[31]

The mere absence of one of the logismoi does not mean that it has been overcome. Even if it is due to the cultivation of apatheia on my part, I do well

29 Brakke, *Antirrhetikos*, 159n2. See Evagrius, *Eight Thoughts* 8.12; Sinkewicz, 87–88; and Evagrius, *Exhortations* 1.6; Sinkewicz, 218.

30 Evagrius, *Eulogios* 15; Sinkewicz, 41.

31 Evagrius, *On Thoughts* 20; Sinkewicz, 167.

to remember that even that would not have been possible without the first stirrings of compunction in me by the active presence of God. The work has always been mine to do, but it is only ever brought to fruition through the ongoing working of the Holy Spirit.

Although there is ample pride in thinking one has succeeded under one's own power, there is also pride involved in the thought that would turn one's attention in the other direction and deny that one has contributed in any way to one's current state. If God is in charge, I might think, then God is in charge even of my sinning. The theory of predestination and its kindred practice of quietism are both to be combated in conjunction with "the blasphemous thought that denied the free will that is in us and said that we sin and are justified not by our own will and therefore condemnation is not decreed justly."[32] Evagrius finds the scriptural response to this thought in Deuteronomy 30:19, where God calls heaven and earth as witnesses that he is setting before his people life *and* death, blessings *and* curses, and telling them to choose wisely. God simply sets the options on the table. That one would then choose death and curses over life and blessings is entirely a matter of one's own doing.

Pride is an obstacle to communion with God, but it is no less an obstacle to communion with one's companions in the renunciant-contemplative life. Filled with pride, one might think it one's job to point out the faults of others and to set oneself up as the moral watchdog of the assembly in light of "the proud thought that derides the brothers on the pretext, 'Look, they are neglecting the service of the commandments.'"[33] As with anger, the issue is not whether it would be *better* for those monks to act differently but whether it is *my job* to see to it that they do: "How can you say to your neighbor, 'Friend, let me take out the speck in your eye,' when you yourself do not see the log in your own eye? You hypocrite, first take the log out of your own eye, and then you will see clearly to take the speck out of your own eye" (Luke 6:42). Pride would have me believe that I have removed my log long before that is actually the case—if indeed I could ever be sure of such a thing in the first place.

Pride, again like anger, puts distance between myself and those around me. But whereas anger involves removing others around me, pride simply places them beneath my regard. "The proud thought that has prevented me from seeing the brothers on the pretext that they are no better than I am in

---

32 Evagrius, *Antirrhetikos* 8.16; Brakke, 162.

33 Evagrius, *Antirrhetikos* 8.31; Brakke, 166.

knowledge"[34] tells me that I have nothing to learn from my spiritual equals. "The thought of pride that advised us to scorn our holy fathers on the pretext that they have not labored in their way of life any more than we have"[35] tells me that they are no more deserving of respect than I am. "The thought of pride that glorifies me on the pretext that I edify souls with a stable way of life and knowledge of God"[36] lets me know that it is others who should be coming to me to learn from my ways and to listen to my wisdom and superior insight. Pride would have me believe that I have spiritually *arrived*.

Vainglory and pride are the last two logismoi that Evagrius enumerates, but they have been present at every stage of the process of coming to stillness. They may have sought support in the conditions of the world through food, sex, money, freedom from harm, and the demands that the world be otherwise and that the renunciant life be stimulating. All the same, it was only ever the maintenance of the self and its primacy over everything else that was ever at stake. Cultivating abstinence, gentleness, joy, gratitude, and perseverance may have disabused one of looking for something to bolster the self in those other conditions, but nothing cuts to the root of self-love like humility; it is the antidote to both vainglory and pride:

> Freedom from vainglory is the working of humility, a defection from obsequiousness, blindness to praises, contemplation of knowledge, a counter to the world, keen perception of the soul, a teacher of lowliness, a hiding place for ascetic works, hostility to fame, a hidden treasure in a corruptible body.[37]

As concerns pride,

> humility is a thankful acknowledgement of God, a true recognition of one's nature, a forceful confession of one's weakness, a fortress for love, a refuge from hatred, an unfallen acropolis, a parting of the diabolic waves, light over the snares of the enemy, the natural overthrowing of Satan, a pleasing life, praise of enemies, a philosophy provided by God, and true friendship with wisdom.[38]

Humility captures all that abstinence and the rest were able to do and more besides.

---

34 Evagrius, *Antirrhetikos* 8.33; Brakke 166.
35 Evagrius, *Antirrhetikos* 8.8; Brakke, 160.
36 Evagrius, *Antirrhetikos* 8.30; Brakke, 166.
37 Evagrius, *Vices* 7; Sinkewicz, 64–65.
38 Evagrius, *Vices* 9; Sinkewicz, 65.

As Burton-Christie points out, "humility, a quality valued so strongly by the early monks, is nothing more or less than a reduction of the concerns and claims of the self, a continual and ever deepening movement of self-emptying that the monks understood to be an extension of Christ's great gesture of *kenosis*."[39] Just as Christ "did not regard equality with God as something to be exploited, but emptied himself" (Phil 2:6–7), so too the monk who empties himself in humility is freed of the delusion of a presumed favor with God. In this respect, Evagrius's claim that "the beginning of salvation is condemnation of yourself"[40] takes on a twofold meaning. The beginning of salvation for all is the self-emptying of Christ; the beginning of my participation in Christ's saving activity is my own self-emptying in humility, the "same mind . . . that was in Christ Jesus" (Phil 2:3, 5).

As at the start of the engagement with the logismoi, so too here at the end: silence and solitude are the test of one's humility. "Set the seal of silence on the spices of your ascetic labors, lest unfastened by your tongue they be stolen by esteem," Evagrius writes,[41] and the surest way to keep that silence is to remain hidden from view: "The prudent person hides a treasure, and the sensible monk the labours of virtue."[42] The cell, which up to this point had provided a kind of firewall between the monk and any unnecessary distractions, now functions as a bulwark for keeping the world free from the displays of the monk's pride and for keeping the monk out of everyone else's business. It also serves as a constant reinforcer of the monk's place as the lowest of all. Hidden from public view, one cuts off any possibility of self-aggrandizement through the praise of others: "Here we must pay careful attention, lest . . . we be seen by people. Since we already have our reward in full, yet another more terrible shipwreck will follow, when the demon of vainglory has blown a contrary wind."[43] Retiring to the cell, the monk fulfills Christ's command, "Beware of practicing your righteousness before others in order to be seen by them, for then you have no reward from your father in heaven" (Matt 6:1). This is particularly important in terms of the monk's prayer life: "Vainglory advises you to pray in the streets, but he who wars against it prays in his chamber."[44] Since prayer is only ever

39 Burton-Christie, "Simplicity," 355.
40 Evagrius, *Maxims* 1.1; Sinkewicz, 229.
41 Evagrius, *Eulogios* 14; Sinkewicz, 41.
42 Evagrius, *Eight Thoughts* 7.10; Sinkewicz, 85.
43 Evagrius, *On Thoughts* 3; Sinkewicz, 155.
44 Evagrius, *Eight Thoughts* 7.12; Sinkewicz, 86.

a "communion of the mind with God,"[45] its proper place is in the silence and solitude of the cell, again consistent with Gospel command: "But whenever you pray, go to your room and shut the door and pray to your Father who is in secret." The rewards of the contemplative life are not given by others; they are given only by God, the one who "sees in secret" (Matt 6:6).

Living and dying unknown and unacknowledged is, for most, one of the most dreaded forms of life. Many put a good deal of effort into ensuring that they leave a legacy of some kind, an ongoing recognition of their uniqueness and efficacy and impact. They try to be known while alive and hope to be remembered when dead. Because making a name for oneself is the very definition of worldly success, entering into silence and solitude is a kind of social death. But, for the monk, that is precisely the point of the exercise—to become untraceable. As John Chryssavgis notes, "the way of the desert elders is that of humility in the *disappearance* or flight to the desert; it is the way of action in the transforming silence and power of prayer."[46] Just as Christ's self-emptying is inseparable from his resurrection, the monk's self-emptying is his birth into the eternal life of God.

The bhikkhu was no less subject to vainglory than the Evagrian monk, and while vainglory is not counted among the nīvaraṇas, safeguards against its possible manifestations were already set down in the training rules. The disciples were to speak of the Dharma only when first asked by someone who showed signs of asking in all sincerity, and even then they were not to speak on matters of practice beyond their respective levels of attainment, nor were they simply to repeat verbatim what they had heard. So strict was the rule against misrepresenting one's attainment—"deliberately lying to another person that one has attained a superior human state"[47]—that it was grounds for immediate expulsion from the saṅgha of the ordained. In addition to shielding the homeleaver from a bhikkhu's displays of accomplishment, such a prohibition also served to strengthen the hearer's confidence in the Dharma, since he or she would know that what was being said was not mere bluster or the stuff

45 Evagrius, *Prayer* 3; Sinkewicz, 193.

46 John Chryssavgis, "Fire and Light in the Egyptian Desert: Aspects of Desert Spirituality," *Cistercian Studies Quarterly* 34 (1999): 456.

47 Bhikkhu Thanissaro, trans., *The Buddhist Monastic Code: The Patimokkha Training Rules* (Valley Center, CA: Metta Forest Monastery, n.d.), 86; cited in Bhikkhu Ariyesako, *The Bhikkhus' Rules: A Guide for Laypeople. The Theravadin Buddhist Monk's Rules* (Kallista, Australia: Sanghāloka Forest Hermitage, 1998), 108.

of deception. Moreover, the disciples were not to prognosticate on things to come or act as matchmakers, nor were they to insinuate themselves in the domestic affairs of everyday people lest they cause scandal.

Of course, no amount of regulation can keep one from thoughts of pride and exercises of vanity when all is said and done. Extolling oneself and looking down on or disparaging others, as it is put in the *Suttanipāta* and elsewhere, is such a perennial obstacle that resolving not to engage in it is the seventh of the Ten Bodhisattva Precepts in the Mahāyāna. Like any of the precepts, it is fully kept only when the conceit of the self underlying their violation has been abandoned. Without a self-concept to rely on, what could possibly serve as a point of differentiation between self and other? Until that point, however, the point of differentiation that most commends itself is the character of one's practice by comparison with the practice of others. Do I spend more time in meditation than they? Do I keep the precepts better? Have I attained some degree of concentration, stillness, and insight that they have not?

The Buddha used such concern with the practice of others as a way to distinguish an untrue person (*asappurisadhamma*) from a true person (*sappurisadhamma*). In the *Sappurisa Sutra*, he lists all the stages in the gradual training from homeleaving to the attainment of the supramundane levels of insight, along with whatever special ascetic practices one might engage in and whatever material gains (renown, food and clothing, and the like) might happen to follow from them. With the attainment of any of them, he points out, the untrue person will entertain the following thought: "I have attained (or received) thus and so, but these other bhikkhus have not." In this way, that person praises him- or herself and disparages others.[48]

The true person, however, does not engage in such comparative exercises. The true person knows that, as far as the mundane attainments go, it is simply a matter of "putting the practice of the way first"[49] and letting things take their course. There is no *status* to be gained by following the precepts and the training rules. Not taking what is not given, for instance, does not turn me into a saint, and developing dispassion and equanimity does not make me a spiritual hero. These are just what happens in conjunction with wholehearted engagement in practice in light of the Dharma.[50] As far as the

48 Ñāṇamoli and Bodhi, *Middle Length Discourses*, 909.

49 Ñāṇamoli and Bodhi, *Middle Length Discourses*, 909.

50 Recall that the Buddha pointed out that anyone who would praise him for being morally upright was only focusing on "inferior matters" (Walshe, *Long Discourses*, 68–73).

meditative states go, such a true person knows that it is a matter of "putting non-identification first," as the Buddha describes it. However one happens to think or feel about these states, in terms of attainment and the like, "the fact is ever other than that."[51] In other words, even advanced meditative states are themselves still conditioned dharmas that do not speak to the true nature of things. As long as I am noting and assessing my meditative accomplishments, no matter how lofty or supramundane, there is still a trace of the self—enough of a self to be doing the assessing. In the very end, the Buddha continues, the aspirant whose attachments to dharmas have been thoroughly destroyed with insight "does not conceive anything, he does not conceive in regard to anything, he does not conceive in any way."[52] No thought of attainment or nonattainment, no conception of better and worse even enters his mind, and certainly no comparison of his own attainment with the attainment or nonattainment of others. Whether in relation to everyday matters or to the finer points of the Dharma, it is enough to know for oneself; one need not be known as "one who knows" on top of it:

> When it was said: "This Dhamma is for one with few desires, not for one with strong desires," with reference to what was this said? Here, when a bhikkhu is one with few desires, he does not desire: "Let people know me to be one with few desires." When he is content, he does not desire: "Let people know me to be one who is content." When he resorts to solitude, he does not desire: "Let people know me to be one who resorts to solitude."[53]

Living the holy life is not at all contingent on whether anyone happens to know I am living it.

Recall that in the process of investigation by which one overcomes indecision in the Buddha, an individual was invited to ask: When the Buddha acquired fame and renown, did he manifest any of the "dangers" connected with these?[54] In the *Nāgita Sutra*, we hear both about the extent of those dangers and how diligent the Buddha was in steering clear of them. It seems the Buddha and a retinue of bhikkhus had stopped to stay in a wooded area near the brahmin village of Icchānaṅgala. Having heard reports of his spiritual accomplishments and eager for a chance to see the Blessed One for themselves, the Icchānaṅgalans gathered up a bunch of fine food and made

51 Ñāṇamoli and Bodhi, *Middle Length Discourses*, 911.

52 Ñāṇamoli and Bodhi, *Middle Length Discourses*, 912.

53 Bodhi, *Numerical Discourses*, 1163.

54 Above, p. XX.

their way toward to the encampment, where they stirred up quite a ruckus to let the Buddha know of their arrival. The Buddha asked one of the bhikkhus, Nāgita, what all the commotion was about: "Who is making such an uproar and a racket, Nāgita? One would think it was fishermen at a haul of fish." Nāgita explained that it was the villagers come to make their offerings, to which the Buddha replied:

> Let me never come upon fame, Nāgita, and may fame never catch up with me. One who does not gain at will, without trouble or difficulty, this bliss of renunciation, bliss of solitude, bliss of peace, bliss of enlightenment that I gain at will, without trouble or difficulty, might accept that vile pleasure, that slothful pleasure, the pleasure of gain, honor, and praise.

Nāgita tried to get the Buddha to consent to their offerings, pointing out that wherever he went he was sure to come upon such admiration and praise due to his wisdom and virtue, just as surely as water flows down a hillside after the rain. But the Buddha simply repeated what he had just said and went further:

> Nāgita, what is eaten, drunk, consumed, and tasted winds up as feces and urine: this is its outcome. From the change and alteration of things that are dear arise sorrow, lamentation, pain, dejection, and anguish: this is its outcome. For one devoted to practicing meditation on the mark of unattractiveness, revulsion toward the mark of the beautiful becomes established: this is its outcome. For one who dwells contemplating impermanence in the six bases for contact, revulsion toward contact becomes established: this is its outcome. For one who dwells contemplating arising and vanishing in the five aggregates subject to clinging, revulsion toward clinging becomes established: this is its outcome.[55]

The outcome of living the holy life is simply the holy life, as Sāriputta had reminded Mahākoṭṭhita. Anything else that others might try to pin on it is wholly beside the point.

With realization, this business that I call "me" neither disappears nor goes elsewhere; it simply leaves no traces or signs by which it might be detected. "The signless liberations," Peter Harvey notes, "not only

55 Bodhi, *Numerical Discourses*, 652–53. Bodhi notes that the commentaries say that these five are five ways of discussing insight (vipassanā) (*Numerical Discourses*, 1725n999). In another version of this interchange, the Buddha uses the occasion to discuss the disadvantages of living in the vicinity of a village and the advantages of living in the forest in terms of the temptations the bhikkhu living near the village will face that will prove detrimental to his practice, temptations that do not beset the forest-dwelling monk (*Numerical Discourses*, 905–7).

undermine ignorance, but also conceit, for they dissolve away any apparently solid basis for I-ness into an insignificant, ephemeral flux . . . which offers no 'signs' as a basis for I-ness."[56] So, when we read concerning the mind of one who has come to signlessness that it "inclines to seclusion, leans to seclusion, tends to seclusion,"[57] this is not a deliberate sequestering or hiding. That, too, would involve a reintroduction of signs—"I am here, far away from the others who are over there." Instead, the person just bumbles along with everything and everyone else. The Buddha himself wandered abroad, sent his disciples into the towns to beg their food, and allowed them to teach the Dharma to others, but they did so tracelessly, signlessly, anonymously. One who has penetrated the signless simply finds no indicator of specialness by which to mark any of those activities as an indication of superiority or honor.

Are there differences between people? Of course there are, but these are of no more significance than saying, "This is an elm; this is a birch," or "The flame is hot; the ice is cold." Difference can be noted without introducing *measure* or *rank* of any kind. In the same way, a bhikkhu is not a cobbler, and one can say as much without implicitly or explicitly elevating the one and denigrating the other. Even the highest level of development in the Dharma, the cessation of tṛṣṇā in nirvāṇa, does not mark one out as a *better person*.[58] When one of the disciples, Cunda, asked about the final liberation or effacement, the Buddha told him:

> Now, Cunda, here effacement should be practiced by you:
>
> "Others will be cruel; we shall not be cruel here": effacement should be practiced thus.
>
> "Others will kill living beings; we shall abstain from killing living beings here": effacement should be practiced thus.
>
> "Others will take what is not given; we shall abstain from taking what is not given here": effacement should be practiced thus. . . .
>
> "Others will be shameless; we shall be shameful here": effacement should be practiced thus.

56 Peter Harvey, "'Signless' Meditation in Pāli Buddhism," *The Journal of the International Association of Buddhist Studies* 9 (1986): 48.

57 Ñāṇamoli and Bodhi, *Middle Length Discourses*, 400.

58 We saw hints of this already in the discussion the Buddha had with Khema and Sumana about measuring oneself with respect to others.

> "Others will have no fear of wrongdoing; we shall be afraid of wrongdoing here": effacement should be practiced thus. . . .
>
> "Others will lack wisdom; we shall possess wisdom here": effacement should be practiced thus.
>
> "Others will adhere to their own views, hold on to them tenaciously, and relinquish them with difficulty; we shall not adhere to our own views or hold on to them tenaciously, but shall relinquish them easily": effacement should be practiced thus.[59]

The content of the full passage (the Buddha lists forty-four such observations) is simply a compendium of the main aspects of practice—the courses of wholesome action, the factors of the Eightfold Path, the five hindrances, the sixteen imperfections, the factors of enlightenment, and the like. Some follow them; some do not. Even here, there is just the seen in the seen and the heard in the heard, and nothing more.

It is one very important aspect of practice not to engage in unwholesome and unskillful actions oneself. The very first steps of the training sequence involved the aspirant submitting to the precepts or the monastic rules, and subsequent steps were aimed at uprooting the attachment and aversion that give rise to all possible unskillful actions and states of mind. But effacement, the definitive overcoming of all self-conceit, is particularly manifested in an utter lack of preoccupation with whether others engage in such actions and practices or not. I am not others. Their behavior is not me. None of that is my self. At the end of the sutra, the Buddha tells Cunda:

> What should be done for his disciples out of compassion by a teacher who seeks their welfare and has compassion for them, that I have done for you, Cunda. There are these roots of trees, these empty huts. Meditate, Cunda, do not delay or else you will regret it later. This is our instruction to you.[60]

"Just live the holy life yourself, Cunda," the Buddha might have said, "and that is enough."

In identifying vainglory and pride as obstructions to prayer and the development of meditative stillness, Evagrius and the Buddha effectively call into question any attempt to assess renunciant-contemplative practice in terms of

---

59 Ñāṇamoli and Bodhi, *Middle Length Discourses*, 125–27.
60 Ñāṇamoli and Bodhi, *Middle Length Discourses*, 131.

its *usefulness*—whether to one's place in the world, to the broader religious community, or to society generally. Such practice is often accused of being out of touch with society, leading some of those who do see value in such a life to counter by trying to demonstrate that the renunciant-contemplative life is, all appearances to the contrary, actually quite useful. Historian of Christian mysticism Bernard McGinn viewed contemplative practice in such terms:

> The [monastic] was committed to the pursuit of contemplative wisdom, and many monks and nuns also were happy to share this wisdom with others through teaching and writing. The monastic prophet felt the call to present God's message to the broader church and world in times of crisis, be it those of the fourth century, or the twelfth, or even the twentieth. In the history of Christianity monasticism has functioned, at least in part, to provide a context in which some humans strive to attain a marginality that enables them both to be free *of* the world and also free *for* the world.[61]

But *monastic prophet*, if we follow Evagrius, is no less a contradiction in terms than *public theologian*. Yes, some of the elder monastics shared with interested and sincere disciples a word or two that might be helpful to them, and some of them served as a focal point for the establishment of a community of renunciants around them. But it is one thing for one more advanced in the renunciant-contemplative life to offer encouragement and correction to a fellow traveler on the path, and it is quite another to broadcast such encouragement and correction to a wider audience of otherwise disinterested persons. God may well be the sower who scatters seed hither and yon, but the monk is not God. The monk is simply one of those seeds fallen on good soil, one who "hears the word and understands it" (Matt 13:23), and who, in all humility, cultivates that understanding as far as humanly possible, leaving the other seeds to fare as they will.

Rita Gross, writing from within the Buddhist tradition, sought to identify a prophetic dimension in the practice of the Dharma in imitation of her Christian counterparts. In her view, "we have responsibilities to use our knowledge to address problems, rather than to leave troubling issues of social and environmental justice to those less knowledgeable, with less respect and good will for diverse and alternative world views."[62] One cannot fail to detect

61 Bernard McGinn, "Withdrawal and Return: Reflections on Monastic Retreat from the World," *Spiritus: A Journal of Christian Spirituality* 6 (2006): 167.

62 Rita Gross, "Buddhist Theology?," in *Buddhist Theology: Critical Reflections from Contemporary Buddhist Scholars*, ed. Roger R. Jackson and John J. Makransky (Surrey, UK: Curzon, 2000), 55–56.

an element of "praising oneself and disparaging others" in such a statement (at least McGinn was talking about others, not himself). Even with that aside, such a view can be held only by overlooking the Buddha's reminder not to concern oneself with the practice of others, a marked lack of concern that even he, for his part, practiced in full measure:

> The Tathāgata has no concern whether the entire world will be emancipated, or half the world, or a third of the world. But he can be sure that all those who have been emancipated, or who are being emancipated, or who will be emancipated from the world first abandon the five hindrances, corruptions of the mind that weaken wisdom, and then, with their minds well established in the four establishments of mindfulness, develop correctly the seven factors of enlightenment. In this way they have been emancipated or are being emancipated or will be emancipated from the world.[63]

It is one of the signs of the "well-taught" Dharma that it is *not* taught with a view to maximizing its reach, saving as many as possible, or fixing this troubled world, but simply to be a refuge for those who happen to seek it out.

It may well be the case that everyday persons might feel some need to press the monastic into service to church, saṅgha, or society. Everyday people, much like Nāgita above, tend to think in such terms. What they do not realize is that it is not the responsibility of the renunciant-contemplative to make others act one way or another, so enlisting them as agents in socially transformative enterprises is misguided from the start. For the everyday Christian generally no less than for the monk, "the word of the commandments is for us the cause of all good things"[64] and not the actions of others. Similarly, the noble disciple of the Buddha recognizes that "it is not the worthy ones that make us act; it is the Dhamma that makes us act."[65] Part of what humility entails is that I do not fancy myself to be in a position of some kind of *service* as a result of my practice, whether that service is offered to some particular individual, to my immediate congregation, or to society as a whole.

It is quite easy not to involve oneself in the affairs of the world; misanthropes of all kinds do this day in and day out. But it is not at all easy to keep one's distance from the affairs of the world when one sees the ills of the world quite clearly but at the same time knows that one is not in a position to fix them. Here, no less than in conjunction with the obstacles of anger and ill will,

---

63 Bodhi, *Numerical Discourses*, 1471.

64 Evagrius, *Eulogios* 15; Sinkewicz, 41.

65 Ñāṇamoli and Bodhi, *Middle Length Discourses*, 882.

patient forbearance and the disposition toward joy and thanksgiving in all things is the order of the day. In the end, individuals must do whatever work needs to be done for themselves, and no amount of assistance can substitute for that. Making as if one *could* do something about it all the same, as one subject to vainglory and pride might think, only bolsters oneself by fueling others' expectations that someone else could or should do the work that is only theirs to do. One who has confronted the logismoi and the nīvaraṇas will have had firsthand knowledge of what it means to do this work for oneself; to then turn around and suggest that one can do for others what they will not do for themselves is tantamount to forgetting much of what has been learned in the process through one's own indispensable effort and endurance.

To the question as to what a renunciant-contemplative who has overcome the obstacles *does* do, the short answer would be: exactly what he or she has been doing all along—living the life of ascesis and prayer or meditation in all humility and anonymity. Now, however, that life is not experienced as an arduous means to an end, as it might have seemed at the outset; instead, it is simply a life lived more and more as a straightforward expression of what one has been seeking all along, communion with God or the unshakable deliverance of mind. The noble disciple no more needs notice or praise from others for living this way than one needs applause for chewing one's food or for having drawn one's own finger from a flame. And just as in the case of eating one's dinner or keeping clear of the burner on the stove, so too with living this life—no talk of self ever need arise in conjunction with such a plain presentation of the truth of things just as they are.

Conclusion

Renunciant-contemplative practice is the journey home, but overcoming the obstacles is still not the end of the prodigal's journey—not by a long shot. Much has been undertaken, of course, but so much more remains to be done. For the noble disciple of the Buddha, the ability to abide in the stillness of jhāna with the overcoming of the nīvaraṇas is marked by the advent of rather pleasant mind states—"rapture and pleasure born of seclusion" with the first state, "rapture and pleasure born of concentration" with the second, "pleasure divested of rapture" with the third, and finally "pure bright mind" with the fourth.[1] But, as rapturous, pleasurable, and refined as these states are, they are not yet the final liberation; the Buddha simply called them "pleasant abidings here and now"[2] because they are still conditioned states, still subject to waxing and waning, and still attended with thought. Next come the supramundane awarenesses—the awareness of the infinity of space and the infinity of consciousness, the base of nothingness, and the base of neither-perception-nor-nonperception—that build on these pleasant abidings, but even these are not the end. The Buddha called these four "peaceful abidings,"[3] again quite tranquil but still subject to rising and falling and, however faintly, still tied up with an idea of the self. These, too, will need to be abandoned, for the final liberation in nirvāṇa lies beyond them still.

For the Evagrian renunciant-contemplative, overcoming the logismoi marks the end of the first and second renunciations, but there is still the third, the separation from ignorance in gnōsis and, with God's ever-present aid, theōsis. This is the full entry into "the kingdom of God [which is] knowledge of the Holy Trinity co-extensive with the substance of the mind and surpassing

1 Ñāṇamoli and Bodhi, *Middle Length Discourses*, 367–69.
2 Ñāṇamoli and Bodhi, *Middle Length Discourses*, 123.
3 Ñāṇamoli and Bodhi, *Middle Length Discourses*, 124–25.

its incorruptibility."[4] One who has attained apatheia and hesychia still has not come to the fullness of the kingdom of God, the "immaterial knowledge, that is, as one might say, the contemplation of the naked Godhead itself";[5] for that, one needs to surrender the self and any of its lingering representations even further. Even though these mental representations no longer have their root in bodily or affective states but only in the mind, they still stand between oneself and the fullest possible participation in the life of God.

The noble practitioner in either tradition is not daunted by any of this. From the very first stirrings of hiri-ottappa or compunction, through the confrontation with the obstacles, and on to the attainment of stillness, one will have encountered firsthand that paradoxical mix of joy and sorrow in the unvarnished acknowledgment of one's delusions. And this is why the logismoi and the nīvaraṇas commend themselves so compellingly for consideration. Confronting delusion is already a form of wisdom; simply prating on about realization, salvation, and the like without recognizing in oneself those things that obstruct them is nothing but delusion decked out in fancy language. It is perhaps for this reason that Dōgen said, "Those who have great realization of delusion are buddhas; those who are greatly deluded about realization are sentient beings."[6] More recently Ajahn Thiradhammo observed, "The result of working with the Hindrances is not simply getting rid of them, but rather the careful and detailed study of them, in order to arrive at the subtle wisdom of knowing how they support self-identification."[7] In coming to know the obstacles for the delusions they are and mustering the wherewithal to overcome them, one can already taste something of freedom that lies at the end of the path even now.

As one will have long surmised, renunciant-contemplative practice is not for everyone. While no one is preemptively excluded from entering into it, few indeed are those who will find within themselves the dedication, resolve, and perseverance to abide in it. If the early training sequences, designed as they are to bridle one's everyday untempered "wildness," are not enough to disincline one to practice at the outset, the nīvaraṇas and the logismoi are certainly powerful enough to thwart all but the most steadfast. This is wholly expected, and both traditions are not at all hesitant to differentiate those who

---

4 Evagrius, *Praktikos* 3; Sinkewicz, 97.

5 Evagrius, *Letter on Faith* 8.7.22–24; cited in Sinkewicz, 249n13.

6 Dōgen, *Moon in a Dewdrop*, 69.

7 Thiradhammo, *Working with the Five Hindrances*, 59.

abandon the journey home from those who keep at it—there are goats and there are sheep, as it is put in the Gospel (Matt 25:31–33); there are donkeys and there are cows, as it is put in the *Nikāyas.*[8] Meditation or contemplative prayer taken up in isolation from a trenchant reassessment and decisive reorientation of one's whole life is not the kind of practice that accords with the Dharma, nor is it one that much accords with the gospel, either.

For some, this will stand as condemnation enough of the renunciant-contemplative life. If the road is not wide and the journey easy, some might think, then too many will be left behind. But this is to fail to understand the nature of renunciant-contemplative life on its own terms. The Buddha was well aware that there would be those who would take up the holy life and still would not attain liberation, and when pressed to account for why that should be the case, he replied:

> Nibbāna exists and the path leading to Nibbāna exists and I am present as the guide. Yet when my disciples have been thus advised and instructed by me, some of them attain Nibbāna, the ultimate goal, and some do not attain it. What can I do about that, brahmin? The Tathāgata is one who shows the way.[9]

In the Christian tradition, many are indeed called, but only few will follow their Lord in his passion to the fullness of life. When asked whether only a few would be saved, Jesus answered the question by posing a challenge to the inquirer:

> Strive to enter through the narrow door; for many, I tell you, will try to enter and not be able. When once the owner of the house has got up and shut the door, and you begin to stand outside and to knock at the door, saying, "Lord, open to us," then in reply he will say to you, "I do not know where you came from." (Luke 13:24–25)

Neither the Buddha nor Evagrius felt the need to defend—much less apologize for—the renunciant-contemplative life. Follow it or not, each might well say, but if you persist in your delusions, do not complain that you do not share in the liberation enjoyed by those who have overcome them.

As I intimated at the outset, I would hope that this exploration of the obstacles can further a certain kind of Buddhist-Christian encounter. Although I have not hesitated to present the material in such a way that parallels between the

8 Bodhi, *Numerical Discourses*, 315.

9 Ñāṇamoli and Bodhi, *Middle Length Discourses*, 878.

two traditions with respect to the obstacles might readily be seen, I have been careful to avoid any attempt to equate them or to somehow split the difference between them. I leave it to the reader to assess how skillful I have been in that regard. In any case, none of this was ever intended as support for any kind of recommendation that the Buddhist be a Christian or the Christian be a Buddhist, or even some kind of hybrid of the two (whatever that could possibly mean). Renunciant-contemplative practice is best viewed as a *human* practice, not a *Christian* or *Buddhist* one, at least not in the narrow sectarian sense in which those terms are so often used. No matter whether one understands them as logismoi or as nīvaraṇas, the obstacles stand in the way of *anyone* who would devote themselves to the attainment of stillness and all that follows from it. All who confront and work to overcome them are *already* brothers and sisters in a shared endeavor.

Because both the Christian and the Buddhist renunciant-contemplative attest, through their concerted practice, to a truth that is liberating for anyone who cares to pursue it, there is no need to shy away from the various expressions of that truth, no matter their source. Paul, for one, recommends such an openness: "Finally, beloved, whatever is true, whatever is honorable, whatever is just, whatever is pure, whatever is pleasing, whatever is commendable, if there is any excellence and if there is anything worth of praise, think about these things" (Phil 4:8). So, too, does the Buddha:

> Those things of which you might know: "These things lead to dispassion, not passion; to detachment, not to bondage; to dismantling, not to building up; to fewness of desires, not to strong desires; to contentment, not to non-contentment; to solitude, not to company; to the arousing of energy, not to laziness; to being easy to support, not to being difficult to support," you should definitely recognize: "This is the Dhamma; this is the discipline; this is the teaching of the Teacher."[10]

The teaching on the obstacles is one of those excellent and worthy things, one that leads to dispassion and the rousing of energy. Columba Stewart saw it as a distinctively Christian quality of Evagrius's teaching on dispassion that apatheia "was not selfish. It meant the opening of the self to others and to God, the unclenching of the hand grasping what it desires or fending off those who are a threat."[11] As we have seen, that opening of the self and that

10 Bodhi, *Numerical Discourses*, 1193.

11 Columba Stewart, "Evagrius Ponticus and the Eastern Monastic Tradition on the Intellect and the Passions," in *Faith, Rationality and the Passions*, ed. Sarah Coakley (Chichester, UK: Wiley, 2012), 75.

unclenching of the grasping and defending hand in openness to others and the truth of things are no less distinctive qualities of the Dharma than they are of the gospel. Each tradition offers a path toward liberation and peace that is more than sufficient for the task of setting ego delusion aside and opening oneself up fearlessly to the plain truth of one's fraught and conditioned nature. There is no need to take sides here.

In fact, when each does what is one's to do, each is then in a position to be for the other the kind of good friend the Buddha had in mind when he said that good friendship constituted "the whole of the holy life."[12] A good friend is one toward whom I feel such a degree of respect that I find moral shame and moral dread, that "first cause and condition that leads to obtaining the wisdom fundamental to the spiritual life,"[13] arising in me and prompting me to further effort and resolve. If good friendship is the whole of the holy life, it is not because it is important that we all just hang out together nicely or engage in some kind of sharing exercise. Good friendship runs deeper than that. When noble practitioners encounter one another in full humility and openness, an occasion arises that serves as the proximate cause for each to muster further the wherewithal to follow the path to which one is committed. The longsuffering patience of the Christian who follows the Crucified is exemplary for the pursuer of the Dharma. The resolve and vigor of the son or daughter of the One who opened the gates of liberation is exemplary for the brother or sister of the Christ. The humility shown by both is a reminder to each of one's own proper rank and station among all beings.

Evagrius offers that "a person accomplished in the gnostic life and one accomplished in the practical life met each other; between the two of them stood the Lord"[14] as a way of indicating the essential unity of contemplation and renunciation. Here at the end of this exploration of the obstacles, we might well venture a slight reworking of that observation: A daughter or son of the Buddha set on overcoming the nīvaraṇas met a sister or brother of the Christ set on overcoming the logismoi; between the two of them stood—*not very much at all.* Having begun to face and work through their most deeply deluded thoughts and unskillful impulses—and, because of what that confrontation will have cost them, no longer holding to any kind of specialness, distinction, or pretense of merit—by what dint of ego could either party think

12 Bodhi, *Connected Discourses*, 1524.

13 Bodhi, *Numerical Discourses*, 1112.

14 Evagrius, *Monks* 121; Sinkewicz, 130.

itself now in a position to look at the other with anything other than a smile of recognition or a knowing wink of the eye, even as they continue their respective ways? Each will know that the holy life, despite everything that stands in its way and every temptation lying in wait to derail it, is still manifest in the world. And that is enough. Should others happen to encounter such men and women—just as those in the past encountered Antony, or as the young Siddhartha encountered that unnamed *śramaṇa* on that fateful evening—and then set out to take up such a life for themselves, that will be just fine. And if not, that is just fine, too. There is nothing here worth adhering to.

Bibliography

Arbel, Keren. *Early Buddhist Meditation: The Four* Jhānas *as the Actualization of Insight.* New York: Routledge, 2016.

Ariyesako, Bhikkhu. *The Bhikkhus' Rules: A Guide for Laypeople. The Theravadin Buddhist Monk's Rules.* Kallista, Australia: Sanghāloka Forest Hermitage, 1998.

Armstrong, Regis J., OFM, J. A. Wayne Hellman, and William J. Short, eds. *The Prophet.* Vol. 3 of *Francis of Assisi: Early Documents.* New York: New City, 2001.

Asaṅga. *The Bodhisattva Path to Unsurpassed Enlightenment: A Complete Translation of the* Bodhisattvabhūmi. Translated by Artemus B. Engle. Boulder, CO: Snow Lion, 2016.

Athanasius. *The Life of Antony and the Letter to Marcellinus.* Translated by Robert C. Gregg. New York: Paulist, 1980.

Bitton-Ashkelony, Brouria. "'More Interior than the Lips and the Tongue': John of Apamea and Silent Prayer in Late Antiquity." *JECS* 20 (2012): 303–31.

———. "Theories of Prayer in Late Antiquity: Doubts and Practices from Maximos of Tyre to Isaac of Nineveh." In *Prayer and Worship in Eastern Christianities, 5th to 11th Centuries*, edited by Brouria Bitton-Ashkelony and Derek Krueger, 10–33. New York: Routledge, 2016.

Bluck, Robert. "The Path of the Householder: Buddhist Lay Disciples in the Pali Canon." *Buddhist Studies Review* 19 (2002): 1–18.

Bodhi, Bhikkhu, ed. *A Comprehensive Manual of Abhidhamma: The Abhidhammattha Sangaha of Ācariya Anuruddha.* Onalaska, WA: Pariyatti, 2000.

———, trans. *The Connected Discourses of the Buddha: A Translation of the Saṃyutta Nikāya.* Boston: Wisdom, 2000.

———. *Dhamma Reflections: Collected Essays of Bhikkhu Bodhi.* Edited by Buddhist Publication Society. Onalaska, WA: Pariyatti, 2016.

———, trans. *The Numerical Discourses of the Buddha: A Complete Translation of the Aṅguttara Nikāya.* Somerville, MA: Wisdom, 2012.

———, trans. *The Suttanipāta: An Ancient Collection of the Buddha's Discourses Together with Its Commentaries.* Somerville, MA: Wisdom, 2017.

Brakke, David. *Demons and the Making of the Monk: Spiritual Combat in Early Christianity.* Cambridge: Harvard University Press, 2006.

———. "Reading the New Testament and Transforming the Self in Evagrius of Pontus." In *Asceticism and Exegesis in Early Christianity: The Reception of New Testament Texts in Ancient Ascetic Discourses*, edited by Hans-Ulrich Weidemann, 284–99. Göttingen: Vandenhoeck & Ruprecht, 2013.

Brock, Sebastian. *The Syriac Fathers on Prayer and the Spiritual Life.* Kalamazoo, MI: Cistercian, 1987.

Brown, Peter. "The Rise and Function of the Holy Man in Late Antiquity 1971–1997." *JECS* 6 (1998): 353–76.

Buddhaghoṣa. *The Expositor (*Atthasālinī*): Buddhaghoṣa's Commentary on the Dhammasaṅgaṇī, The First Book of the Abidhamma-Piṭaka*. Translated by Pe Maung Tin. Delhi: Motilal Banarsidass, 2016.

———. *Manorathapūraṇī* (*Aṅguttaranikāya-Aṭṭhakathā*). Pali ed. N.p.: Theravada Tipitaka, 2010.

———. *The Path of Purification: Visuddhimagga*. Translated by Bhikkhu Ñāṇamoli. Kandy, Sri Lanka: Buddhist Publication Society, 1999.

Bunge, Gabriel. *Despondency: The Spiritual Teaching of Evagrius Ponticus on Acedia*. Translated by Anthony P. Gythiel. Yonkers, NY: St. Vladimir's Seminary Press, 2011.

———. *Dragon's Wine and Angel's Bread: The Teaching of Evagrius Ponticus on Anger and Meekness*. Translated by Anthony P. Gythiel. Crestwood, NY: St. Vladimir's Seminary Press, 2009.

———. *"Évagre le sage." L'image d'Évagre le Pontique dans l'Histoire de l'Église*. Sankt Ottilien, Germany: EOS, 2022.

———. *Spiritual Fatherhood: Evagrius Ponticus on the Role of the Spiritual Father*. Translated by Luis Joshua Salés. Yonkers, NY: St. Vladimir's Seminary Press, 2016.

Burton-Christie, Douglas. "Evagrius on Sadness." *Cistercian Studies Quarterly* 44 (2009): 395–409.

———. "Simplicity, or the Terror of Belief: The Making and Unmaking of the Self in Early Christian Monasticism." *Cistercian Studies Quarterly* 40 (2005): 353–64.

———. *The Word in the Desert: Scripture and the Quest for Holiness in Early Christian Monasticism*. New York: Oxford University Press, 1993.

Carter, J. M. "The Prodigal Son in Its Buddhist Shape." *JRAS* (1893): 333–34.

Cattoi, Thomas. "Holy Anger, Holy Wrath: The Role of Anger and the Emotions in Early Christian Spirituality and the Mahayana Buddhist Tradition." *Buddhist-Christian Studies* 39 (2019): 53–66.

Chang, Garma Chen-Chi, ed. *Treasury of Mahāyāna Sūtras: Selections from the Mahāratnakūta Sūtra*. University Park: Pennsylvania State University Press, 1984.

Chryssavgis, John. "Fire and Light in the Egyptian Desert: Aspects of Desert Spirituality." *Cistercian Studies Quarterly* 34 (1999): 455–67.

Clement of Alexandria. *Les Stromates. Stromate VII*. Translated by Alain Le Boulluec. Paris: Cerf, 1997.

Conze, Edward, trans. *The Perfection of Wisdom in Eight Thousand Lines and Its Verse Summary*. San Francisco: City Lights, 2006.

Corrigan, Kevin. *Evagrius and Gregory: Mind, Soul and Body in the 4th Century*. New York: Routledge, 2009.

Corrigan, Kevin, and Gregory Yuri Glazov. "Compunction and Compassion: Two Overlooked Virtues in Evagrius of Pontus." *JECS* 22 (2014): 61–72.

Crislip, Andrew. "The Sin of Sloth or the Illness of Demons? The Demon of Acedia in Early Christian Monasticism." *HTR* 98 (2005): 143–69.

Derrett, J. Duncan M. "Monastic Masturbation in Pāli Buddhist Texts." *Journal of the History of Sexuality* 15 (2006): 1–13.

Diem, Albrecht. "The Limitations of Asceticism." *Medieval Worlds: Comparative & Interdisciplinary Studies* 9 (2019): 112–38.

Dōgen. *Moon in a Dewdrop: Writings of Zen Master Dōgen*. Edited by Kazuaki Tanahashi. New York: North Point, 1977.

Driscoll, Jeremy, OSB. "Gentleness in the *Ad Monachos* of Evagrius Ponticus." *StMon* 32 (1990): 295–321.

Epictetus. *The Handbook (The Encheiridion)*. Translated by Nicholas P. White. Indianapolis: Hackett, 1983.

Evagrius of Pontus. *Chapitres des Disciples d'Évagre*. Translated by Paul Géhin. Paris: Cerf, 2007.

———. *Evagrius'* Kephalaia Gnostika*: A New Translation of the Unreformed Text from the Syriac*. Translated by Ilaria L. E. Ramelli. Atlanta: SBL Press, 2015.

———. *The Greek Ascetic Corpus*. Translated by Robert E. Sinkewicz. New York: Oxford University Press, 2003.

———. *Talking Back: A Monastic Handbook for Combating Demons. Antirrhêtikos*. Translated by David Brakke. Collegeville, MN: Liturgical, 2009.

Fischer, Norman. "Acupressure Point of the Heart." In *All the Rage: Buddhist Wisdom on Anger and Acceptance*, edited by Andrea Miller, 68–77. Boston: Shambhala, 2014.

Frost, David L., trans. *The Divine Liturgies of Saint John Chrysostom and Saint Basil the Great*. Cambridge: Aquila, 2015.

Gavin, John. "'The Grief Willed by God': Three Patristic Interpretations of 2 Cor 7:10." *Greg* 91 (2010): 427–42.

Gethin, R[upert] M. L. *The Buddhist Path to Awakening*. Oxford: One World, 2007.

———. "Cosmology and Meditation: From the Aggañña-Sutta to the Mahāyāna." *HR* 36 (1997): 183–217.

———. *The Foundations of Buddhism*. New York: Oxford University Press, 1998.

Giustarini, Giuliano. "Faith and Renunciation in Early Buddhism: Saddhā and Nekkhamma." *Rivista di Studi Sudasiatici* 1 (2006): 161–79.

Gold, Jonathan C. "Freedom through Cumulative Moral Cultivation: Heroic Willpower (*Vīrya*)." *Journal of Buddhist Ethics* 25 (2018): 741–66.

Gross, Rita. "Buddhist Theology?" In *Buddhist Theology: Critical Reflections from Contemporary Buddhist Scholars*, edited by Roger R. Jackson and John J. Makransky, 53–60. Surrey, UK: Curzon, 2000.

Guillaumont, Antoine. *Un philosophe au désert: Évagre le Pontique*. Paris: J. Vrin, 2004.

Harmless, William, SJ. *Desert Christians: An Introduction to the Literature of Early Monasticism*. New York: Oxford University Press, 2004.

Harmless, William, SJ, and Raymond R. Fitzgerald, SJ. "The Sapphire Light of the Mind: The *Skemmata* of Evagrius Ponticus." *TS* 62 (2001): 498–529.

Harvey, Peter. *An Introduction to Buddhism: Teachings, History and Practices*. New York: Cambridge University Press, 2013.

———. "'Signless' Meditation in Pāli Buddhism." *The Journal of the International Association of Buddhist Studies* 9 (1986): 25–53.

Hausherr, Irénée, SJ. *Les leçons d'un contemplatif. Le Traité de l'Oraison d'Evagre le Pontique*. Paris: Beauchesne, 1960.

———. *Spiritual Direction in the Early Christian East*. Translated by Anthony P. Gythiel. Kalamazoo, MI: Cistercian, 1990.

Heim, Maria. "The Conceit of Self-Loathing." *Journal of Indian Philosophy* 37 (2009): 61–74.

———. "Shame and Apprehension: Notes on the Moral Value of Hiri and Ottappa." In *Embedded Languages: Studies of Sri Lankan and Buddhist Cultures*, edited by Carol S. Anderson et al., 237–60. Colombo: Godage International, 2012.

Hevelone-Harper, Jennifer L. L. *Disciples of the Desert: Monks, Laity, and Spiritual Authority in Sixth-Century Gaza*. Baltimore: Johns Hopkins University Press, 2014.

Hill, Jonathan. "Did Evagrius Ponticus (AD 346–99) Have Obsessive-Compulsive Disorder?" *Journal of Medical Biography* 18 (2010): 49–56.

Holland, Glenn. "Celibacy in the Early Christian Church." In *Celibacy and Religious Traditions*, edited by Carl Olson, 65–84. New York: Oxford University Press, 2008.

Horner, Isabel Blew, ed. and trans. *The Book of the Discipline*. Oxford: Pali Text Society, 1938.

van der Horst, Pieter W. "Silent Prayer in Antiquity." *Numen* 41 (1994): 1–25.

Ireland, John D., trans. *The Udāna and the Itivuttaka*. Onalaska, WA: Pariyatti, 2018.

Joest, Christoph. "The Significance of *Acedia* and *Apatheia* in Evagrius Ponticus Part I." *American Benedictine Review* 55 (2004): 121–50.

Laird, Martin. "The 'Open Country Whose Name Is Prayer': Apophasis, Deconstruction, and Contemplative Practice." *Modern Theology* 21 (2005): 141–55.

Largen, Kristin Johnston. "Introduction to Liberation Theology and Engaged Buddhism." *Buddhist-Christian Studies* 36 (2016): 51–53.

Linge, David. "Leading the Life of Angels: Ascetic Practice and Reflection in the Writings of Evagrius of Pontus." *JAAR* 68, no. 3 (September 2000): 537–68.

Loori, John Daido. *Invoking Reality: Moral and Ethical Teaching of Zen*. Boston: Shambhala, 1998.

Louth, Andrew. "Evagrius on Anger." *StPatr* 47 (2010): 179–85.

Luibhéid, Colm. "Antony and the Renunciation of Society." *ITQ* 52 (1986): 304–14.

Maugans Driver, Lisa D. "Apophatic Theophanies: Incarnational Knowledge of God in Early Eastern Christianity." In *The Routledge Handbook of Religion and the Body*, edited by Yudit Kornberg Greenberg and George Pati, 52–68. New York: Routledge, 2023.

McGinn, Bernard. "Withdrawal and Return: Reflections on Monastic Retreat from the World." *Spiritus: A Journal of Christian Spirituality* 6 (2006): 149–72.

Misiarczyk, Leszek. *Eight* Logismoi *in the Writings of Evagrius Ponticus*. Turnhout: Brepols, 2021.

———. "*Impassibilitas et impeccantia*: Jerome's Misunderstanding of Impassibility and Sinlessness in Evagrius Ponticus." *Bogoslovni vestnik* 81 (2021): 271–81.

Muller, A. Charles, and Kenneth K. Tanaka, trans. *The Brahmā's Net Sutra*. Moraga, CA: BDK America, 2017.

Nāgārjuna. *Letter from a Friend: A Bodhisattva's Advice to an Indian King on Right Living and the Buddhist Path*. The Suhṛllekha. *An Epistle Composed for King Śatakarṇī by Ārya Nagarjuna (circa 200 CE)*. Translated by Bhikshu Dharmamitra. Seattle: Kalavinka, 2009.

———. *Nāgārjuna on the Six Perfections: An Ārya Bodhisattva Explains the Heart of the Bodhisattva Path: Exegesis on the Great Perfection of Wisdom Sutra Chapters 17–30*. Translated by Dharmamitra. Seattle: Kalavinka, 2009.

Ñāṇamoli, Bhikkhu, and Bhikkhu Bodhi, trans. *The Middle Length Discourses of the Buddha: A New Translation of the Majjhima Nikāya*. Boston: Wisdom, 1995.

Nattier, Jan. *A Few Good Men: The Bodhisattva Path according to the* Inquiry of Ugra (Ugraparipṛcchā). Honolulu: University of Hawai'i Press, 2003.

Nault, Jean-Charles. *The Noonday Devil: Acedia, the Unnamed Evil of Our Times*. Translated by Michael J. Miller. San Francisco: Ignatius, 2015.

Newhauser, Richard, ed. *In the Garden of Evil: The Vices and Culture in the Middle Ages.* Toronto: Pontifical Institute of Mediaeval Studies, 2005.

Norris, Kathleen. *Acedia and Me: A Marriage, Monks, and a Writer's Life.* New York: Riverhead, 2008.

Nyanaponika Thera, trans. *The Five Mental Hindrances and Their Conquest: Texts from the Pali Canon and the Commentaries.* Kandy, Sri Lanka: Buddhist Publication Society, 2018.

Nyanaponika Thera and Hellmuth Hecker, trans. *Great Disciples of the Buddha: Their Lives, Their Works, Their Legacy.* Edited by Bhikkhu Bodhi. Somerville, MA: Wisdom, 2003.

Nyanatiloka. *Buddhist Dictionary: Manual of Buddhist Terms and Doctrines.* Onalaska, WA: Pariyatti, 2019.

Opperwall, Daniel G. "Chained to Grievance, Rotten to the Roots: Evagrius and John Cassian on Sadness." *StPatr* 115 (2021): 367–74.

Palladius of Aspuna. *The Lausiac History.* Translated by John Wortley. Collegeville, MN: Cistercian, 2015.

Parmentier, M. "Evagrius of Pontus, 'Letter to Melania.'" *Bijdr* 46 (1985): 2–38.

Pine, Red, trans. *The Diamond Sutra: Text and Commentaries Translated from Sanskrit and Chinese.* Washington: Counterpoint, 2001.

Ramelli, Ilaria L. E. "Evagrius and Gregory: Nazianzen or Nyssen? Cappadocian (and Origenian) Influence on Evagrius." *GRBS* 53 (2013): 117–37.

———. "Gregory and Evagrius." *StPatr* 101 (2021): 177–206.

Regnault, Lucien. *The Day-to-Day Life of the Desert Fathers in Fourth-Century Egypt.* Petersham, MA: St. Bede's, 1999.

Rhys Davids, [Caroline], trans. *A Buddhist Manual of Psychological Ethics: Translation of the First Book of the* Abidhammapiṭaka *Entitled* Dhammasaṅgaṇī *(Compendium of States or Phenomena).* Delhi: Motilal Banarsidass, 2016.

Rivas, Rubén Peretó. "Dreams in Evagrius Ponticus' Life and Teaching." *Vox Patrum* 37 (2017): 523–42.

Russell, Norman, trans. *The Lives of the Desert Fathers: The Historia Monachorum in Aegypto.* Collegeville, MN: Cistercian, 1980.

Sayadaw, Mahāsi. *Manual of Insight.* Translated by Vipassanā Mettā Foundation Translation Committee. Boston: Wisdom, 2016.

Senauke, Hozan Alan. "Right Anger and the Path to the End of Caste." Clear View Project, November 4, 2014. https://www.clearviewproject.org/2014/11/right-anger-and-the-path-to-the-end-of-caste/.

Snell, R. J. *Acedia and Its Discontents: Metaphysical Boredom in an Empire of Desire.* Kettering, OH: Angelico, 2015.

Soma Thera. *The Way of Mindfulness: Being a Translation of the Satipaṭṭhāna Sutta of the Majjhima Nikāya; Its Commentary, the Satipaṭṭhāna Sutta Vaṇṇanā of the Papañcasūdanī of Buddhaghosa Thera; and Excerpts from the Līnatthapakāsanā Ṭīkā, Marginal Notes of Dhammapāla Thera on the Commentary.* Whitefish, MT: Kessinger, 2010.

Stadel, Seth M. "Prayer without Anger and Sadness: The Syriac Adaptation of Evagrius' *Chapters on Prayer.*" *ParOr* 45 (2019): 341–62.

Stewart, Columba, OSB. "The Desert Fathers on Radical Self-Honesty." *Vox Benedictina* 8 (1991): 7–53.

———. "Evagrius Ponticus and the Eastern Monastic Tradition on the Intellect and the Passions." In *Faith, Rationality and the Passions*, edited by Sarah Coakley, 67–80. Chichester, UK: Wiley, 2012.

———. "Evagrius Ponticus on Prayer and Anger." In *Religions of Late Antiquity in Practice*, edited by Richard Valantasis, 65–81. Princeton: Princeton University Press, 2000.

Strousma, Guy G. "From Master of Wisdom to Spiritual Master in Late Antiquity." In *Religion and the Self in Antiquity*, edited by David Brakke, Michael L. Satlow, and Steven Weitzman, 183–96. Bloomington: Indiana University Press, 2006.

Tan, Piya. "Nīvaraṇa: Mental Hindrances." The Minding Centre. https://www.themindingcentre.org/dharmafarer/sutta-discovery/sutta-discovery-vol-30-39.

Thanissaro, Bhikkhu, trans. *The Buddhist Monastic Code: The Patimokkha Training Rules*. Valley Center, CA: Metta Forest Monastery, n.d.

Thiradhammo, Ajahn. *Beyond I-Making. A Contemplative Investigation of the Concept of* Anattā *and the Path to Its Realization*. Hertfordshire, UK: Amaravati, 2002.

———. *Working with the Five Hindrances*. Northumberland, UK: Aruno, 2014.

Tilby, Angela. *The Seven Deadly Sins: Their Origin in the Spiritual Teaching of Evagrius the Hermit*. London: SPCK, 2002.

Tiso, Francis V. "Evagrius of Pontus and Buddhist Abhidharma." *Religion East & West* 5 (2005): 41–71.

Trungpa, Chögyam. *The Truth of Suffering and the Path of Liberation*. Boston: Shambhala, 2009.

Vernezze, Peter J. "Moderation or the Middle Way: Two Approaches to Anger." *Philosophy East and West* 58 (2008). 2–16.

Vivian, Tim, trans. *Four Desert Fathers: Pambo, Evagrius, Macarius of Egypt, and Macarius of Alexandria. Coptic Texts Relating to the* Lausiac History *of Palladius*. Crestwood, NY: St. Vladimir's Seminary Press, 2004.

Von Balthasar, Hans Urs. "The Metaphysics and Mystical Theology of Evagrius." *Monastic Studies* 3 (1965): 183–95.

Vos, Nienke. "Seeing *Hesychia*: Appeals to the Imagination in the *Apophthegmata Patrum*." *StPatr* 64 (2013): 33–45.

Walshe, Maurice. *The Long Discourses of the Buddha: A Translation of the Dīgha Nikāya*. Boston: Wisdom, 1995.

Ward, Benedicta, trans. *The Sayings of the Desert Fathers: The Alphabetical Collection*. Kalamazoo, MI: Cistercian, 1975.

Watson, Burton, trans. *The Lotus Sutra*. New York: Columbia University Press, 1993.

Wendebourg, Dorothea. "Luther on Monasticism." In *The Pastoral Luther*, edited by Timothy J. Wingert, 327–54. Minneapolis: Fortress, 2017.

Wortley, John. *Anonymous Sayings of the Desert Fathers*. New York: Cambridge University Press, 2017.

———. "What *hêsychia* Meant to the Desert Fathers." *Cistercian Studies Quarterly* 54 (2019): 159–70.

Zöckler, Otto. *Das Lehrstück von den sieben Hauptsünden*. Munich: Beck, 1893.

Index